For Dan
Best Wishes
Christine Brinkley
Jan 16, 1997

HABITATIONS OF THE GREAT GODDESS

Cristina Biaggi, Ph.D.

Knowledge, Ideas & Trends
Publisher
Manchester, Connecticut

Cover design: Bob Josen
Book design and production: Cindy Parker

First Published in 1994 by:

Knowledge, Ideas & Trends, Inc.
1131 Tolland Turnpike, Suite 175
Manchester, CT 06040

Library of Congress Cataloguing-in-Publication Data

ISBN: 1-879198-18-5

Includes bibliographical references and index.
1. Neolithic period—Malta. 2. Neolithic period—Scotland-Orkney. 3. Religion, Prehistoric—Europe. 4. Goddesses—Europe. 5. Malta—Antiquities. 6. Orkney (Scotland) — Antiquities. I. Title.

GN776.22.M35B53 1994
291' .042'09378—dc20   CIP: 93-30386

10 9 8 7 6 5 4 3 2 1

First Edition
Printed in the United States of America

TABLE OF CONTENTS

FOREWORD BY MARIJA GIMBUTAS

Cristina Biaggi's book on the temples of Malta and of the Orkney and Shetland islands north of Scotland is a study grounded in factual archaeological finds. It is an analysis of temple architecture and art dating from the period some 6000-4000 years ago (*i.e.*, from an era which is "beyond God the Father"). Malta and the Orkney and Shetland islands offer an unmatched range of well-preserved temples of stone, and this description and interpretation of architecture and artifactual finds sheds much precious information on the temples themselves and on the sculpture, painting, engraving and symbols associated with the temples and with the divinity worshipped within them. Though the Maltese temples have been known throughout this century and though very useful general books exist about them, for instance, *Malta*, by J.D. Evans,[1] 1959, his *The Prehistoric Antiquities of the Maltese Islands*, 1971, and *Malta: An Archaeological Guide*, by David Trump, 1972, no work before Cristina Biaggi's has analyzed the findings within the context of a theacratic society worshipping a goddess as its main deity. The author's attempt to evoke from physical remains the spiritual lives of our ancestors is praiseworthy: she offers much to the decipherment of the ways in which the Goddess was worshipped and what powers She possessed over life, death and regeneration. The title of the book, *Habitations of the Great Goddess*, is a perfect choice. The temple plans themselves are anthropomorphic and the supporting symbolism expressed by sculptures, engravings and pottery is indeed inseparable from the regenerating and life-giving body of the Goddess.

Dr. Biaggi's pioneering examination of the temples of the Orkney and Shetland islands, so far hardly known to the wider public, has confirmed their unquestionable relationship to the Maltese temples and has shown the far-flung extent of the same Goddess religion between the Mediterranean and northwestern Europe. Here, in the far Northwest, the temples and the worship of the Goddess continued for nearly a millennium longer than in Malta.

The book is richly illustrated with the author's original photographs and plans, many published for the first time. This study provides solid evidence for the existence of the Goddess religion in Europe; it will remain a valuable reference work in the field of the earliest temple architecture.

Marija Gimbutas

Marija Gimbutas
1993

PROLOGUE

The Great Goddess and Her role in human history as a life-producing, life-nurturing force have won increasing recognition in recent years. The pioneering work of women prehistorians and artists has done much to reverse centuries of neglect; these scholars and thinkers have cleared away accumulated layers of misrepresentation. Slowly these women are restoring the Goddess to Her rightful rank and dignity as the earliest of humankind's deities. Sympathetic and sensitive interpretation of ancient sculpture, painting, myth and symbol provide new insights into the Goddess and Her powers, particularly Her central role in the cycle of birth, death and rebirth.

Today the Great Goddess is a symbol and a focus for many groups within the women's movement that seek to build a more cohesive, peaceful and caring society. Yet this role has led to a universalization of the Goddess and Her nurturing qualities that often obscures Her historical origins and humankind's reflection of Her powers through art, sculpture and myth. Too often the permanent record of Her shrines and temples with their many clues to ceremony and worship is neglected.

The power and personality of the Goddess flow through the early history of *Homo sapiens*. She is a constant presence throughout the Paleolithic and Neolithic eras. The grave-sites and shelters of Neanderthal people furnish signs of her presence and power; they continue to be abundant in the shelters, camps and cave-sanctuaries of the Cro-Magnon peoples of Paleolithic Europe. The layperson will probably know the Goddess best from the rich troves of image and artifact prehistoric Europe has yielded. Many of the most striking of these have been photographed and published. The enthusiast will know that Her domain extended beyond Eurasia. Prehistorians have found Her images and symbols throughout the world. The scholar will be familiar with the large and specialized literature that deals with Goddess figurines and images from Siberia and the North American Arctic and from lands as distant and different as Africa, Australia and the Americas.

How, then, we can ask, was the Great Goddess overthrown? Why has She been eclipsed to become less well-known than the gods and goddesses of the Egyptians and the Greeks? The answers to these questions are partly found in the myths and legends of Sumer and its successor civilizations and in those of Egypt and Greece. They tell of the Goddess' overthrow and dispossession by male warrior gods. Though overthrown as a primary public deity, the Great Goddess survived as a continuing power linked to the mysteries of birth, death and rebirth. She lived on within the spiritual core of women, Her intercession sought, Her rites celebrated, Her images honored. But She was always secondary to the male deities of organized religion.

This book is designed to present and evoke the Goddess through the most tangible of all mediums, the enduring architecture and art of Her habitations. The temples and tombs of Malta and the Orkney and Shetland islands offer a challenging and rewarding topic where geography has imposed natural limits yet where recent archaeology and scholarship are giving rise to a rapidly expanding recognition of the Goddess and Her religion.

"To present and evoke the Goddess" are carefully chosen terms. Malta and the Orkney and Shetland archipelagoes present architectural sites of the very greatest interest. The many parallels that architectural design, symbol and artifact offer demand a reconsideration of the Goddess and Her role in the life of the northern islands. I chose Malta because Maltese tombs and temples offer perhaps the richest single concentration of physical evidence of the Goddess. I chose the Orkney and Shetland islands because the structures found there offer compelling even if less clear-cut evidence of Her presence. Moroever, as the archaeologist Alexander Calder pointed out in the 1930s, over half a century ago, extensive physical evidence points to a relationship between Maltese and Scottish structures. In this book, I will seek to expand upon and confirm this relationship.

Though the architectural record in Malta and the Orkneys and Shetlands speaks powerfully, its language is that of symbols. The societies of the third millennium B.P. were pre-literate. The archaeologists and the historians of architecture, art and religion must tread with great care as they attempt to evoke from physical remains the inner lives and thoughts of civilizations long since passed away. The emphasis in this book is therefore on the tangible and the finite, on the tombs and temples themselves. I hope that the numerous photographs and plans, many of which are new, will convey the human commitment to the Goddess' religion and worship.

The investigation of tombs and temples and the analysis of artifacts and art (sculpture, painting, image and symbol) illuminate the Goddess' many roles. The interpretation given to the images and symbols created to honor the Goddess illustrate the powers She possessed over life, death and fertility. They also help us develop insights into how She was recognized and worshipped. If the Maltese tombs and temples confirm the power of the Goddess, those of the distant Orkneys and Shetlands indicate the far-flung extent of Her religion.

DEDICATION

To my Mother and Father

LIST OF FIGURES

List of Plates

ACKNOWLEDGMENTS

This book, based on research I did for my doctoral dissertation, grew out of my passionate interest in the Great Goddess — who I believe was the earliest anthropomorphic embodiment of the spiritual yearnings of human beings — and out of my fascination with caves and megalithic structures. As a sculptor, I harbor strong aesthetic feelings for these earliest sites and centers of numinous energy.

The writing of this book, including the research for the earlier dissertation, required several enjoyable and rewarding field trips with lengthy visits to Malta, the Orkney and Shetland islands and mainland Scotland. These trips, the research and compilation of data, and correspondence with scholars and museum curators in many nations were extremely rich and exhilarating experiences.

During the eight years this book was in the making, a number of people helped and encouraged me. Their enthusiasm and commitment did much to sustain me. I owe much gratitude to Professor Janice Gorn, a dedicated and supportive member of my dissertation committee. I thank her for her sincere interest, her continued encouragement, and for the long hours of time and effort that she expended on my behalf.

I am very grateful to Dr. Francis Mallia, the former director of the National Museum of Archaeology, Valletta, Malta, for his helpful suggestions, for entrusting me with the keys to various sites, and for helping locate others. I would like to especially thank Mr. Anthony Paca and Dr. Tancred Gouder of the National Museum of Archaeology, Malta, for their help in gathering the Maltese illustrations. Thanks go also to the National Museum of Antiquities in Edinburgh, Scotland. I wish to express my gratitude to the Malta National Library in Valletta, and the National Library of Scotland in Edinburgh. The staffs of these institutions went beyond the call of duty to locate needed source materials for me and to ensure that I could make the fullest possible use of them during my time abroad. I owe similar thanks to the staff of the New York Public Library, the Bobst Library at New York University, and the Rockland Community College Library. Special thanks are extended to Helen Waldron of the Rockland Community College Library; she was invaluable in locating and making available a number of crucial sources which I was unable to find elsewhere.

I would particularly like to express my most enthusiastic thanks to Professor Marija Gimbutas. Her pioneering work on the Great Goddess was a crucial source of inspiration for this book, and I wish to thank her especially for reading my manuscript in its various forms and making insightful suggestions and comments.

Other special thanks also go to Riane Eisler who read my manuscript in its latest drafts and made helpful suggestions. I wish to thank the following scholars who have read the work with a critical eye and added their comments: Eleanor Gadon, Giulia Sorlini, Miriam Dexter, Kristina Birgen, and Buffie Johnson, and I especially want to thank Mimi Lobell for her inspiration and support.

I am also deeply indebted to Dr. Audrey Henshall and to Michael Dames for their valuable comments, suggestions and advice. Both willingly shared the fruits of their personal research and knowledge.

Sincere thanks are extended to the following individuals: Anna Maria Quaiat, for locating needed sources in Italian libraries; Gail Dunlap, for doing essential research; Marina Harrison, my sister, and Virginia Dare, my good friend, for reading the original manuscript and making important suggestions; Kamado for reading the latest version of the text with a critical feminist eye; and my mother, my daughter Diana Green, my son John Anderson, and Grace Shenell — all of whom have provided inspiration and support.

A number of friends and colleagues shared the burden of preparing the manuscript and ensuring that this book saw the light of day. I owe much to them, particularly to Robin Mooring-Frye for extensive library research and expert word-processing; to Connie Kane for finding important bibliographical material; to the Minuteman Press for their continued help; and to Ray at Paragraphics for the production of charts. I owe a debt of gratitude to Galowitz Photographics for the great care they took to produce high quality reproductions. My thanks go to Peter Skinner, whose constant enthusiasm, many suggestions, and perceptive comments have done much to transform an academic thesis into an accessible book.

And last, I would like to thank my dearest friend Patricia Walsh for reading the work in its various stages and for her heartfelt enthusiam and encouragement and her continued help with the illustrations.

Cristina Biaggi
Palisades, New York
March 8, 1994

Glossary

Alignment. Single or multiple rows of standing stones.

Apse, apsidal end. A semicircular recess in a building.

Architecture. The art of designing structures that have a functional as well as an aesthetic purpose.

Artifact. Anything that has been constructed or modified by humans.

Baetyl. A small pillar of stone thought to have been a venerated object.

Barrow. "An artificial mound of earth, chalk or turf built to cover burials. Long Barrows, often with timber or stone-built chambers were customary during the Neolithic period in many parts of Britain. Round Barrows, circular mounds with no entrance or chamber, slowly replaced the long forms after 2500 B.C. and remained popular throughout the Bronze Age."[1]

Beakers. "Coil-built pots, probably used as drinking vessels, which were made by people from the mainland who first entered the British Isles around 2600 B.C. These vessels were flat-based and decorated all over with cross-hatched patterns."[2]

Bookan-type chamber. Scottish tomb chambers which are roughly oval and divided into compartments by radial slabs.

B.P. "Before Present" is used throughout the book instead of B.C. ("Before Christ"), except in quotations from authors who have used the B.C. form.

Brachycephalic. "Short-headed or broad-headed humans with a cephalic index of over 80."[3]

Cairn. A mound of stone, sometimes covering a chamber.

Capstone. A large stone laid across the top of other stones, usually to form the roof of a chamber or dolmen.

Cardial or Impressed ware. Pottery which is decorated by impressing the edges with cardium shells. The distribution of this ware in the Mediterranean is strongly coastal both in the eastern and western Mediterranean.[4]

Causeway camps. "Large scale constructions, some started before 4000 B.P. in the British Isles. The camps consisted of rings of earth, banks and ditches, with a central enclosed area. Broad causeways of level earth run from the perimeter to the central enclosure. The use of the camps has caused controversy . . . It may be that farmers of the area wintered here and sheltered their cattle behind the embankments. Some people may have lived in the camps the whole year. It is quite likely, however, that they were gathering places for the people . . . around the times of the seasonal festivals. . . ."[5] They are also called earthworks.

Chambered mound. An earth mound or barrow with a chamber, usually of stone, inside it.

Chalcolithic. The transitional stage between the Neolithic and the Bronze age in which some copper was used.

Chthonic. Underground, subterranean.

Collective burial. "The burial of the members of a community in a large tomb. It describes a custom whereby burial chambers were used and re-used over many generations, the older bones being stacked on one side to make way for fresh interments. Collective graves were cut into rock or constructed of wood as well as built of megaliths and drystone walling."[6]

Corbelled. "In megalithic construction, a roof formed by horizontal layers of stone which overlap each other as they rise and are closed off at the top."[7]

Coralline limestone. A hard type of limestone found in Malta which varies in color from white to red, cream or grey and is harder than globigerina, but less even in texture.

Cro-Magnon. An early form of *Homo sapiens* that appears about 40,000 B.P. and is associated with Upper Paleolithic tools and art.

Culture. "The sum total of procedures by which humans adapt to their environment and which is learned by one generation after another. A specific culture is an instance of such procedures at any given place and period of time. Archaeologically, a culture is the total assemblage of remains belonging to a people or group of related peoples."[8]

Cultural evolution. "Cumulative change resulting from one or more historical processes including local inventions of new traits (be they tools, beliefs, or social institutions), the borrowing of traits by way of diffusion, the amalgamation of peoples by way of trade or other forms of contact, or the stratification of society by way of conquest."[9]

Cupmark. A rounded depression carved in the face of a stone, also called a cupule.

Cup-and-ring marks. Concentric rings carved around a cupmark, often with another line penetrating from outside the rings to the cupmark in the center.

Cyclopean construction. A type of drystone building consisting of successive layers of *large* irregular stones fitting closely to each other and forming a wall.

Daub. A kind of mortar or plaster made of mud.

Dendrochronology. "The science of dealing with the study of the annual rings of trees determining the dates and chronological order of past events. In 1929, A.E. Douglass showed how this method could be used to date archaeological material. Recent studies based on the California bristlecone pine established a floating chronology going back to 7210 B.P. which is applicable for the Neolithic. This method checks the validity of radiocarbon dating."[10]

Diffusion. A process by which cultural change observed in a society is brought about by the influence of one culture over another, usually by means of migration.[11]

Dolichocephalic. "A type of human being having a relatively long head with a cranial index of less than 75."[12]

Doorjamb. The vertical side of a door.

Dressed stones. Stones which have been modified or shaped by tools.

Drystone building. Construction without the use of mortar or adhesive of any kind between the stone layers. Also known as drystone walling.

Eurafrican type. "An assumed Prehistoric subrace or type from which originated Mediterraneans of Europe and certain North African peoples, as in Algeria, Egypt, and Ethiopia . . .".[13]

Excarnation. A method of burial whereby the body was kept outside the tomb until the flesh disappeared, then the bones were collected and placed in the tomb. This was practiced at Çatal Hüyük and also in Scotland.

Ex-voto figures.   Statues which are offered or erected in fulfillment of a vow and often in gratitude for deliverance from distress. They are also called Votive Statues.

Fiddle-shaped idols.   Small schematic sculptures, particularly prevalent in the Bronze Age Aegean, which are shaped like fiddle instruments.

Flintknapper.   A person who manufactures stone tools out of flint.

Gallery grave.   "A megalithic chamber consisting of one long space, as against the passage plus the broader chamber arrangement of a 'passage grave' . . . called *Allée couverte* in French."[14]

Globigerina limestone.   "A soft limestone found in Malta, . . . composed almost entirely of minute fragments of the shells of mollusks, [it] is soft, and of a deep yellow color. It yields blocks that can be pared into shape with the aid of a suitable instrument, like lumps of cheese. When exposed to the weather, they quickly develop a protective patina on the surface which is quite resistant to weather until it is broken off at any point. Once this happens, however, the stone decays rapidly."[15]

Great Goddess.   The principal deity worshipped in Paleolithic and Neolithic times in Europe and in the Near East, who was the personification of fertility, of life and of death. She is also known as Mother Goddess or Great Mother.

Grooved ware.   Later Neolithic pottery made after 3200 B.P. in the British Isles. It is ". . . flat-based, profusely decorated either by incision or by applied strips of dots or both. The design consists generally of geometric shapes especially triangles, lozenges; and filling parts of the patterns with dots and other rustication is a diagnostic feature."[16]

Gylany.   A term coined by Riane Eisler to represent a balance and equality between the sexes. *Gy* is from the Greek root *gyne* meaning "woman," *an* is from *andros,* "man," and the letter *l* stands for linking.[17]

Gynocentric.   Woman centered as in a woman-centered society. *Gyno* is from *gyne* meaning "woman" in Greek. [18]

Henge.   An enclosure usually formed by a roughly circular earthwork ditch and bank. Henges often had circles of standing stones or timber within the earthworks.

Hypogeum.   An underground tomb, usually with one or more egg-shaped chambers. The largest is the Hal Saflieni Hypogeum in Malta, in which the dead were buried from the 4th millennium to 2500 B.P. Hypogea are also found in Sardinia, Sicily and in France.

Independent invention. "The belief that similar innovations or inventions found in distant regions, which had no contact with each other, are due to independent invention which is probably a result of similar psychic processes shared by mankind."[19]

Indo-European. "A group of languages, first recognized by William Jones in 1786, originating in the Kurgan homeland and carried out from there by folk movements during the second millennium B.P. Now also a specific group of cultures with a communal heritage."[20]

Inhumation. Burial by placing the body in the earth.

Kerb. A ring of large stones around the bottom edge of a mound.

Kurgan tradition. Proto-Indo-European (PIE) traditions linked with the Kurgan culture which spread into Europe during the period 4300-2800 B.P. The Kurgans were seminomadic patriarchal pastoralists who worshipped a sky god. Their contact with the matristic Goddess-worshipping peoples of Old Europe changed the egalitarian Old Europeans forever.

Lobe. Any rounded or projecting part. See Apse.

Long-Short building technique. Use of alternating rectangular blocks set horizontally with blocks set upright; it is aesthetic and adds strength to the wall.

Marmite image. Carvings on French megaliths, having the appearance of an earthenware casserole with a cover; also called Box images. (*Marmite* means casserole in French.)

Matriarchy. A social system in which the dominant authority is held by women.[21]

Matrilineal. A social structure in which the ancestral descent and inheritance is traced through the female line.[22]

Matrilocal. The home territory of a matrilineal kin group.[23]

Matristic society. A matrilineal "partnership" society in which women are honored but do not subjugate men.[24]

Mediterranean type. A subrace or type of human being ". . . characterized by medium or short stature, slender build, dolichocephalic, and dark complexioned." The other two Caucasian types are Alpine and Nordic.[25]

Megalithic. Composed of or built with large stones.

Mesolithic. A transitional period between the Paleolithic and Neolithic (c. 10,000 to 7,000 B.P.) characterized by the dog as the first domestic animal, pottery and the bow and arrow.

Midden. An ancient rubbish heap, usually of household refuse.

Menhir. A single vertical standing stone.

Myth. An archetypal event described in words. "Its functions are: aetiological or to justify an existing social system or to account for traditional rites or customs."[26]

Neanderthal or *Homo sapiens Neanderthalensis*. An early type of human being existing from 200,000 to 40,000 B.P., during the Middle Paleolithic period who made tools and worshipped.

Neolithic Period. A phase of prehistoric history, which occurred at different time intervals in various parts of the world, characterized by agriculture, by the domestication of animals and by fixed settlements.

Oculi. Oculus, singular. An architectural or decorational detail resembling or suggesting an eye; also called Eyebrow motif.

Omphalos. Navel, central part, focal point; from the Greek word meaning navel. It was a special stone in Delphi, pre-eminent as the most sacred spot in Greece.

Orthostat. Upright megalithic slab forming part of a structure.

Ossuary. "Tomb or other site for the deposition of bones. Neolithic ossuaries functioned as sacred communal centers, providing a link between the living kin and the ancestors."[27]

Oversailing courses. A series of stone or brick courses, each one projecting beyond the one below it, as in corbelled megalithic construction.

Ovoid. Having the shape of an egg.

Paleolithic Period. A prehistoric phase characterized by stone implements. It is generally subdivided into three stages: Lower and Middle (200,000 - 40,000 B.P.), during which Neanderthal Man was prevalent, and Upper (after 40,000 B.P.), which marks the appearance of *Homo sapiens*.

Passage grave. "A megalithic chamber consisting of a large passage leading to one or more central chambers which are structurally separate from the passage; also called *Dolmen à couloir.*"[28]

Patriarchy. A form of social organization in which the father (*pater*) is the supreme authority in the family, clan, or tribe.[29]

Patrilineal. Tracing the descent and inheritance through the male line.[30]

Patrilocal. The home territory of the husband's family or tribe.[31]

Pilaster. A shallow pier or rectangular column projecting slightly from a wall.

Pit marks. A typically Maltese decorative motif or pattern, found on architecture, sculpture and pottery, that consists of small holes drilled into a surface, a few centimeters apart, seemingly at random. Also called drilled holes.

Pleistocene. An early epoch, 2 million to 10,000 years B.P. marked by the emergence of *Homo erectus*, an early human being.

Porthole slab. A slab of rock into which a door has been cut, as in the Maltese temples.

Prehistorians. In this text, refers to archaeologists, anthropologists, historians.

Pythia. The Greek prophetess who sat on a sacred tripod in a special room at Delphi to give her prophecies which were then interpreted for the faithful by the priestesses or priest.

Quern. A primitive hand mill for grinding grain, consisting of two stone disks, one upon the other.

Radiocarbon dating. A method for dating organic remains up to 50,000 years old by measuring the amount of radiocarbon decay in carbon 14, which gradually disappears at a known rate from the moment life ceases. The method was devised by the American chemist William L. Libby in 1946.

Rock-cut tomb. Tombs that were cut out of the living rock. Rock-cut tombs are essentially Mediterranean in origin with the earliest examples, from the 5th millennium, occurring in peninsular Italy and in the central Mediterranean islands. The earliest examples were of simple form and were used for single or double burials. "The most elaborate and unusual occur on islands - Malta, Sardinia and Mallorca; they represent the end-products of separate specialized insular traditions. . .".[32]

Ropeholes. Also called V- or U-shaped holes with two mouths. Some, because of their positions on the jambs of doorways ". . . show that they were intended to hold the hinges or fastenings, probably of leather, of doors and screens."[33] Others, occurring on horizontal surfaces, often in paving slabs, were fitted with stone plugs; these probably had a ritual function.

Schematic art. Art which has conformed to a style of expression often extreme in character rather than to the appearance of nature; also called stylized art.

Schist. A metamorphic crystalline rock that can be split easily into layers.

Sculpture. The art of designing structures whose only function is aesthetic.

Sign. Something material which stands for or signifies something spiritual.

Skerry. A rocky island or reef.

Slash and burn. "A primitive type of agriculture in which fields are cleared from forest by cutting trees, burning them and permitting the ash to wash into the soil. Since the land is not irrigated and, in Europe, is confined to light soils, the fertility lasts only a few years, whereupon those who work the land move onto a new patch of forest. This was the method employed by the first farmers of Europe, the Danubians."[34] This system was also known as swidden.

Stab and drag technique. A technique for decorating pottery in which the tool is employed in a pecking motion on the pot surface and then dragged along to create the design.

Stele. An upright stone slab or pillar used as a monument or grave marker. It is also called stela, plural stelae.

Steatopygia. "An excessive development of the fat on the buttocks especially in females that is common among the Hottentots or some Negro people."[35]

Stimulus diffusion. "Process whereby the idea of a culture trait is communicated to another."[36]

Structure. Something made up of more or less interdependent elements or parts. In this book this word is used to designate architecture and sculpture.

Symbol. Something that stands for or suggests something else by reason of relationship, association, convention, or accidental but not intentional resemblance. "Symbolization arose from the need to give perceptible form to the imperceptible."[37]

Tellurian. Pertaining to the earth.

Theacratic. A social structure organized around the worship of a Goddess, guided by a queen, assisted by a council of women.[38]

Tomba a forno. "An oven-shaped rock-cut tomb which was the predominant type of tomb during the Late Neolithic and the Bronze age in southern and western Italy."[39]

Torba. A cement-like flooring material made from the local Maltese globigerina limestone by crushing, watering and pounding.

Trefoil. Having three cusps in a circle; resembling a threefold leaf.

Trilithon. An arrangement of two megaliths set upright into the ground, with a third placed across the top of both.

Trilobate. Having three lobes.

Triune. Have three aspects.

Tuff. A rock composed of the finer kinds of volcanic detritus usually more or less stratified and in various states of consolidation — also called tufa.

Undressed stones. Rough, unworked stones which have not been modified or shaped by tools.

Unstan ware.   Early Neolithic pottery which appeared around 4000 B.P. in the British Isles; shallow pots with upright decorated collars. The designs consist of ". . . zones of upright or slanting lines, or hatched triangles, or variations of these themes."[40]

Wattle and daub.   A framework of woven rods and twigs covered and plastered with clay and used in building construction.

INTRODUCTION

Malta and the Orkneys and Shetlands, the former a minute and arid island in the Mediterranean and the latter windswept, lightly populated islands lying beyond Scotland's northern shore, may seem a strange focus for a book on the Great Goddess. Surely mainland Europe or Asia Minor or India would offer more in tombs and temples, in traces of the Great Goddess and Her habitations. Names and places associated with the Great Goddess spring to mind. Lascaux and Altamira, Çatal Hüyük and Hacilar, Knossos and New Grange are among them. The art treasures of the French and Spanish caves have been reproduced in fine illustrated books. The Anatolian cities with their remarkable shrine rooms, Knossos in Crete and New Grange in Ireland are major tourist attractions.

The case for an examination of Malta and the Orkneys and Shetlands is twofold. First, Malta has an unmatched range of well preserved and near-complete tombs and temples — yet no single modern work presents all the more recent archaeological and artifactual findings and analyzes them within the context of a *theacratic* society worshipping a female deity. Second, given their number and range of types, the tombs and temples of the Orkneys and Shetlands are far too little known, despite the valuable work of Audrey Henshall, Alexander Calder, Colin Renfrew and other pioneers. Their work has been primarily archaeological; Ms. Henshall, for example, in her unrivalled survey of Scottish prehistoric tombs and structures, has focused primarily on chronology and structural types and forms rather than on analysis of religion and artistic issues.

Henshall, Calder, Renfrew and their colleagues offer a small but meaningful amount of reconstruction of the movements, thought and religious concerns of the population. Though serious students will value the analyses and interpretations of recent archaeological work in the Orkneys and Shetlands and in Malta that these and other specialists offer, much more demands to be done.

This book, however, is for readers with an interest in the Great Goddess and the feminine principle, who want answers to questions about life, death and rebirth, about the concept of deity and the role of religion in ancient society. Nearly a decade of personal fieldwork and research has convinced me that a unique religious vision produced the cohesive and continued force that led Neolithic peoples to devote huge amounts of energy to the construction of enduring and deeply impressive tombs and temples. In Malta that vision strikes the sympathetic student of prehistory with a particular force. Only when the Great Goddess is moved from the margin of prehistory to the center do we recognize a context and an explanatory power that gave rise to the structures that even now, across the centuries, amaze us.

We cannot make the non-stop journey from Malta to the Orkneys and Shetlands without being painfully aware of the vast expanse of Europe that we pass over. Sardinia, Southern Italy, the Mediterranean and Atlantic shores of Spain, the Breton peninsula, Ireland and the Scottish mainland are rich in megalithic tombs and shrines. Here too the literature ranges from the recent and accessible to the specialized and scarce. The Goddess has left her imprint throughout this vast swath of territory. Tombs number in the thousands, and those above ground represent a challenging array of type, construction and alignment. Because illustrations of megalithic tombs and temples, including those of the Orkney and Shetland structures, are scattered throughout many different monographs and specialized publications, I thought it important to illustrate this text in full as few readers have access to research libraries or can make trips to the sites.

We recognize the presence of the Goddess through the myriad of incised symbols on rock faces and on the megaliths used in tomb construction. Without difficulty we can track the Goddess in a comprehensive progress north. To do so captures an undeniable kernel of truth, and at the same time poses many questions. Central among these is that, barring perhaps one or two exceptions, we do not see any single clear-cut evolution of architectural type from the archetypal Maltese temple structure to other sites on the European mainland. Indeed, it would be demanding much to expect this since all forms evolve, and every region and local population puts its own stamp on any basic design. Evolution and change is of course found in symbols incised on rock faces and on megaliths — but here the underlying design is generally more consistent and easily recognized.

The central and most puzzling issue that this book addresses is the re-appearance in the Orkneys, and especially in the Shetlands, of structures that reflect major elements of classic Maltese temple design. This fact is the more puzzling because we do not find a continuing and clearly marked evolution of the form on mainland sites. Why, we may ask, did Neolithic peoples journey so far north and settle on islands presenting at best a harsh environment of little sun, constant wind and long winters? It is difficult to imagine the Orkneys and Shetlands as a trade entrepôt or as producing an exportable excess of foodstuffs. We must question how populations limited in size by available food resources could devote the time and energy required to construct the tombs and build and maintain the temple structures.

Ironically, we can ask the same questions of the Maltese. We have to divorce ourselves from the image of a sun-kissed, fertile island. Malta is composed entirely of limestone. The topsoil is at best scant and of no great fertility. Water resources are minimal and tree cover nil. We have no evidence of Neolithic Maltese industries; the island did not possess such valued resources as obsidian or dyestuffs. Though easily accessible from the Aegean, Sicily, Sardinia, the Italian mainland and the North African littoral, Malta offers no evidence of having been a point at which trade routes met or crossed.

The island-as-sanctuary is a recurrent fact in human history. Islands too small for economic value have frequently become religious sanctuaries. Lindisfarne, Iona and Holy Isle, all off the shores of Great Britain, demonstrate this. Mont St. Michel off the northern coast of France and Delos in Greece are also part of the sacred island tradition. Mount Athos, a peninsula rather than an island, is another example. Malta and the Orkneys and Shetlands are of course much greater in extent and in economic potential than the islets just noted. But they are distant from the mainstream of human movement and commerce. We can surely ask whether they owe their rich archaeological heritage in part to this fact. Were they indeed "islands of sanctuary," remote places where life centered on religion and ritual?

If this is the case, as I believe, then Malta and the Orkneys and Shetlands merit major reassessment. Where religious activity is most concentrated, we might reasonably expect to find it in its purest and most pervasive forms. A sympathetic consideration of the role of the Great Goddess in the life of these island societies can contribute much to our understanding of Neolithic peoples.

To commence this account of the Great Goddess with the tombs and temples in which people celebrated the great recurring cycle of birth, death and rebirth puts the lay readers at a disadvantage, asking them to accept the Goddess at the height of Her power without evidence of the earlier growth of Her religion. Space does not allow for a retelling of the complex and many-faceted story of humankind's earliest images of the Goddess. The most famous "Venus" images — the Willendorf Venus, the Lespugue Venus and the Venus of Laussel — can be found in many reference books and will provide the reader with at least a starting point and a basic reference for personal explorations of the earlier evolution of the Great Goddess.

Marija Gimbutas' recent book, *Civilization of the Goddess*, traces the development of the Goddess religion and culture from the Paleolithic through the Bronze Ages. Riane Eisler, Merlin Stone and others have greatly contributed to the analysis of the change from the early egalitarian Paleolithic and Neolithic societies to the later hierarchical ones. The bibliography lists further accessible works now available that will provide some background to the Goddess and to this book.[1]

BOOK ONE

MALTA: AN ISLAND RICH IN MYSTERY

INTRODUCTION

Much of the quest for the Great Goddess is a search for elusive evidence. When found, it is often fragmentary and always challenging in its possible interpretations. The sculpted figurines found at habitation sites, the painted animals deep within the labyrinthine cave systems, and other findings, albeit often limited and ambiguous, provide clues about the ceremonies, belief systems and daily lives of our Paleolithic forebears. Only later, in the period 6500 B.P. to c. 3000 B.P., with the great wealth of European, African and Middle Eastern figurines,[1] do we have fully convincing evidence of the religion of the Great Goddess and the worship of Her in Her many manifestations during the Neolithic period. Yet tantalizing questions remain as to the types of rituals, the places of worship — for though altars of many sorts have been found, the huts and caves in which they probably stood have most often perished, collapsed or been put to other uses.

There are very few equivalents of Gothic cathedrals or Indian stupas — places in which divinity and faith are palpable — to aid us in our quest. When we look for such centers of worship in Anatolia, in the Aegean or in the well-populated Danubian basin and its hinterlands, we come away with numerous indications of the Great Goddess and many clues as to the role She played in the daily lives of the people of those regions. With the concrete evidence of the megalithic temples of Malta, we will have full and convincing confirmation of Her presence and power.

Even when sites such as Çatal Hüyük and Hacilar provide dramatic tangible evidence of shrines and places of religious observance, much of the story they tell may escape the untrained visitor. But the evidence offered by two small Mediterranean islands — Malta and Gozo — is so dramatic and clear-cut that even the layperson leaves deeply impressed.

To the trained archaeologist, prehistorian or historian of religion, the Maltese temples are of compelling importance in providing evidence of a fully developed religion of the Goddess. Every visitor bears witness to their power and presence. The temples number twenty-four in all, but none stands alone. Five sites have pairings of two temples, two sites have groupings of three, and two sites have complexes of four temples.

Plate 1. Interior View of Xemxija Tombs. Note the carved pillars and apse.
Diameter 6 m, approximately 1.50 m high.

Plate 2. General View of Ta Hagrat North.
Overall dimension 8 m x 6 m, trilithons, 1.5 m high, wall 1 m high.

Plate 3. Shape comparison between Maltese deity figure, temple models, and temples.

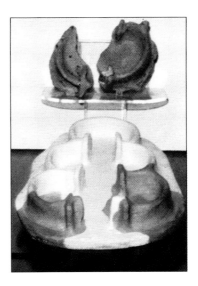

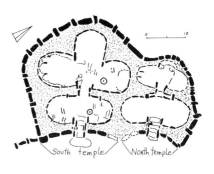

a. Seated deity figure from the Hypogeum seen from the back. The head is missing. Globigerina limestone, approx. 24 c high.

b. Terracotta temple models from Hagar Qim. The white part has been reconstructed. Approx. 28 c high.

c. Plan of Ggantija South and North.

d. Model of Mnajdra temple complex.

Plate 4. Eastern view of Ggantija temple. Facade approximately 53 m wide.

Plate 5. Ggantija South temple, west outside wall. Note the long-short building technique.

Plate 6. Overall view of Ggantija South. Total apse area: 25 x 25 m.

Plate 7. Pubic triangle at Ggantija South, Room 6.
Approximately 1.5 m.

Plate 8. Triple altar in Ggantija South.

Plate 9. Back wall in Room 7, Ggantija South. Wall is 5 m high.

Plate 10. Bar holes in Ggantija South at the entrance of Room 6.

Plate 11. View of Mnajdra Temple site. On the left is the Center temple; on the right, part of the South temple.

Plate 12. Facade of Mnajdra South temple. End orthostats, approximately 3.5 m high.

Plate 13. Entrance to Mnajdra South. View from the outside.
A baetyl can be seen to the left of the orthostat.

CHAPTER ONE

MALTA: GEOGRAPHY, ENVIRONMENT, POPULATION

It is indeed an irony that tiny, out-of-the-way Malta provides the most significant evidence of the Goddess. Here, in Malta and Gozo — its adjoining isle — tomb, temple, and figurine cast powerful light on the religion and worship of the Goddess (FIG. 1).

Malta and Gozo lie some 80 km² due south of Sicily and 335 km northeast of Tunisia. While the thought of Malta as a stepping stone or crossroads springs immediately to mind, careful consideration of Mediterranean geography and early trade routes will confirm that the islands existed almost in limbo. They lay too far north of the African littoral to have been a likely stopping place for coast-hugging shipping; they lay too far west to have participated to any great extent in the seaborne trade of the Aegean and Adriatic. Only Sicily, visible on a clear day, can be considered a natural trading partner. Pantelleria, Malta's source of obsidian during the Neolithic period, lies some 210 km to the west.

But to this unlikely site for a concentration of tombs and temples we must add further elements of unlikelihood. Malta and Gozo are small, dry and rocky. Malta measures no more than 28 km by 13 km and has an area of only 153 sq. km; Gozo is barely one third of this size. The tiny islets of Comino, Cominotto, and Filfla yield less than 3 sq. km among them. With no natural springs, no great abundance of carob and fig trees — certainly no wooded areas offering timber of any size — and poor, stony soil, it is difficult to believe that Malta ever provided the constant abundance of food to support even a modest population. Yet Malta did, during the Neolithic period, before desiccation set in. Renfrew estimates that Malta supported about 11,000 people during the temple-building period (compared with a contemporary population of 340,000), and, based upon the location of the major temples, hypothesizes that the land was divided into six territories of about 2,000 inhabitants each.[3] Despite the lack of actual hard evidence about a hierarchical society and rulers, Renfrew has suggested that these

1. Santa Verna
2. Ggantija
3. Xemxija-Tombs
4. Tal Qadi
5. Bugibba
6. Ta Hagrat (Mgarr)
7. Skorba
8. Zebbug Tombs
9. Hagar Qim
10. Mnajdra
11. Ghar Dalam
12. Borg-in -Nadur
13. Xrobb il-Ghagin
14. Tarxien
15. Hypogeum
16. Korbin

Fig. 1
Map of Malta and Gozo

territories were ruled by chiefs who owed allegiance to a supreme ruler.[4]

Renfrew, if he is correct in his surmise (which I do not accept), is depicting what may well be termed a *theocratic* state — one in which religion played the leading role and in which a large part of the population's work and endeavor went to support it. Though we cannot be sure of the politico-religious system of Neolithic Malta, we have to admit that it promoted a great surge of creative activity. "By a little after 4000 B.C. [the Maltese] were building the rock-cut tombs; then between 3500 B.C. and 3200 B.C. all the 'great' temples were built. Almost all the burials in the tombs associated with the temples are earlier than 3000 B.C. and by 2500 B.C. the whole local civilization was apparently extinct." Such is the summary of events offered by Service and Bradbery.[5] They raise the central question of what happened to the temple-building Maltese; this is a question we shall try to answer in this chapter.

Malta has impressed travelers forcibly. Patrick Brydone, in his *Tour through Malta and Sicily* (1773), commented that: "The industry of the Maltese in cultivating their little island is inconceivable. There is not an inch of ground lost in any part of it; and where there was not soil enough, they have brought over ships and boats loaded with it from Sicily, where there is plenty and to spare. The whole island is full of enclosures and free-stone, which gives the country a very uncouth and very barren aspect; and, in summer, reflects such light and heat, that it is extremely disagreeable and offensive to the eyes."[6] A modern traveler, D. H. Lawrence, also noted the dry heat: "Malta is a strange place — a dry bath-brick island that glares and sets your teeth on edge and is so dry that one expects oneself to begin to crackle."[7] Given these conditions, the dark, cool interiors of the temples must have provided welcome relief in ancient times.

Malta provided an abundance of workable stone; harder, more rugged coralline limestone, and softer, easily worked globigerina limestone. Using these materials of timeless durability, the people of ancient Malta built the monumental tombs and temples that continue to astonish and mystify all who investigate them in search of their innermost meaning. The twenty-four megalithic ("big stone") temples scattered throughout Malta and Gozo bear mute witness to an immense expression of faith that pervaded the population and dominated the life of Malta between 3800 and 2500 B.P. Before exploring the territory in quest of the Goddess, it will be of benefit to draw a basic working map — sketching in chronology, architectural developments and other key facts that will illuminate and assist our explorations of Malta's unrivalled wealth of history and sustained human endeavor.

The chart that follows (FIG. 2) lists only the major temples that most dramatically contribute to the evolution of the unique architectural setting

Suggested Calibrated Dates B.P.	Phase	Tombs	Houses	Temples	Sculpture & Pottery
5200-4500	Ghar Dalam	Collective burial in caves	Huts-*Skorba*		Impressed Ware
4500-4400	Grey Skorba				
4400-4000	Red Skorba			Shrine-*Skorba*	Female figurines in stone & clay
4000-3800	Zebbug	*Zebbug tombs* *Xemxija tombs*			Stylized figures on pot sherds *Zebbug head*
3800-3600	Mgarr	*Hypogeum*			Temple models
3600-3300	Ggantija			Skorba W. *Ta Hagrat S.* *Mnajdra E.* *Ggantija N.* Tarxien Far E. Korbin III E. Korbin III W. Bugibba Santa Verna	*Sleeping Priestess* *Venus of Malta*
3300-3000	Tarxien			Ta Hagrat N. *Hagar Qim* Tarxien S. *Tarxien E.* Mnajdra S. *Mnajdra C.* Skorba E. Bor in-Nadur Xrobb il-Ghagin *Tarxien C.*	Stone & clay figurines Carved phalli in small shrines
2500-1500	Tarxien Cemetery				

Fig. 2
Maltese Chronological Table

Note: Temples whose names are printed in italics are discussed and illustrated in the text.

in which the worship of the Goddess and the forces She symbolized took place. The brief notes on type or style of temple or tomb will be included as our quest focuses on each temple in turn (FIG. 3). The archaeological findings, taken in their totality, are too numerous to allow for comment on every find. Similarly we cannot follow all the possible avenues of inquiry concerning the evolving architecture. The major point of concern is to determine the extent to which the evidence of the tombs and temples and of the artifacts found within them point to the worship of the Goddess.

Basic chronological comparisons are of interest in establishing a context

Class	Sites	Phase
1. Lobed	Korbin III E.	Ggantija (3800-3600) or 3000 B.P.
2. Trefoil	Korbin III W. Mnajdra E. Skorba W.	Ggantija Ggantija Ggantija
3. Five Apse	Ggantija S. Tarxien Far E. Hagar Qim N.	Ggantija Ggantija Tarxien (3300/3000-2500 B.P.)
4. Four Apse	Ggantija N. Tarxien S. Tarxien E. Mnajdra S. Mnajdra C. Skorba E.	Ggantija Early Tarxien Early Tarxien Early Tarxien Tarxien Tarxien
5. Six Apse	Tarxien Center	Tarxien

Fig. 3
Table of Temple Development in Malta

for these awe-inspiring megalithic monuments. Given that the Great Pyramid was built in c. 2757 B.P., Stonehenge c. 2300 B.P., and the palaces of Crete c. 2000 B.P., then the Maltese temples are the oldest free-standing monuments in the world. Dendrochronology and calibrated carbon dating techniques have led prehistorians to revise most temple construction dates back a millennium earlier from traditional dates. As a result, it is clear that the assumption that Maltese building and decorative forms derived from those of Mycenaean Greece or Minoan Crete must be abandoned. Prehistorians now agree that Maltese architecture and decoration sprang from indigenous forms,[8] and probably inspired in some measure by earlier Middle-eastern influences.[9] Indeed, it is more likely that Maltese forms inspired the later classic Cycladic and Minoan forms.

The earliest Maltese almost certainly came from Sicily. We can say this with some confidence. The oldest impressed pottery found in Malta (the Stentinello type) is almost identical with that made and used by the earliest agricultural communities of Sicily.[10] "Once settled in the Maltese islands, the early colonists began to go their own way, and soon were in the process of developing a culture with many special features of its own, and only a general resemblance to those in the areas whence they originally came."[11]

THE MYSTERIES OF CONSTRUCTION TECHNIQUES

What continues to defy easy acceptance is that the Neolithic Maltese had neither copper nor bronze. The fact that the Maltese built their temples and shaped and incised the limestone blocks using the very simplest of flint tools reflects the tremendous power that the religion of the Goddess exercised over an entire people for more than two millennia. Even flints had to be imported, as did obsidian which also provided a hard cutting edge.

CHAPTER TWO

ORIGINS OF TEMPLE ARCHITECTURE:
GHAR DALAM, THE ZEBBUG AND XEMXIJA TOMBS

In the earliest phase described in the chart, the Ghar Dalam phase, the Neolithic Maltese practiced collective burials. The Ghar Dalam (the word Dalam means "cave") was used for both living and sepulchral purposes, with the dead being buried in kidney-bean-shaped tombs carved out of the rock of the cave walls with stone mallets and bone and antler picks.[12]

The oldest examples of round-based pottery were found in the cave, decorated almost casually with rough indentations.

John Evans, who spent many years studying Maltese prehistory, described the site: "The Ghar Dalam (or Dalam Cave) opens in the left bank of the Wied Dalam, a small *wadi*, or dry river bed which is situated in southeast Malta. . . . The cave itself, a long water-worn tunnel, is easily accessible for the first 80 meters or so, after which it narrows and divides itself into various narrow fissures, opening here and there into larger spaces."[13] These extend for at least another 135 meters. Ghar Dalam contains stalactites and stalagmites. Even though researchers have not uncovered any evidence to date that the stalactites and stalagmites of Ghar Dalam played a recognizable role in ritual or ceremony or were the site of offering or sacrifices as in the French Paleolithic caves and the Anatolian Neolithic caves, it is possible that they did. Ghar Dalam has yielded large quantities of animal bones, including those of the dwarf elephant, hippopotamus and red deer, which belong to the Pleistocene period.[14] According to Evans, there is no trustworthy evidence of the presence of human beings in Malta before the Neolithic period.[15]

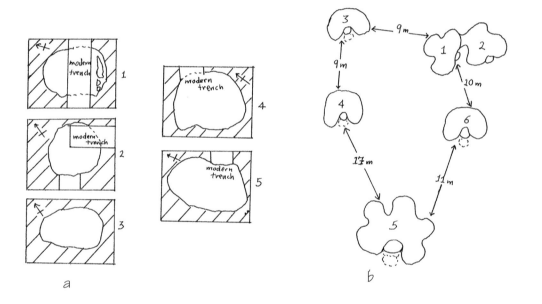

Fig. 4
Plan of the Zebbug and
Xemxija tombs

a) Zebbug tombs (before 4000
B.P.); average dimensions:
3.5 m wide, 1.20 m deep
b) Xemxija tombs

It is interesting to note that the kidney-shaped ("womb-like" or "bean-shaped") contour of the tombs endures throughout the whole of Malta's millennium of intense religious activity. This shape is found in the rock-cut tombs at Zebbug and Xemxija which date from 4000 to 3800 B.P.[16] The five Zebbug tombs (FIG. 4), though partly collapsed and showing signs of later use on top of earlier, provide significant clues about the lives of the early inhabitants of Malta. The tombs are small, about 1.90 m in diameter and 0.6 m in height. They have yielded a variety of pieces of pottery (generally broken), shaped beads and worked flints. Lumps of red ochre and human bones bearing traces of red ochre, symbolizing life and fertility, were also found. Powdered ochre was presumably sprinkled on the bodies at the time of burial. Some of the animal bones that were found probably represent offerings to the deity.[17] Among the grave goods, which included shells and buttons,[18] a small stylized limestone head with a face engraved in low relief was found — the oldest piece of sculpture unearthed in Malta (FIG. 5). It too bore traces of red ochre. Though in its almost flat, minimally finished form the sculpture has affinities with the free-standing menhirs of megalithic Western Europe (Iberia, France and Ireland), its dating is problematic. Prior to the revision of Maltese archaeological chronology, the statue was considered to represent an artistic borrowing from the Western Mediterranean. This borrowing now seems less possible; however, the piece is the only one of its kind in Malta and so far it has proved impossible to provide a supporting context for it.

Fig. 5
Zebbug head (4000 B.P.), height, 18.5 cm

The second group of important early tombs, the Xemxija tombs (FIG. 6), are chronologically later than the Zebbug examples. Located in north-eastern Malta overlooking St. Paul's Bay, they have small, almost unnoticeable entrances cut into the soil and offer nothing dramatic to the passerby's eye. I spent five hours searching for the tombs before I fell into the smallest, thereby discovering all of them. The interiors are rough-hewn, as though scooped out by a giant hand. The tombs are slightly larger than those of the Zebbug group, averaging about 3.5 m in width and about 1.20 m in height. They are generally kidney-shaped with domed ceilings and floors of hard packed clay-like soil of which the top few centimeters were impregnated with red ochre. The six tombs, all within an area of about 200 sq. meters, are womb-like. Given their underground silence and apartness and a size seemingly larger than needed, they hint at something more than simple burial places. Tomb 5 is of particular interest owing to the degree to which its formation prefigures the architecture of the temples. This tomb is over 6 m wide at its broadest point and has a substantial central pillar of unexcavated rock left in to support the roof. Five distinct lobes radiate out, providing an illustration of the basic temple architectural form in embryo (PLATE 1). Tombs 1 and 2 are connected by an underground passage.

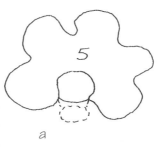
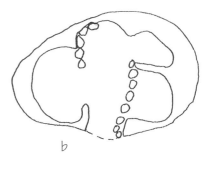

Fig. 6
Xemxija Tomb 5 and Ta Hagrat Temple

9

As was the case with the Zebbug tombs, those at Xemxija provide only a limited amount of specific evidence of religious activity except for the grave goods and large amounts of red ochre found in them and the lobed shape that is reflected in the early Maltese temples. The discovery of skeletons in fetal positions in them suggests that these human-made caves were used primarily as tombs. Certainly they cannot be said to provide irrefutable evidence of the consistent worship of a particular deity or of the Goddess. However, sparse evidence does not mean the lack of religious ceremonies. Much of the importance of the lobed tombs in the quest lies in their prefiguring the temples with their lobed interiors. They are links in a chain — one whose later links provide the strongest evidence of the Great Goddess and of Her religion.

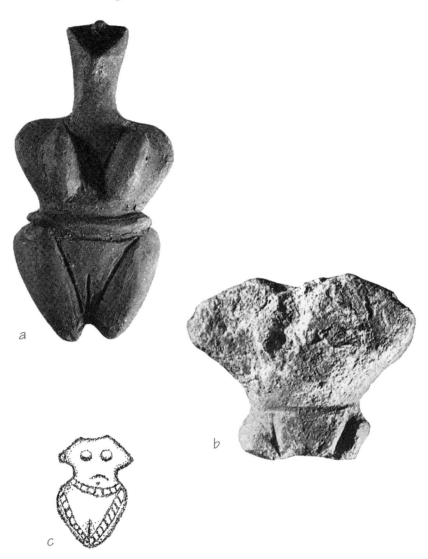

Fig. 7
Figurines from Skorba shrine and from Hacilar

a) Reconstructed figure in plastelline. Original: 4400 B.P., clay, 5.7 cm high
b) Figure in globigerina limestone (4400 B. P.), 8.7 cm high, 9.8 cm wide
c) Clay fiddle figure from Hacilar I (5000 B.P.), 6 cm high

CHAPTER THREE

THE EARLY TEMPLES: SKORBA, MGARR AND GGANTIJA

One of the oldest temples is Skorba. Its importance derives from the sculpture found at the site. The temple itself is too ruined to offer much visual or architectural information to the visitor. The figurines found at the Red Skorba shrine are extremely evocative (FIG. 7). The very fleshy thighs and upper arms of the more complete figurine hint at Paleolithic forms; the tapering neck and highly stylized head look forward to the Cycladic and Danubian figurine types, with the deeply incised vulva reflecting the Paleolithic concern for fertility. Moreover, such characteristics as the cinch belt, the necklace, the static frontal pose, the minimal legs, the long neck, and the emphasis on reproductive and nurturing attributes strongly suggest the figurines function as female deity figures. The small headless stone figurine also has the massive and pronounced fertility characteristics that reflect Paleolithic influences.

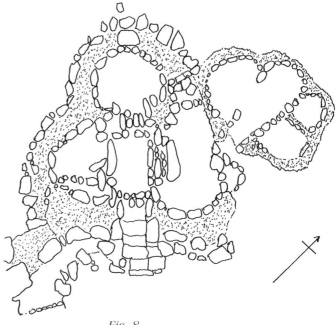

Fig. 8
Plan of Ta Hagrat Temple, Mgarr

a) South Temple (c. 3600 B.P.),
18 m x 15 m, b) North Temple
(c. 3300 B.P.), 8 m x 6 m

An early transition from sepulchral site to true temple is found at Mgarr. Here the paired Ta Hagrat temples are a true, above-ground place of religious ceremony and worship, as opposed to a subterranean place primarily used for interment (FIG. 8). Prehistorians consider the larger temple, trefoil in shape, to belong to the Ggantija ("early") phase; they assign the smaller four-apse temple to the Tarxien ("late") phase (PLATE 2). The temples are of interest primarily in presenting the positive (or constructed) use of the womb-like, bean-shaped or ovoid form of the tombs which were negative (or excavated) in formulation.

Evans believes that the temples were copies of the rock-cut Zebbug and Xemxija tombs and adds that the Hypogeum ("underground chamber") copied the temples since it functioned as both temple and tomb.[19] The trefoil and quatrefoil apse patterns are architectural formulations we will meet in the later temples. Similarly, the crescentic ("horned") forecourt, the floors of large flagstones or torba (a sort of cement of crushed limestone), and the walls made of dressed outer and inner large or megalithic stones with rubble fill between them will be constants. The small model of a temple found at Ta Hagrat (FIG. 9) is of exceptional interest in providing an early "architect's model" of a temple. As the figure shows, the Ta Hagrat temples have another prototypical aspect; they are paired, providing a tenuous link with another attribute of the Great Goddess, that of duality,

11

Fig. 9
Small model of a megalithic temple
from Ta Hagrat, Mgarr.
Globigerina limestone, 4.5 cm long,
3.7 cm wide

whether expressed as a mother-daughter, a goddess-lover, or a double-egg source-of-life feature.

The fact that the tombs were imitations of caves and that the temples were imitations of tombs suggests the close link between the propitiation of the forces with whom the dead would have to contend and the worship of the forces of life. Thus, these earliest structures of the Neolithic Maltese provide evidence, perhaps not as dramatic as that of the later temples, of a substantially compelling context and likelihood of the religion of the Goddess.[20]

As we investigate the temples, a number of constant factors will become strikingly apparent: (1) the size, sophistication and artistic elements of the temples, (2) the consistent placement of altars and the presence of oracular cells and niches containing altars, (3) the presence of libation holes and ritualistic objects such as horns and pendant axe amulets in or near the niches and obsidian knives near the altars,[21] (4) the presence of naturalistic and figurative sculpture, both large and small, (5) animal reliefs and geometric designs on stonework, and (6) the variety of pottery sherds and remains in the temples. All of these suggest a highly evolved religion with a wealth of rituals and ceremonies. Other factors too must be taken into consideration. The large paved forecourts extending from the crescentic facades of the temples and the water cisterns frequently found by the temples suggest that the religious ceremonies of the Neolithic Maltese were large-scale and participatory, probably involving the entire community.

Ugolini, an early investigator of the temples, believes that they functioned not only as spiritual centers but also as social centers, like the cathedrals of medieval Europe.[22] It is of interest and importance that researchers have found no human bones within the temples;[23] this strongly suggests that they were indeed places of worship, not places of interment, even though their configuration reflects the shape of the tombs.

Rachel Levy and Michael Dames are among the historians who have considered this last point forcefully. They read a compelling meaning into the linked architecture of tomb and temple. Levy considers that the shape of the Maltese temple (essentially a uniform lobed structure despite modifications within the basic pattern) resembles a seated Goddess viewed in profile. "Each temple resembles a seated figure, with head at the axial dolmenic shrine, and shoulders and knees formed by the pairs of lateral apses. The enormous, nearly always monolithic, threshold-stone then resembles the base of the statue, and the whole calls to mind the small seated figurines found before the altar of Hagar Qim . . . . It is possible that these edifices were erected as bodies of the gods, their habitation in the Egyptian sense, by which form called up divinity."[24]

Levy's belief that the shape of the Maltese temples was inspired by the seated deity figures establishes a convincing link between the art and architecture of the Neolithic Maltese. However, the early temples (those of the Ggantija phase) predate the appearence of seated goddess figures. As the Neolithic Maltese made terracotta models of temples, they must have been constantly aware of the architectural potential of the form they had adopted. They even may have realized that the configuration resembled their highly stylized seated deity figures. This might have inspired them to stylize their sculptures to echo the temples, rendering them more effective as sacred images (PLATE 3).

Michael Dames adds to this concept: "Entering the Maltese temple . . . would doubtless have meant a return to the Goddess and issuing forth a kind of renewal or rebirth. To sleep within such a goddess shape, as the votaries apparently did at Malta . . . would itself have been a ritual act, an analogy for the actual death which would have implied its own kind of immortality since it meant a return to her."[25]

The duality of the temples has also drawn analytical comment. Mimi Lobell, an architectural historian, suggests that the Great Goddess may be represented symbolically in the pairing of temples, the familiar two temples within the same enclosure, one always larger than the other. "The Goddess is consciously linked with both birth and death, sun and moon, sexuality and intelligence, earth and heaven."[26]

GGANTIJA

Ggantija is the oldest of the major temple complexes and is very well-preserved. It is also the largest and most classically shaped. While traditional in that two temples — a larger and a smaller — share the site and that both have crescentic facades (totalling some 53 m in length) and trefoil aspidal chambers within, the Ggantija site also offers unique features (FIG. 10). The temples occupy a low hill top, one of sufficient height to dominate the surrounding countryside. They face east toward the rising sun. Above all, because of their huge size, their obvious age and their classic shape, they give the visitor a sense of their absolute power and permanency (PLATES 4 & 5).

Ggantija, whose name conjures up the impression of immensity, is located on the small island of Gozo (about 7 km long and 5 wide) and occupies an inland site near the modern village of Xaghra. Gozo and the sea that washes its beaches were known in classical myth as the realm of Calypso,

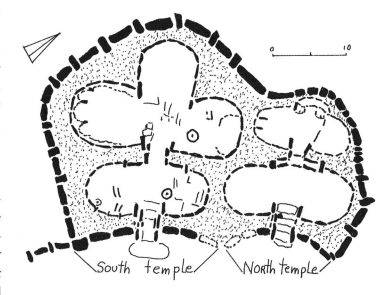

Fig. 10
Plan of Ggantija Temple (3600 B.P.)
South Temple, 30 m x 30 m; North
Temple, 23 m x 23 m

daughter of Oceanus. Homer has told of the seven years' sojourn of Odysseus, and inhabitants of Gozo will point out the cave in which Calypso dwelt. It lies below and close to Ggantija, just above the warm Mediterranean waters. Legend identifies Calypso with the Great Goddess in one of Her manifestations.

Given the sparsity of crop-bearing land, the lack of water, and other limitations that Gozo places on human habitation, one can ask the following question: How came the temples to be? Ggantija's very size makes the question the more intriguing and demanding. Perhaps, as suggested earlier in this chapter, Gozo and Malta were islands of pilgrimage where religious life and practices took absolute primacy over other concerns such as trade and commerce. The building of the temples may have been a decade-long community endeavor, having the same power over the inhabitants as did the cathedral-building drive in early medieval Europe.

Folk-memory in Gozo clings to the belief that a woman, with baby at her breast, was the creator of the temples. Von Cles-Reden tells it thus: "Strengthened by a meal of magic beans, she is said to have taken the huge blocks of stone to the site in a single day, and then to have built the walls by night."[27] Since the chambers of the trefoil within the southern temple each have a long axis of about 10 meters, this creator was a goddess of great power.

In the Ggantija temples, considered to be prime examples of Maltese megalithic architecture, we witness the changes which mark temples of a later period. Although the South Temple is probably older, both temples were built during the Ggantija phase.[28] The North Temple with its niche-like trefoil apse is a good example of the later type of temple which we will see at Mnajdra and other sites.[29] In the South Temple, the central trefoil apse is pronounced as it was in all other early trefoil temples (PLATE 6). However, there are indications ". . . that some building or buildings existed at the [Ggantija] site at an earlier period, since pottery of earlier types was found in some of the trenches."[30] Direct comparison between the southern temple and its northern neighbour reveals a strange reversal of balance. In the northern temple, the central lobe of the trefoil is truncated, shortening the long axis of the temple; in addition, the outer chamber is significantly larger than the opposing two chambers of the trefoil.

Also awe-inspiring is the vast stone outer wall that surrounds the whole complex. As the figure shows, the section of the wall enclosing the southern temple is pentagonal (reflecting the pentagons painted on a chamber wall in the Hypogeum, discussed on page 31), while the section surrounding the northern temple is *ovoid*, and has much the same curvature as the tumuli above many of the megalithic tombs of northwestern Europe. The outside wall consists of rough, undressed coralline limestone blocks; a long-short building technique was used in the construction. This is a use of alternating rectangular blocks set horizontally with blocks set upright. It is aesthetic and adds strength to the wall (see Plate 5).

The early Maltese architects made internal walls and doorways of dressed globigerina slabs. Their deliberate use of different types of limestone for different purposes was a marked feature of later temple architecture. Workers rough-plastered the inside walls to give them a more finished look; the plaster also formed a base for a layer of red ochre.[31] Here again, the immense scale strikes the visitor. Some of the outside blocks measure 4 x 5 m and weigh 50 tons. They are among the largest ever used on the Maltese islands.

The walls of Ggantija show that Maltese masons understood corbelling, but this does not appear to have been carried upward or inward to any great extent. In fact, it is hard to believe that the temple walls could have supported the weight of a corbelled or beehive vault in stone. "At a certain level the temple was probably completed with a flat roof of beams, brushwood and clay."[32] Indeed, the model found in the temple at Mgarr bears out this belief (see Fig. 9), as does the relief carving of a small temple model found at Mnajdra Central (see Fig. 14).

What do we know of the ceremonies and rituals that took place within Ggantija? Though the Ggantija site has yielded less artifactual and contextual evidence than we will find at such sites as Hagar Qim and Tarxien, what has been found is important in establishing or confirming the basic decorative motifs noted in almost all the later temples. The two Ggantija structures have a strongly defined shape; they clearly reflect the female morphology on which Levy and Dames comment. We can indeed say that the temple *was* the Goddess. When we add to this consideration the presence of the yoni, the baetyls (or phallic stones), and the snake relief — all to be discussed hereafter — the underlying connection of the temple to fertility and rebirth becomes very convincing.

The major finds at Ggantija include the impressive snake relief found in Room 6 of the South Temple (FIG. 11). The snake has been looked upon with awe and as a powerful spirit since the Paleolithic age. At Rouffignac in central France, in the recently discovered Dome of Serpents, we come face to face with the hundreds of intertwining, serpentine lines scored repeatedly all over the soft surface.[33] Snakes are a powerful force in the mythology and belief systems of peoples the world over. The Ggantija relief is of great importance in confirming the chthonic and telluric aspects of the Great Goddess. The snake was also a significant avatar of the Great Goddess in Neolithic Europe.

Other finds at Ggantija include the "Pubic Triangle" in the South Temple,

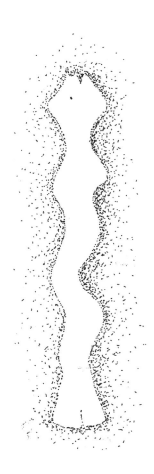

Fig. 11
Snake relief at Ggantija (c. 3600 B.P.). Globigerina limestone; approx. 1.20 m high

to the left of and facing the altar (PLATE 7). This is a large freestanding trapezoidal slab set upright like a pillar, its wider side up. "Pubic triangles" are found in the innermost chambers of most of the Maltese temples. Facing this slab, on the ground on the far side of Room 6, was a square stone that probably served as a pedestal for a second significant stone, the Phallic Stone, now in the Gozo museum. Their presence adds to the emphasis on rebirth and renewed life we associate with the Goddess. Room 2 of the South Temple has spiral decorations. These will be found in more dramatic form at Tarxien, the last of the temples we will examine.

The great triple altar of Room 6 (PLATE 8), the nearby libation holes and the remains of a fireplace in Room 5 speak convincingly of intensive use of the shrine and suggest ceremonies and rituals. When one enters Room 7 with its centrally located altar and its high walls, one truly has the sensation of being enclosed in a sacred structure. The walls of Room 7 are rough boulders interspersed with smaller stones and show slight corbelling toward the top (PLATE 9). From the end of its walls two pillar slabs jut, clearly separating this central apse and signaling its importance. Besides the truly impressive altar of Room 7, other rooms in both the South and the North temples have altars as a main focus. Room 6 of the South Temple, like the rooms of the North Temple, display an important feature, bar holes in the door jambs (PLATE 10). These suggest that at least some ceremonies were held behind locked doors, hinting at the presence of religious specialization. One additional feature should be noted: the presence of pit marks in temple stonework (small circular indentations gouged out at random). They can also be seen to advantage in the threshold slab of Room 4 of the South Temple. We shall see the continuing appearance and evolution of this indigenous Maltese design in other temples.

Today, however, the massively constructed and well-preserved South Temple seems almost stark and bare. Almost nothing remains of the red ochre-washed plaster that once clad and smoothed the inner walls. The somewhat later North Temple has not yielded much additional evidence of design or decoration but confirms that the basic elements of temple design did not change dramatically within the temple-building period. The trilithon doorways, the long-and-short construction technique apparent on the encircling outside walls, the paved temple rooms and forecourt, and the crescentic facade all persist, as does the basic interior layout.

One tantalizing clue remains. Sybille von Cles-Reden noted in her description of Ggantija that, "There is an account by an eighteenth-century antiquary of his discovery and exploration of a labyrinth under the temple."[34] This may prove to be true. There may indeed be a second "Hypogeum" near the Ggantija temples. During the past five years a team of archaeologists has been excavating the Brochtorff Circle. This structure consists of a series of natural caves with numerous interconnecting chambers used for burial purposes.[35]

CHAPTER FOUR

THE LATER TEMPLES: MNAJDRA, HAGAR QIM

The ancient Maltese built Mnajdra on a dramatic site in southeastern Malta, on a promontory that overlooks the ocean. This was the first temple I visited on Malta. The experience was so impressive and memorable for me that I trust the readers of this book will allow me to recount it. It was

dark on the night of my visit; there was no moon and the site was deserted. I had to grope my way along the straight path, a causeway going directly down from Hagar Qim to Mnajdra, using my night vision. As I approached the site, the outline of the temple stood out like a ghostly sculpture against the dark hollow in which it nested. I entered the temple through the portal stones and found myself inside the first double apses of Mnajdra South. The only sounds were the wind, the sea and my breathing. The feeling that this was a sacred place inhabited by some powerful force was absolutely palpable. Without any alcohol or mind-altering drugs in my system, I spent a good deal of time invoking the

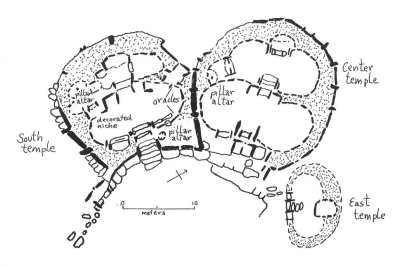

Fig. 12
Plan of Mnajdra temple complex
External measurements: South Temple (c. 3000 B.P.), 17 m x 18 m; Center Temple (c. 3000 B.P.), 20 m x 21 m; East Temple (c. 3600 B.P.), 7 m x 9 m

Goddess and feeling Her presence. This was the most spiritual moment of my first trip to Malta. I am confident that anyone else making a night visit to the Mnajdra site will experience equally powerful feelings.

Mnajdra is a three-temple site on an almost circular forecourt (FIG. 12 and PLATE 11). The two large temples with their shared crescentic facade are shaped like two giant horseshoes. Again there is the sense of supreme fit between site and building, with Mnajdra looking out over the open sea onto the tiny island of Filfla. In fact, Mnajdra South is separated from the sea only by a terrace and a steep slope that plunges down to the water 100 meters below. Although wind and water have somewhat eroded the temple facade, it is still very impressive. The stillness of Ggantija is replaced here by the restless sounds of the sea.

Within the encircling wall, within the temples, we must note significant changes from the archetype. The trefoil has become a cinquefoil as a result of the virtual omission of the 'waist,' the corridor that connected the trefoil to the ovoid chamber just within the temple entrance. As in Ggantija North, the apse at the top of Mnajdra South is truncated, being only a large niche. But what most clearly differentiates Mnajdra from Ggantija and other temples is the reflection of a sort of tension between change and adherence to established forms. Mnajdra South deviates from the formal patterns of a cinquefoil through the addition of a number of mini-chambers and niches. Despite the fact that it is chronologically the newest, the Center Temple adheres to a simple, more traditional form, with far fewer mini-chambers.

The East Temple, much smaller and substantially older than the other two (dating from the Ggantija phase), is a simple trefoil. The masons built, as they did at Ggantija, with undressed coralline stones of various sizes. The East Temple has an unusual triple entrance that is found again in the Center Temple. The small central apse is horseshoe-shaped, cut off from the other two by a line of three slabs and flanked by two pillars that the masons decorated with pit marks.

As the illustrations show, the South Temple is extremely well preserved. Its concave facade faces the east and the rising sun that dramatically bathes the cream-colored stones in a resplendent rosy hue every sunny morning (PLATE 12). The vertical slabs forming the trilithon doorway incline inward, imparting the feeling of massive and timeless strength (PLATE 13). On the north side of the first room are five courses of corbelled walls, curving inward noticeably. Here I felt I was inside a building rather than wandering through its ruins (PLATE 14).

Such features as the trilithon doorways, the orthostats lining the passage-ways, the altars and the torba floor, and the extensive concave forecourt are now familiar and need little commentary. At Mnajdra, the rope holes in the entrance slabs, one near ground level, the other near the top of the slab, merit a mention. They allow a rope to pass through that could ensure the secure tethering of an animal. They could also be receptacles for liquids offered in worship during religious ceremonies to the Goddess in Her underworld aspect. Also noteworthy is the baetyl on the left of the entrance to the South Temple; it replicates the baetyl before the South Temple at Ggantija and may represent the pillar avatar of the Goddess. Two trapezoidal pit-marked free-standing slabs, or "pubic triangles," of substantial proportions flank a pit-marked doorway that leads into the second set of apses (PLATE 15). To the right of one is a low altar also covered by fine, closely spaced pit marks. The vertical slabs forming the trilithon doorway incline inward, as they do in the central doorway. This inclination and the tooled pit marks that cover them give the feeling of *élan vital* combined with tremendous strength. The well-executed and closely spaced pit marks at Mnajdra are particularly impressive in light of the intensity of effort in the gouging process and the regular, balanced appearance of the finished surfaces. We noted this form of stone-marking or engraving in our discussion of Ggantija and will refer to it in greater detail in the description of the Tarxien temple complex.

Of particular interest are the oracle holes in the South Temple (Room 1), giving onto the smaller Rooms 5 and 6. These are spaces outside the basic, organic architecture of the temple. Oracle holes allow a priestess to make pronouncements or to chant in Rooms 5 and 6 from a point out of sight of assembled worshippers, adding to the drama of a ritual or ceremony in the much larger Room 1.

In the Center Temple, a porthole entry (PLATE 16) leads off Room 8 into a small chamber containing a pillar altar; two others are in Rooms 3 and 5 of the South Temple (PLATE 17). This type of altar has its ancestry in the stalagmite altars found in Paleolithic caves, many of which bear signs of having had red ochre painted on them and food sacrifices placed at their base.[36] The decorative use of stalactitic fragments at Tuc d'Audoubert[37] and at the pillar altars found at Jericho, together with a similar example in the Maltese temples, reflects the continuity of this element in the religion of the Great Goddess.

Rooms 5 and 6 of the South Temple and the niche at the left of Room 8 in the Center Temple clearly reflect a growing specialization or ritualization of ceremony at Mnajdra. Just as in a Gothic cathedral where the small side chapels in the apse are devoted to special ceremonies and services, it is logical to assume that the small rooms beyond the main chambers of the temples likewise served special purposes. Incubation, the practice of sleeping within a shrine in order to receive divine communications and healing through dreams, appears to have been among these special purposes. Such practices and the preparation and facilities they required reflect an increasingly developed religion which may have required a group of priestesses with specialized roles. The two priestess figures discussed in the section on the Hypogeum will provide us with an opportunity to explore this topic.

The case for the temple as a place in which the healing power of the Goddess could be invoked is strongly supported by the ex-voto figurines found below the floor of Room 4 of the South Temple. One such figurine (FIG. 13) has large, pendant breasts, a swollen belly, and a deeply incised vulva. Perhaps pregnancy was desired through the agency of this figure. Another figurine found in the Hypogeum appears to be a medical case: the figure, a female with pendulous breasts hanging over a swollen abdomen, has a protruding backbone and ribs and a hollow iliac region.[38]

At Mnajdra we face a situation similar to that noted at Ggantija: though the temples constitute the expected setting for the worship of the Goddess, the artifactual evidence is slight. But the setting, the structure, and the decorative motifs of the temples, including their extensive pit marking, all provide a strong supporting context for the religion of the Great Goddess.

a   b

Fig. 13
Ex-voto clay female figurines

a) clay female figure seen from the back. One arm rests on the head, the other hangs down with the hand pointing to the genitalia. Her abdomen is enlarged and her ribs are clearly marked on the back. Small bits of shell have been stuck in various parts of her body and head. Found at Tarxien, c. 3000 B.P., 7 cm high. b) Clay female figure with large breasts and abdomen and deeply incised vulva. Found under the floor of Mnajdra South, c. 3000 B.P., 5.1 cm high

19

Fig. 14
Small temple model relief (c. 3000 B.P.). Relief carving of small temple model from Mnajdra Central. Globigerina limestone, 24 cm high

However, this lack will be more than remedied at Hagar Qim and Tarxien, both later temples from the Tarxien Period (3000-2500 B.P.). Both of these temple complexes will display now familiar features: oracle holes opening onto small, inner chambers and holes drilled into door jambs suggesting that bars were inserted behind the doors to keep them closed while ceremonies and rituals were performed in secrecy. These facts help confirm our earlier supposition that intense and organized religious activity took place. It is conceivable that valuable or important images were brought from one temple site to another or that smaller images were abandoned or ritually destroyed as larger ones were sculpted.

But a mystery remains. Why should Hagar Qim and Tarxien be so rich in artifactual evidence of the Goddess while the predecessor temples are so sparse? It could be that as they were built later, they were used more, and perhaps they even took over some of the statuary that had belonged to the earlier temples.

The Mnajdra site provides a significant clue about an important architectural concern — how the builders roofed the temples (FIG. 14). In the Center Temple, the builders engraved a model of a temple on an upright in the corridor between the two sets of apses. Trump considers that it depicts a beamed roof covered with brushwood and clay,[39] adding to the accepted belief that the corbelling of temple walls did not continue upward to form a beehive dome. Such domes would have been of immense weight.

I had to politely ask a couple engaged in amorous dalliance on the slab below this engraving to move for a moment so that I could photograph it.

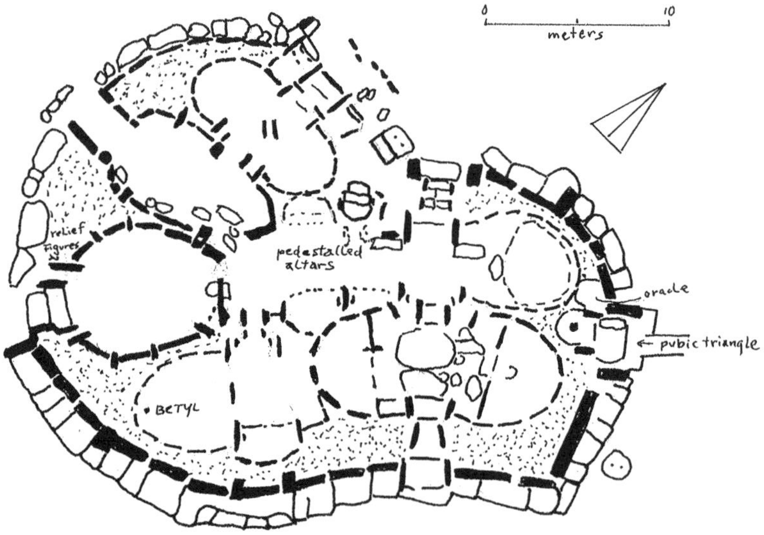

HAGAR QIM

Hagar Qim — the Stone of Prayer — sits on a sloping rock shelf about 200 meters farther inland and a little higher than Mnajdra. From the air, the site resembles the paw print of a gigantic dog (FIG. 15).Visitors who drive along the desolate road from Valletta to the southern coast of Malta will see the immense ruined blocks of Hagar Qim long before they reach the site. The honey-colored tints of the soft globigerina limestone contrast subtly with the greyer tones of the harder, more weather-resistant coralline limestone. Today, much of the upper course stonework has decayed, cracked or collapsed because of the effects of wind and weather. This is strikingly evident in the great stones of the seaward-facing section of the encircling wall.

Fig. 15
Plan of Hagar Qim temple (c. 3000 B.P.). External measurements: 25 m x 30 m

Nothing, however, can prepare the visitor for the central entrance in the main facade facing the southeast (PLATE 18). Here the crescentic facade with its huge squared blocks (2 m high in front and 3.5 m high at the ends) rising from long, well-finished base stones, with trimmed stone courses above, presents a simple and powerful sight. The entrance slabs have notches that helped the builders position and secure the top two courses of horizontally laid blocks. Only the entrance to the south temple at Mnajdra can rival it. While there, the cream-colored facade with its great curving entrance court framed by the sea offers a romantic and impressive sight; here, the emphasis is the simplicity and power of the massive vertical and horizontal slabs framed by the sky.

Looking into the Hagar Qim entrance, one has a clear-through view since the vestigeal cinquefoil has been traversed by another entrance beyond Room 4. As the plan indicates, Hagar Qim has exploded out from a basic cinquefoil plan (Rooms 1-5) and the double-chambers of Rooms 11 and 12, and has expanded with energy, adding entrances and using spaces between the temples for religious purposes.

Taken as a whole, Hagar Qim reflects all the architectural elements and ceremonial arrangements we have noted so far, but in freer, less constrained forms because the accretions seem to have been dictated by need. At the same time, one has the feeling of a complicated spatial arrangement — a maze. It suggests that the religious energies of the Neolithic Maltese had reached some sort of exuberant, bountiful peak and that the costs and labor of creation were not considered a burden. The central corridor beyond the entrance and Room 1 has become an assembly space. The chambers to the left and right (Rooms 2 and 3) have been reduced in size and are entered via portholes. Both porthole slabs leading into these rooms have small bar holes on either side, suggesting the use of some sort of doorway to close off the rooms. Room 5 has an oracle hole (PLATE 19) running obliquely through the slab and opening into Room 16. This is a small room behind the apse wall (Room 15) which can be entered only from the outside of the temple. What is distinctively new at Hagar Qim is a semicircular niche — an *external* shrine — containing two pairs of upright slabs (one of which is pitted) with a trapezoidal stone, a pubic triangle, planted between them (PLATE 20). This stone, which is about knee high and also pitted, could have served as an altar.

Within the main entrance to the temple is a delicately sculptured freestanding altar with carving representing a stylized, symmetrically leaved plant growing out of a pot. Obviously, this is the indication of an active Tree Cult[40] (FIG. 16).

Fig. 16
Pitted altar with plant in flower pot (c. 3000 B.P.). Found at Hagar Qim, globigerina limestone, 73 cm high, 43 cm wide

In what can best be described as an inner courtyard (Room 6) are two more free-standing altars, both mushroom-shaped and sculpted out so that they could contain liquid within the shallow concavity. On the north-west end of Room 6 are two rooms that contain two pitted altars and a stone pillar; a third chamber, adjacent to these, is entered through a porthole. Room 10 contains a niche to the south, entered through a porthole, and a pillar to the west. Rope holes on the corners of the porthole indicate that the niche could have been closed off. The architect designed all these rooms and niches so that they connect with each other in some way.

The free-form, or developmental, aspects of Hagar Qim are powerfully illustrated by Rooms 11, 12 and 13. These have entrances set directly in the encircling wall. In contrast to the Room 6 cluster described above, they do not interconnect nor can anyone enter them from within the temple complex. This formulation hints at specialization, at specific ceremonies for specific groups and suggests at first glance a "separate entrances" policy. All three rooms contain altars. One wall of Room 13 has the worn remains — the feet and part of the legs — of two figures in relief. Room 13 has an oracle hole. Behind it lies a small chamber, almost a secret room. We do not know the specific purpose of this little room; however, a person standing within it would command an extensive view of the main passageway of the temple complex — from Room 13 through Rooms 6, 4, and 5.

Almost in keeping with the complex anomalies of its architecture, Hagar Qim boasts an impressive baetyl, 4.5 m high, which stands in the encircling wall just beyond Room 5. This could represent both the "Pillar Goddess" and the "Phallus Stone." Powerful symbols can have several meanings; multiplicity adds to power (PLATE 21). This wall, like that encircling Mnajdra, was roughly plastered on the inner side with the plaster then painted with red ochre. Fragments of this plaster can be seen in the Archaeological Museum in Valletta.

What makes Hagar Qim unique in the quest of the Great Goddess is the wealth of artifacts and figurines that directly represent or reflect upon the Goddess. As a gallery of images, they are indeed impressive, yet each has a strongly individualistic character. As a starting point to analysis, we can divide the figurines into two categories: nude and clothed. The nude figures share certain characteristics, particularly the massive hips and thighs that have been virtually constant since Paleolithic times although their manifestation and stylization has differed from culture to culture.

CHAPTER FIVE

FIGURINES FROM THE TEMPLES AND THE HYPOGEUM

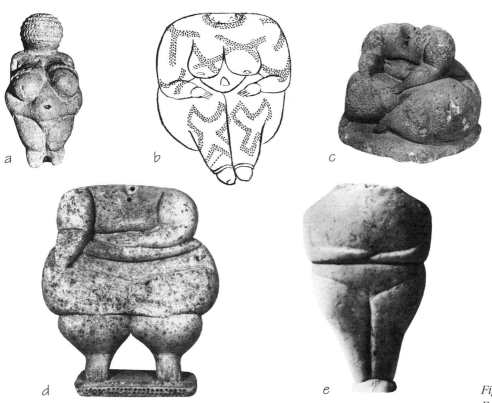

a

b

c

d

e

Fig. 17
Paleolithic and Neolithic figurines

a) "Venus" of Willendorf, Austria, Aurignacian period (c. 32,000 B.P.), limestone, 5 cm
b) Painted clay figure from Çatal Hüyük, Anatolia, 5250 B.P.
c) Seated nude figure from Hagar Qim (c. 3000 B.P.), globigerina limestone, 20 cm
d) Standing nude figure from Hagar Qim (c. 3000 B.P.), globigerina limestone, 38.2 cm
e) Marble figure from Borets, Central Bulgaria, (4000 B.P.), 10 cm

In all, prehistorians have found about 30 Goddess figurines, ranging in size from 20 cm to almost 3 m, in the Hypogeum and in the Late Maltese temples. Some are nude, others clothed; some seated, some standing; some without primary sexual characteristics, but all obese — or, at least, very heavy. They represent the continuation of a philosophical idea given visual form in the Paleolithic Age, as exemplified by the Willendorf and Savignano 'Venuses' (FIG. 17). The Neolithic peoples carried the tradition of this obese Goddess of life, death, and regeneration forward as the figurines from Çatal Hüyük and Hacilar and from the Danubian and southern European sites have shown. The illustrations that follow indicate the extent to which the European Paleolithic and Anatolian Neolithic artistic impulses can be traced in Maltese Great Goddess figurines as well as the extent to which they incorporated unique indigenous qualities.

This array of Hagar Qim figurines is particularly important for several reasons. First, all are found within the narrow confines of one temple complex that is clearly within a consistent religious tradition exemplified by the earlier temples. Second, they are indigenous, and their locational associations are particularly rich. And third, they fall into two primary categories, nude and clothed, though both types are obese. Although a few clothed figures have been found in Siberia, the vast majority of Paleolithic figures are nude. It may be helpful to summarize the major conclusions scholars and historians have drawn about the figurines.

The nude figurines, like the clothed ones, were sculpted from globigerina limestone. They all represented an immensely fat deity— huge torsos, buttocks, thighs, legs and arms — but with tiny hands and feet. They lack sexual characteristics, female or male. Whether standing or seated, the Goddess figurines are sculpted in the stylized poses shown in the illustrations. The seated Goddess figurines average 22 cm in height. They are headless but have hollow sockets between the shoulders for a separate head that could be attached by a dowel. Small holes around the neck indicate that the head could be made to move by means of strings.[41]

The production of heads separately from the figurines for which they were intended also occurred at Hacilar.[42] Here, too, the reason was probably that a separate head, seated in the socket between the shoulders, allowed movement and thus a more impressive and active participation of the Goddess in ceremonies and rituals.

Goddess figures appear in stylized but comfortable positions, seated on what appears to be a large cushion. When standing, the Goddess appears

Fig. 18
Figure from Hagar Qim and temple model from Starčevo

a) Clothed figure from Hagar Qim (c. 3000 B.P.) The figure has a necklace and deep holes (for a head). There are traces of red ochre. Globigerina limestone, 23.5 cm high. b) Reconstructed clay temple model from Porodin, Yugoslavia, Starčevo culture (6000 B.P.), 16 cm

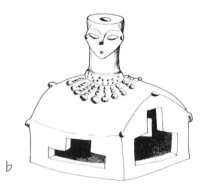

a   b

in a far more formal frontal posture with almost stylized rolls of fat across her torso (on which the breasts are not depicted at all) and with truly immense hips from which almost triangular thighs and calves end in tiny feet. The horizontal line between hip and thigh could almost be taken to indicate that the Goddess was wearing a highly stylized skirt. The pedestal on which the Goddess stands is deeply pit-marked. We shall see a different and more interesting form of pedestal decoration in the Great Goddess statue from Tarxien. Almost certainly the major emphasis and mimetic power of the nude Goddess figurines were directed to fertility and abundance, a theme we will return to in the conclusion to this chapter.

The clothed Goddess figurines are dressed in bell-shaped skirts that reach half-way down the leg. They appear to be seated on stools or low thrones (FIG. 18). Seven of these clothed figures, some complete and some fragmented, have been found in the lower chambers of the Hypogeum and in the sacred inner areas of the temples. They range in height from 23 cm to about 2.75 m. Some display a necklace, or a *décolleté*, reminiscent of earlier deity figures along the Mediterranean littoral. A fragment of a statue found at Tarxien consists of part of a calf and a fringed skirt; the Goddess is seated on a stool, and four small obese nude figurines are represented below Her skirt (FIG. 19). These could be Her acolytes, or they could represent Her power of protection.

The largest of all the Maltese figures is the seated Great Goddess of Tarxien (PLATE 22). The statue is cut off at about knee level leaving massive calves that project below a pleated skirt to end in tiny feet. If not mutilated, the Goddess would have had a height of about 2.75 m. She stands on a pedestal decorated by a relief reminiscent of the "egg and dart" pattern of Classical Greece but more likely represents querns and wheat or barley grains.[43] Considering the importance of agriculture, especially in the limited land area of Malta, the fertility aspect of the Maltese Goddess must have included agriculture. The quern interpretation is of particular interest. The Neolithic Maltese built a seven-compartment quern into the limestone of Kordin Temple and left other free-standing querns on raised bases, suitable for placing before the Goddess. This Tarxien design representing the wheat or barley grain, taken together with the querns, strongly suggests that in addition to Her other attributes "Our Lady of Tarxien" was a goddess of grain and fertility, a precursor of Demeter. Fergusson considers that this grain-related interpretation is completely compatible with the Neolithic Maltese farming community and its concerns. He notes too that the ovoid interpretation is untenable because the "eggs" predate the introduction of the chicken into Malta. However, this does not fully exclude the possibility that the eggs of gulls or some other bird were represented. The larger gulls were apparently as big as the chickens of antiquity.

Here, for the first time, we meet the Great Goddess in a dramatically tangible form in a familiar and expected context. The large, often larger than life-size, sculpture of a deity is central to the historic tradition of religious art and sculpture. We are accustomed to the impressively large Christ figure or the figure of a saint. We are accustomed too to the very large and sometimes colossal Buddha statues. Now, for the first time, we are seeing a larger than life-size statue of a female deity within a shrine, a deity prefigured in miniature for some 20,000 years. That this powerful image should have been created in the tiny and remote island of Malta adds to its power.

Fig. 19
Clothed seated goddess with acolytes, Tarxien (c. 3000 B.P.).
Lower half of a draped figure seated on a stool from Tarxien. Part of one calf and half of the fringed skirt are preserved. Below, on the left side (not seen) are three small figures of the fat type. A fourth (seen) sits below the skirt to the right of the leg.
Globigerina limestone, 20 cm high

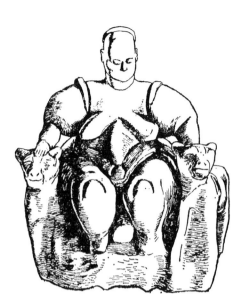

*Fig. 20
Enthroned Goddess from Çatal
Hüyük supported by leopard while
giving birth (6050 B.P.). Clay, 16.5
cm*

That Goddess figurines and statues appear both clothed and nude has attracted scholars' attention. Clothing and adornment clearly reflect rank and status. Nudity has traditionally been associated with magical powers and sanctity. Its use as an erotic or sexual stimulus developed only in much more recent patriarchal times. It is likely that the nude and the clothed figurines represented different numinous aspects of the Goddess. In the case of the clothed Goddess figurines and statues dressed in bell-shaped pleated skirts, wearing necklaces, and seated on a stool, the separate, movable heads might have been operated to nod in command or assent during ceremonies or rituals, thus heightening their impact. These trappings of rank — full or pleated skirts, necklaces and stools — suggest a special numinous quality. We find them in other recognized deity figures around the Mediterranean such as the Enthroned Goddess giving birth and flanked by lions at Çatal Hüyük (FIG. 20).

The nude figures could represent the deity as the Goddess of Vegetation, the ensurer of fertility, fecundity, and generous harvests, Her obesity emphasizing Her opulence. These figurines could have evoked erotic-mystical emotions in both sexes in the Neolithic Maltese society which was unencumbered by later patriarchal sexual codes that objectify and therefore preclude the mystical in the female body.

Some scholars ascribe the significance of the figurines' obesity to the long tradition dating from the Paleolithic period in which many Goddess figurines had exaggerated or "monstrous" proportions. ". . . The 'Monstrous Venus' of prehistory was one manifestation of a long-standing tradition of cosmogonic myth as old . . . as human culture . . . the 'Monstrous Venus' is a religious representation — the reification of the Life Genetrix."[44] It seems feasible that the obesity of the Maltese figures may well have been a measure of their sanctity.

Themistocles Zammit, the dean of Maltese archaeologists, inclines to this opinion, believing that obesity was associated with power, wealth and fertility; that it was related to sanctity and was considered a desirable and beautiful condition.[45] Battaglia suggests that the obese Goddess figures were inspired by living models who were considered special in their societies.[46] But in general, the majority of scholars broadly interpret the obese figurines in keeping with the law of mimetic magic, i.e., to increase the volume of the Goddess is to increase the intensity of the powers which emanate from Her.

Perhaps the clothed figures could represent another aspect of the Goddess which the Neolithic Maltese invoked at different times and for different reasons. The clothed figure could represent the Goddess as queen, sitting properly gowned and adorned on Her earthly throne. Perhaps the clothed Goddess or Her priestesses should be approached and addressed in a devout manner after certain preliminary rituals had been completed, much like the Pythia of Archaic Greece. (The Pythia, or Pythoness, of Delphi was the oracle of the Goddess at Delphi, Greece's oldest, most famous oracle, " . . . where Mother Earth was worshipped under the name of Delphyne, the Womb of Creation, along with her serpent-son and consort Python. . . Eventually the patriarchal god Apollo took it over, retaining the Pythoness, but claiming to have placed the Serpent in his underground uterine cave, whence came the oracle's inspiration").[47]

Gertrude Levy's belief that the seated Goddess inspired the shape of the temples (or, given the dating of temples and figures, the contrary opinion that the figures derived their shapes from the temples) remains of great interest. The temple *was* the deity in ancient religion, just as today the cruciform church is far more than a mere structure — the shape reflects the body of Christ on the cross and the cupola represents the vault of heaven.

In an earlier published work I noted, "Even though Levy's theory is valuable because it establishes a link between Maltese sculptures and architecture, I believe that the sculptor was inspired by the architect and not the other way around. There is a strong and undeniable affinity between the shape of seated Goddess figures and the shape of the temples. This becomes apparent when one compares the temple shape with the little clay temple model and then compares it with the Goddess figure, especially as seen from the back. Because Maltese sculptors could see the contour of the models at one glance, they may have realized that the shape of temples resembled seated deity figures. This may have inspired them to stylize their sculptures so that they echoed the temples, rendering them more effective as sacred images."[48]

The Goddess figurines' lack of primary sexual characteristics has elicited diverging opinions concerning their sexuality. Some scholars have said that they represent males,[49] others have even suggested that they might be eunuchs.[50] After lengthy examination of the figures, I believe that they appear more female than male. Their ambiguous sexlessness might be due to extreme stylization and to a change in ideology. "The lack of sexual characteristics might represent the result of a process of evolution from figures whose power as sacred images lay in well-defined sexual characteristics, to figures whose power lay in their opulence. The sex of the figures may have been deliberately left out to concentrate on the most important thing — the fatness and therefore the opulence and sanctity of the figures. The lack of sexual delineation in the late figures might also be interpreted as a recognition of the similarities between the sexes, as in medieval angels, whose sexuality was not apparent. But because they are the product of Maltese religion, which was female-oriented, these nude figures were more female than male. The medieval angel, on the other hand, is assumed to be male, because he is the product of the patriarchal Christian religion. The Maltese figures seem to embody cosmic power and overflowing fullness on a superhuman scale which is beyond dualism, beyond sex."[51]

One additional figurine, the "Venus of Malta," requires mention (FIG. 21). Its distinctive beauty of line and form and the absence of the characteristic stylized obesity suggest that the figurine was probably an ex-voto, quite possibly modelled from life. The left hand is folded across the torso below the large breasts and rests upon the abdomen, perhaps indicating a concern for pregnancy; the right hand rests on the upper thigh. This positioning allows for interpretation as a goddess posture, and the full bosom has a hint of the old Paleolithic tradition. Perhaps "Venus" is an image of a real person, or a "fetish" figure designed to ensure fertility for a particular individual. The body of the "Venus" bears traces of red ochre; this may certainly reflect special importance or even indicate deity.

A small number of Maltese figurines do not fall within the characterization and interpretation offered above. Chief among them are the "Red Skorba" figurines. These fiddle-shaped figurines reflect a southeastern European tradition; some of those from Hacilar have the same quality (see Fig. 7). They were created during the early period of colonization, before the religion of the Neolithic Maltese took on its own special characteristics.

Fig. 21
"Venus" of Malta. The figure was found at Hagar Qim and is from the Tarxien period (3000-2500 B.P.). Clay with traces of red ochre, 12.9 cm high, 6.5 cm wide

The remaining figure that has attracted much interpretive comment is the Sleeping Priestess, found in the Hypogeum (FIG. 22). The Sleeping Priestess is not the Goddess; she is a priestess engaged in dream incubation. This process allows her, in her sleep, to accept instructions, information, or messages from the Goddess. As a result of this activity, she is able to make oracular utterances, interpret dreams and omens, or provide advice on cures and healing for the sick.

Fig. 22
Sleeping Priestess of Malta (c. 3000 B.P.). She is sleeping on a bed, is naked to the waist and has a fringed skirt. Found in the Hypogeum. Brown clay with traces of red ochre. 12 cm long

CHAPTER SIX

THE HYPOGEUM: TEMPLE-TOMB

The Hypogeum at Hal Saflieni, one of the most remarkable sites of sculptural architecture anywhere, is an underground catacomb-like structure that seems to have been both temple and collective tomb. Encompassing some 600 sq. m and extending downwards for 10.6 m, the Hypogeum consists of three levels of subterranean chambers hewn out of soft globigerina limestone (FIG. 23). The three levels, excavated throughout the period 3800 B.P. to c. 2500 B.P., are remarkable for the extent to which they reflect the architectural developments and advances in above-ground temple architecture. In fact, we can confidently say that every architectural feature, every design motif, and almost all the sculptured art of the temples we have described have analogs in the Hypogeum and the artifacts it has yielded. Each level requires careful examination. All are rich in artifacts, design elements, and reflections of the religion of the Great Goddess.

The visitor enters through a modern trilithon doorway, passes through to the back of a small museum, and takes a spiral staircase directly to the middle level of the Hypogeum. At the bottom of the stairs, a passageway to the right leads to the upper level (the oldest), a series of irregularly shaped rooms very much like the rough-hewn lobed configurations of the Zebbug and Xemxija tombs (PLATE 23). The original trilithon entranceway to the Hypogeum northeast of these chambers, which may have been in part natural caves extended through excavation, probably suffered its final damage early in this century when houses and a street were being built in Pawla. The modern town exists above and around the Hypogeum.

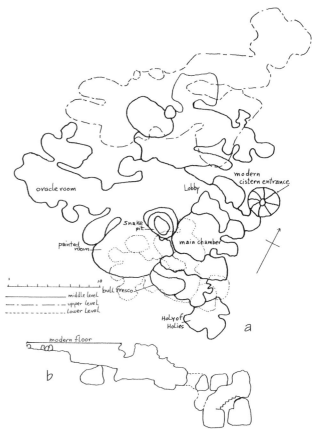

Fig. 23
Plan and cross section of the Hypogeum (3800-2500 B.P.):

a) Plan of the Hypogeum
b) Cross section of the Hypogeum

Sybille von Cles-Reden described them as "crudely hewn upper chambers, round which the burial cells peer at one like empty eye sockets. . ."[52] She also notes that "The Hypogeum consists entirely of curved lines, concave surfaces and rounded vaults. In the flickering light of little oil or grease lamps — there is no sign that torches were ever used — these caverns must have suggested the protective darkness of the maternal womb in which the dead were laid out like seeds to be regenerated and made fertile again."[53]

A passageway leads down to the middle or "temple" level of the Hypogeum, famous for its dramatic and finely finished excavated chambers. Carved concave walls give the impression of masonry built in the typical upright-and-lintel style Maltese builders used in constructing the temples. Several of these halls merit brief description because of their outstanding constructional or decorative features and because they furnish links in our quest. Many of these carefully carved rooms show a high level of finish, and traces of red ochre still adhere to walls and ceilings. Some of the ceilings are of special interest as they bear the remains of several types of spiral decoration.

The biggest of the subterranean chambers — the Main Hall — is roughly circular (PLATE 24). This chamber with its concave walls most strongly gives the impression of the typical upright-and-lintel megalithic masonry pattern found in the temples. High on one wall is an area of black-and-white checkerboard work, a pattern that has also been found on a pottery sherd from the Xemxija tombs and on some pottery vessels from southern France.[54] In describing the spirals, von Cles-Reden comments: " The Great Goddess of the primitive Mediterranean world left her mark here,"[55] suggesting that western Mediterranean influences reached Malta in the earliest period of its settlement, between 5000 and 4000 B.P.

From the Main Hall one descends into two smaller chambers where the two little statuettes of the sleeping priestesses were found. The posture of both these figurines suggests that *incubatio*— sleeping within a sacred shrine in order to receive dream messages from the deity — was among the rituals practiced by worshippers of the Great Goddess. The underlying religious considerations the Sleeping Priestesses give rise to have been poetically expressed: "Are (the sleeping women) . . . seeking omens or dreams, or cures from illnesses by sleeping in a holy place? Are they worshippers, priestesses or the goddess herself? . . . What is implied is that the divinity is the same as that of the built temples, but that this divinity is here, quite naturally below ground, more concerned with death than fertility."[56] Though we cannot prove our supposition about the purpose of the Sleeping Priestess figurines, their location within the temple level of the Hypogeum (and the pleated skirt similar to those of clothed Goddess figurines) confirms at least a religious intention and thus reflects on the power of the Goddess.

Also from the Main Hall, the visitor descends through a roughly carved room into the rectangular Oracle Room (PLATE 25). On the ceiling of this chamber are four stylized trees bearing red balls on their branches. These may be the pomegranates that symbolize the Goddess as a goddess of death (PLATE 26). On the right as one enters are two oval niches (about 1 m high, 0.5 m wide and deep), one called the Oracle Hole. A deep voice projected through this niche will reverberate throughout the entire Hypogeum. This effect is produced by the voice bouncing back from inside the Oracle Hole to a ceiling-high groove with a projecting ledge below it on the adjacent right wall. The groove becomes wider on the right side of the wall, an inverse funnel effect. This is presumed to cause the amplification and distribution of the sound. One must marvel at the Neolithic Maltese for this dramatic device, both as a triumph of acoustics and of the management of people and ceremonies.

"Tour guides to the Hypogeum always stress the fact that only a deep male voice is effective in the Oracle Hole. This seems to imply that the male must have assumed a certain exclusive importance in Maltese religious ceremonies — perhaps as the intermediary voice of the Goddess. Does this mean that the Goddess suddenly made use of a male voice to transmit Her utterings? We can assume that in a female-identified society such as Malta the male became included in this way — that the Goddess could choose to speak also in a male voice as well as in the female voice of Her priestesses, just as She also contained male elements such as the phallus in Her gynandrous repertoire of attributes . . .The significance of the Oracle Hole needs further exploration. . .That it has only been used effectively by a deep male voice may have a number of explanations including the fact that no trained female voices have sufficiently tested the acoustical properties of the Oracle Hole. It would be interesting to test the voice of a Bormliza[57] — a specialized Maltese female singer of ancient tradition with a wide range and a very loud voice"[58] (FIG. 24).

Another small circular chamber near the Oracle Room is noteworthy for its finely finished, inwardly sloping walls and its paintings. Both walls and ceiling are painted, the ceiling bearing spiral patterns loosely interwoven with a honeycomb pattern (PLATE 27). High on one of the walls, the spiral pattern appears within a pentagon. All are painted in red ochre. This may be a stylized rendering of seed within the egg,[59] a symbol of rebirth emphasizing a basic aspect of the Great Goddess. In this chamber is an opening into a 3 meter-deep pit with sloping walls and a sloping shelf around it, probably used to keep snakes or to collect alms.[60]

From this chamber one enters the Holy of Holies that commands every visitor's awed attention (PLATE 28). Upon entering, the visitor has a sense of monumentality, but also a feeling of intimate enclosure. The massive carved facade exactly reproduces the features of the above-ground temples, including the standard entrance of a porthole slab under a center lintel supported by four pillars. These are framed by an even larger trilithon above which is a course of corbelled stone-work — all carved from the enveloping rock. The ceiling is domed but with concentric setbacks imitating the corbelling of the outer part of temple roof. No single illustration can capture the full effects of the brilliant use of concave lines, the sense of strength and balance the carved uprights and lintels give, or the bold curvature of the ceiling. Studying the various features, one is aware of a rhythm stemming from the combination of concave and convex curves. The vertical pillars framing the hollow niches intersect the horizontal corbelling as it moves in a dynamic curve from floor to ceiling. The Holy of Holies is indeed a sacred place. It continues to project its mystery silently down the ages.

Fig. 24
A Maltese Priestess. Reconstructed by the author, clay, 60 cm high.

A pillar on the right side of the room slants inward following the curvature of the wall with three deep circular holes — probably for the hinges of doors that once controlled access to the Holy of Holies. Near the pillar is the very faint painting of a bull, outlined in black pigment. Soot can still be seen on some of the pillars near the Holy of Holies. On the ground in front of the porthole doorway are two interconnecting holes, about 20 cm apart (PLATE 29), libation holes, or tethering holes for animals. It is of interest that the builders left the internal walls of the Holy of Holies somewhat less finished than the great external facade as though to retain the sense of its possible origins as a sacred subterranean cavern.[61]

The room adjacent to the Holy of Holies to which the porthole leads is a small, roughly carved chamber. There are hinge holes on the inside doorway, suggesting that the door could be closed and made fast from within, possibly because the chamber was used for very special rites for the initiated.[62] Also adjacent to the Holy of Holies lies a chamber of the traditional kidney shape. It appears to have been both burial place and shrine — with the latter purpose leading to enlargement of the chamber. The altar niche is clearly apparent, and the floor close by has a hollow that suggests the positioning of some sacred object.[63]

From the Holy of Holies, seven steps lead to the lower level of the Hypogeum. This contains a series of rooms of various sizes, some of which were tombs. They tend to be narrow and high with pilasters jutting from the walls at various intervals, creating a segmented feeling. Though this level is about 10.6 m below ground level, the air is fresh and clean, as it is throughout the Hypogeum. This 10-meter height, curiously enough, is that to which the great temples rose above ground.

On my initial visit, I experienced overwhelming feelings of awe and reverence which delayed my plans to study the Hypogeum's structure. However, once embarked on my study, I noticed that the structure did not represent one building effort in time, but was the product of many generations of continued building. Moving from chamber to chamber through the various levels, I became aware of an evolution of style from simple to complex. The surface of the Hypogeum ranges from roughly carved to a finely tooled finish. This combination of simple and complex strengthens the feeling of progression, of the passage of time. Thus the upper level with its roughly hewn walls seems to be the oldest. Most of the middle level shows an advance in technique and planning. Then the Holy of Holies, as integrated and technically sophisticated a construction as any of the Maltese temples, forms the final stage of this evolution.

Archaeologists estimate that the excavation of the Hypogeum must have taken the Neolithic Maltese some hundreds of years, and that, all in all, the Hypogeum was in use for perhaps a millennium.[64] The bones of about 7,000 persons were found within the catacomb areas, causing much comment among prehistorians. Some suggest the bones are those of the priestly elite and were buried in the Hypogeum over a long period of time.[65] Others believe that at some late stage in the Maltese Neolithic period mass reinterments occurred, with bones being brought to the Hypogeum from other sites.[66] Though the number is impressive as a total at one time and in one place, when averaged out, it represents 70 burials per year. Over a span of 1000 years, this represents one burial every 19 days out of an assumed population of 11,000. A convincing final answer to this mystery would tell us much about Maltese life, particularly about the inhabitants' religious and political life and their thoughts and practices.

As the Hypogeum reaches both back into the era of the earliest tombs and forward to that of the later temples, the artifacts and other evidence it yields in support of the worship of the Great Goddess are of special interest. All the physical aspects of the tombs and temples we have discussed — hewn chambers, internal pillars, altar niches, libation holes and other manifestations — though compelling evidence, are mute. They do provide the environment and context against which the figurines and images must be considered. As an introduction to the evidence the Hypogeum yields, it will be helpful to recollect briefly the record to date.

We noted that the earliest caves — those of Ghar Dalam — were generally womb-like in configuration. Moreover, they served as collective burial places and places of worship. The earliest tomb-chambers excavated by the Neolithic Maltese — the Zebbug tombs and the contemporaneous Xemxija tombs —reflect the Ghar Dalam caves in general configuration. The Zebbug tombs contained animal bones and grave goods, including shells and pearls[67] and, more important, the anomalous menhir statue. The Xemxija tombs were more fully a necropolis, with porthole entry, kidney-shaped tombs and double chambers. Already death had acquired its own power and demanded ceremonial and ritual usages. The most immediate interpretation this fact suggests is that death was not final and that the dead had a continued importance, even a future existence, that demanded recognition by the living.

In the Hypogeum, all the evidentiary traces of the earlier tombs are manifested in fully fledged forms in the uppermost and lowest levels: we see again the lobed caves, the supporting pillars. The Hypogeum's unique architectural and topographical sequence of tombs-temples-tombs reattests to the concern with an afterlife or future rebirth and the need for propitiatory or facilitating ritual and ceremony to ensure that these states come about. The red ochre traces on many walls and ceiling areas; the crescentic forecourt to the Holy of Holies with its hint of the spread of the bull's horns; the tree painted in red on the ceiling of the Oracle Room, with red fruits that might be pomegranates symbolizing death and rebirth (or which might be some other life-giving fruit unknown to the historians of ancient art and religion); the painting of the bull in the holiest part of the temple are all evidence of established religion and organized ritual.

Yet the shrines on the middle level speak to the outside world. The carefully sculptured upright-and-lintel facades of the Great Hall and the Holy of Holies both prefigure and reflect the megalithic construction of the great temples at Ggantija, Mnajdra, Hagar Qim and Tarxien. Similarly, their corbeled roofs and, in the case of the Holy of Holies, the distinctive facade with its crescentic curve, reflect the great above-ground temples.

As we will note, other features such as the trilithon entrances to the great temples and the use of cut-through-the-rock porthole doorways also reflect features found in the middle-level chambers of the Hypogeum. What is surprising is not that the architects so consistently maintained their key architectural motifs but that they so fully and powerfully expressed the connection between life above ground (life) and life below ground (death and rebirth).

RITUAL FEATURES AND ARTIFACTS IN THE HYPOGEUM

Pillars found throughout the Hypogeum are ancient inanimate embodiments of the Goddess. Their analogs have been found in Jericho, in Ghar Dalam, in Căscioarele (Yugoslavia), in Mesopotamia and in Crete, to name only a few sites. The libation holes found in front of the Holy of Holies (see Plate 29) are another not fully explained indicator of ritual. Archaeologists cannot be sure that these shallow holes, only 20 cm apart and connected underneath the floor by a small tunnel, were used for the ceremonial placement of food or liquids. In the latter case, water, wine or some other liquid poured into one hole would naturally rise to an equal level in the other. An alternative use might have been to provide a strong anchorage for a rope used to tether a sacrificial animal for a ceremony that combined worship with supplication for continued fertility.

 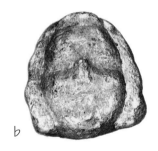

a   b

Fig. 25
Figure and limestone head from the Hypogeum (c. 3000 B.P.)

a) Headless globigerina limestone figure. Part of a head hole is found in the back, 38.9 cm
b) Globigerina head with traces of red pigment, 10.9 cm high

As the excavation of the Hypogeum took many years, we can expect artifacts from a number of different periods. Brief mention should be made of major finds. These include a number of important items of sculpture in addition to the "Sleeping Priestess" already described. Three standing figurines of the nude Goddess, one with the small, very lightly finished head intact, and two headless ones have been found. All three figurines display the characteristic obesity and lack of clearly defined breasts or vulvas noted in the description of the Hagar Qim figurine. Particularly interesting as clues to the depiction of the Great Goddess are two small detached heads, both carved from limestone (FIG. 25). These heads are small in proportion to the bodies to which they would have been attached. This can be seen by examining the proportions of the standing Goddess whose head is present.

Plate 14. Entrance to Mnajdra South Oracle chamber from
Room 1. Walls approx. 5 m high; vertical slabs 1.60 m to 2 m;
horizontal blocks 1.20 m to 3 m; door 1 m x .50 m;
oracle hole 15 c x 25 c.

Plate 15. Pit marked altar and pubic triangle in Room 1, Mnajdra South. Approx. 1.60 m.

Plate 16. Mnajdra Center temple entrance seen from Room 7.

Plate 17. Porthole doorway leading to pillar altar from Room 8, Mnajdra Center temple. Opening 1 m x .60 m.

Plate 18. Main facade and entrance into Hagar Qim, facing southeast. I stand at the left of the doorway. End slab on left 3.5 m high. Note the notch on the end stone on the left which holds the second course of horizontals in place.

Plate 19. Oracle hole in Room 5 at Hagar Qim. Hole is 36 c from the ground and approx. 16 c in diameter.

Plate 20. Pubic Triangle niche at Hagar Qim. East exterior of temple is 82 cm high.

Plate 21. Large baetyl in outside southeast wall of Hagar Qim. Slabs are from 2.5 m to 5 m in height.

Plate 22. Seated great goddess from Tarxien West and wheat and barley frieze.

a) Globigerina limestone. Fragment is 1 m high.

b) Low relief depicting wheat and barley motif from the base of the seated Goddess. Globigerina limestone, 1.30 m long, 16.5 c high.

Plate 23. Upper level of the Hypogeum. This is 3 m below ground.

Plate 24. Main Hall, north, Hypogeum. Middle level; the room is approximately 6 m wide and is 5.5 m below ground level.

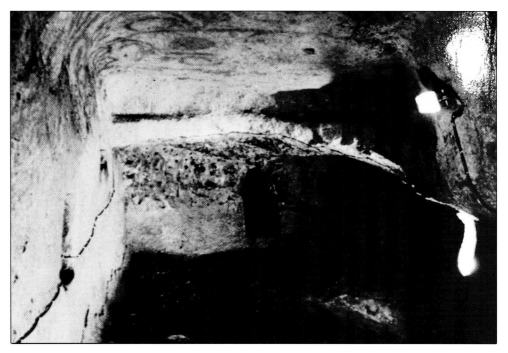

Plate 25. Oracle Room, middle level, Hypogeum. Note the Oracle hole on the left.
Oracle hole is 60 cm high, 44 cm wide, 44 cm deep.

Plate 26. Detail of ceiling of Oracle Room. Note the stylized trees and fruits in red ochre.

Though the two heads differ markedly, they share several basic features. Both are oval, with the hair close to the head, the eyes small and set horizontally, the noses wide and showing a definite ridge, the mouths small but the lips full, and the chin only slightly indicated.

ANIMAL AVATARS AND GRAVE GOODS

The Goddess is also reflected through other images in the Hypogeum, though these animal representations are not sculpted in the round but are images on pottery. Images of the bull, which in Çatal Hüyük is a primary avatar of the Goddess, seem to follow suit here. They occur in the Hypogeum in black outline paintings on the ceiling of the Bull Fresco Chamber. They also occur on a terracotta plate in an incised pattern in which both red ochre and white pigment have been used to highlight the design. This same "bucrania" theme occurs in a striking abstract design on a bowl cover from the Hypogeum (FIG. 26). The curving of the bulls' horns calls to mind both the shrine rooms of Çatal Hüyük and the facades of temples such as Ggantija and Mnajdra.

Grave goods found in burial chambers are among the other important artifactual discoveries made within the Hypogeum. These include many bird pendants made from shell or stone, aerial embodiments of the Goddess (FIG. 27a). They were probably placed on the dead as protective amulets. The bird image dates far back into the Upper Paleolithic age and became very common in the Danubian and Balkan regions in the Neolithic period.

a

b

Fig. 26
Bucrania images: bowl cover and priestess covered with a pelt (both c. 3000 B.P.)

a) Bowl cover from the Hypogeum covered with rectilinear and curvilinear designs executed in fairly broad and deep incisions. The spaces in between are filled with rows of oval jabs, all of which are filled with white pigment. Diameter 15 cm
b) Incised pottery sherd depicting a priestess found at Tarxien. Clay, 4.5 x 5 cm

The pendants provide one more link between the Goddess in Malta and Her earlier manifestations during the Paleolithic period. Other pendants are in stylized "fiddle figure" form (FIG. 27b). They prefigure the Cycladic type that became common throughout much of the eastern Mediterranean in the third millennium B.P. (FIG. 27c). Just as these seem forward looking in time, a double-bead pendant found in the Hypogeum (FIG. 27e) appears to

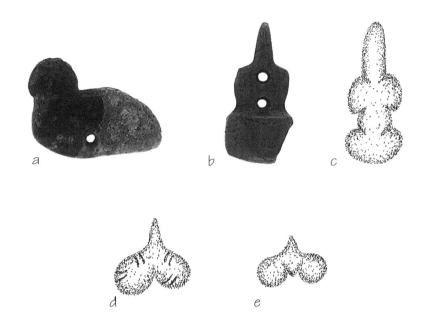

Fig. 27
Pendants and figurines

a) Bird pendant from the Hypogeum carved from hard green stone (c. 3000 B.P.). A hole has been drilled at the bottom. 1.7 cm high, 2.2 cm long
b) Stylized figure pendant from the Hypogeum (c. 3000 B.P.), bone, 3.8 cm
c) Early Cycladic marble figurine from the 3rd millennium, 20 cm high
d) Ivory bead from Dolní Věstonice, Upper Paleolithic (28,000-22,000 B.P.), 2 cm wide
e) Double bead of dark green stone from the Hypogeum (c. 3000 B.P.), 1.6 cm wide

capture the essential form of the ivory breast bead from Dolní Věstonice, which dates from the Upper Paleolithic, c. 30,000-22,000 B.P. (FIG. 27d).

Snake pits are another curious discovery in the Hypogeum. Just as the libations holes did, the snake pits pose problems of explanation. The snakes may have been kept in their shadowy underworld home as symbolic representations of the Goddess' chthonic aspects or may have been used to provide a venom capable of inducing a hallucinatory state that added to ceremony or ritual worship.[68]

Images of fish have been found in the Hypogeum. In one instance, the fish is modelled in clay and is lying flat on a bed, recalling the posture of the Sleeping Priestess figurines (FIG. 28). Perhaps the interpretation is that the fish constituted part of the offerings made at the altars and, as such, symbolized the Goddess in Her aquatic state.

Such, then, is the deeply impressive and powerfully moving subterranean world of the Hypogeum. Tomb and temple; womb and grave; place of rituals held in the very depths of earth. Surely no more numinous seat of religion could be conceived by the worshippers of the Great Goddess. The Hypogeum remains a compelling world apart, removed from the burnt surface soil and brilliant skies of Malta.

Fig. 28
Clay fish on a bed, Hypogeum (c. 3000 B.P.), 8 cm long, 5.5 cm wide

CHAPTER SEVEN

TARXIEN: THE TRIUMPH OF THE TEMPLE BUILDERS

The Tarxien temple complex, with its unrivalled wealth of architectural, design and artifactual remains, provides a fitting close to our investigation of temples (FIG. 29). The complex lies on the northeastern shoulder of Malta, close to the Hypogeum. The site, enclosed by a modern wall, is in

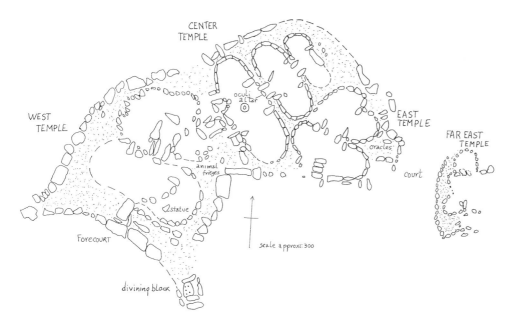

Fig. 29
Plan of Tarxien temple complex (c. 3000-2500 B.P.). External measurements: West Temple, 26 m x 27 m; Central, 23 m x 18 m; East, 19 m x 15 m; and Far East, 13 m x 10 m

the center of the modern village of Pawla. The visitor enters the site through the custodian's house where a small collection of artifacts is on display. Three of the structures within the four-temple group are from the Tarxien Period, having been built between 3300 and 2500 B.P., and one is from the Ggantija Period, 3600-3300 B.P. Tarxien is the most elaborate group of megalithic remains on Malta. Architecture and sculptural reliefs reach their finest flowering. Historically, it seems that the greatest flowering of a faith or form, and its most varied range of expression occur on the eve of its decline. The two and a half acre Tarxien temple site bears this out.

The Tarxien temples were not known about until 1913. "In that year Themistocles Zammit, who was then completing work at the Hal Saflieni Hypogeum, was approached by the tenant of a Government field in the same district, Lorenzo Despott, who said that he struck large blocks of stone whenever he dug deeper than usual."[69] As a result, Zammit started to dig, completing the work only in 1919 because of the delays occasioned by World War I. The temples had been covered by soil for centuries. They have not attracted plunderers and are in a good state of preservation. The foundation courses of most walls are intact and in some areas several courses are preserved, showing the expected corbelling. The Tarxien temples are amazingly rich in very high-quality altar stones, reliefs and design elements. In fact, all the design motifs we have encountered earlier achieve their finest forms. They are also rich in figurines, and more than any other site provide dramatic and compelling physical evidence of the Great Goddess.

FAR EASTERN TEMPLE

The Far Eastern temple, small and fragmentary, is the oldest of the four structures, and dates from the Ggantija phase. It is separated from the other temples by a courtyard on the east. It is the smallest and has five apses although only the scanty remains of the western and central apses survive. The floors are torba. Where the right apse would normally be, there is only an irregular cavelike hollow in the rock (PLATE 30). Despite the collapse of the roof at several points, this cavelike hollow resembles an early rock-cut chamber like those of the Hypogeum. *In fact, we are looking at what may be a conscious architectural link between Maltese tomb and temple structures.* While the Ta Hagrat temple complex may have been a deliberate copy of the tomb configuration, appearing as a temple above ground, Tarxien Far East reflects some below-ground tomb elements.

Fig. 30
Divining block, Tarxien (c. 3000-2500 B.P.). The block is approx. 3 m square; the holes are about 30 cm deep, 25 cm in diameter

THE WEST TEMPLE

The West Temple is approached through an ample semicircular forecourt floored with torba. In the center of the forecourt is a cistern near some large spherical stones that were probably used as ball bearings. If the temple builders placed them under blocks of limestone, they would be able to maneuvre the blocks with far greater ease. If this was in fact the use to which the stone balls were put, they are the earliest tools of this sort on record. On either side of the "horns" of the temple facade are two horizontal slabs pierced by five holes (FIG. 30). Two V-shaped holes of similar dimensions are located on a block in front of the entrance. The holes are about 30 cm deep and 25 cm in diameter. They may have been used in a divination process, for libations, to hold offerings or for some form of game or gambling.

At the entry to the West Temple is a modern concrete replica of the traditional trilithon doorway. Once the visitor is within the West Temple, the palatial scale and the harmonious proportions of the interior restore the sense of being in a numinous place. The apsidal chambers on the immediate left and right (Rooms 2 and 3) are separated from the entrance hall by curving facades, both bearing finely carved reliefs. Of overpowering impact — and of great importance to the quest of the Goddess — is the lower part of a huge statue of the Goddess (see Plate 22). If the complete statue were present, it would measure 2.75 m in height.[70] It may well be the oldest piece of monumental sculpture in the western world. Above small feet, bulbous calves swell out, cut off at midpoint by the hemline of the Goddess' pleated skirt. The pleating is almost identical to that on the statuette of the Sleeping Priestess from the Hypogeum, already described.

To gaze upon the mammoth calves and broad spread of the skirt of the Goddess is thrilling. Here in almost unreal hugeness is that potent force, that pervasive deity, in whose worship a whole people labored for millennia, building temples for which the logistics of construction still baffle the modern engineer. The temples remain. The homes of those who worshipped in them are gone. While the huts of ordinary members of the population were almost certainly no more than perishable simple mud-brick or daub-and-wattle structures, we would expect the population to have built some more substantial structures such as homes for the priestesses or buildings for the storage of grain or other foods. The absence of any such buildings serves to emphasize the centrality of religion in Neolithic Maltese life. It alone merited permanent forms and structures.

Upon viewing this huge fragment questions flood the visitor's mind. Why is the statue of the Goddess truncated? Where is the upper half? Was it, as Fergusson suggests, "quarried away," or was She demolished in some disempowering ritual? Only Tarxien and Hagar Qim, both built in the last phase, possess statues of this magnitude. Did some ceremonial destruction of lesser statues occur that would account for the sparsity of images found in other temples? At present we have no answers to these questions. Strangely, they seem to fade in the face of the rich array of artifacts and other evidentiary material the Tarxien site offers to the historian and artist. Designs, reliefs, altars, portholes, oculi, spirals and other decorative and architectural features are the most numerous and varied of any site. From them and from the architecture of the temples, we can deduce much about the growth and fullest flowering of the religion of the Goddess.

The size of the site (10,000 sq. m) and the number of chambers (32) confirm that religious activity had reached a very high level of intensity and significant complexity. The variety and richness of the architecture and art suggest a flowering of the faith, perhaps an elaboration of ritual and ceremony. Typically, we could expect some lessening of earlier purity and austerity, as is often found in the later development of forms and symbols. Yet we can only assume that both form and ceremony had lost something of their earlier purity and austerity. Indeed, the decoration and the motifs so apparent within the temples are warm and immediate. Whereas Ggantija impresses the visitor with its hugeness, its rough-finished quality and its starkness, at Tarxien the sensation is of a building scaled down to human proportions, reassuring in its almost contemporary concern for well-finished surfaces, cleanly incised reliefs, and elaborate designs. All these characteristics are important to the quest, with most symbolizing some aspect of birth, death or fertility, reflecting the power of the Goddess in these spheres.

Before leaving Tarxien West and going on into Tarxien Center, let us take note of an unusual looking shrine in Room 5. Tucked away in a narrow recess is a pillar-supported altar, flanked by additional pitted pillars (PLATE 31). The interesting thing about this shrine is its two different styles of pit marking. The pillars flanking the altar are decorated with archaic pit marks (PLATE 32), but the single pillar in front of the shrine is decorated with more modern pit marks (PLATE 33). Archaic pit marks are shallow and close together; modern ones are deeper and further apart.

TARXIEN CENTER

In Tarxien Center Temple, the building technique of the Maltese is at its finest. The massive stone paving and the carefully fitted wall give the structure a feeling of simplicity, elegance and power. With its six apses, Tarxien Center is unique and represents the culmination of the architectural development of the Maltese temples.

One is drawn into the temple visually by means of the long corridor, focusing attention on the Oculi Altar, the only design that is seen immediately (PLATE 34). There is a repetition of vertical elements back in space, toward and beyond the Oculi Altar. The altar first arrests attention, then draws one into the temple as though into a vortex, and the round hearth in the center echoes the circularity of the oculi and creates a feeling of greater distance as well as creating a sense of the holy with its suggestion of sacrificial rites.

As the plan of the temple clearly indicates, the position of the Oculi Altar is such that it acts as a screen or halting point between the larger chambers just within the Center Temple and the seemingly more sacrosanct chambers beyond (Rooms 14-19). The Oculi Screen, 62 cm in height, set dramatically between two monoliths and allowing for a long view down the central axis of the temple, also serves as a block to entry. To step over the screen would seem sacrilegious. The sense of watching eyes of basilisk quality is enhanced by the chevron or inverted triangle that divides them. This triangle could represent the generative yoni of the Great Goddess in Her aspect as the cosmic creative principle — the Paleolithic is replete with sacred Goddess triangles.

The visitor who has experienced the silent power that the Oculi Altar projects will have no difficulty in accepting that the spiral was among the most common symbols of the Goddess. Indeed, it is found throughout the western flank of Europe, that broad north-thrusting swath of territory rich in megalithic monuments (FIG. 31). Gavr'inis (Brittany), New Grange (Ireland), Bryn Cellidu (Wales), and Eday Manse (Scotland), and also Fuente de la Zarza (Canary Islands) are among the chambered mounds and other megalithic structures where spirals and spiral-based designs have been found.

a

b

c

d

The Maltese spiral in its many manifestations is related to spiral designs found universally in Neolithic art and pottery. These may have symbolized the spiraling movements of atmospheric and earth currents such as the swirling patterns so often seen in moving water or wind-whipped dust, leaves or snow. Early farmers would have constantly noticed these natural motions.

The Oculi Altar is by no means a single example of oculi as gatekeepers or as guards against the uninitiated or the trespasser. Beyond the altar, in the heart of the Central Temple, screens with four oculi divide the central hallway from the two sidechambers (Rooms 14, 15 and 16; see Fig. 31a). Though at first the design appears entirely similar to that of the Oculi Altar, a glance at the placement of the chevrons reveals the subtle differences between the two forms. The four spirals of the design give it a more cosmic quality. Behind these stone screens are double-shelved niches. An hour-glass-shaped corridor leads into Room 17, which contains a large table niche. On the floor is an enormous slab with low ridges, carved to fit the slabs and pillars of the passage. One of the pillars has five shallow holes,

Fig. 31
Spirals in Europe

a) Spirals on a pit marked background, Tarxien Center (c. 2600 B.P.).Traces of red ochre are visible. Globigerina limestone, 1.40 x 1.10 m
b) Carved stone from New Grange passage grave, Ireland (3200 B.P.). Entire kerbstone is 3.2 m long
c) Cliff face carved with concentric arcs and circles at Fuente de la Zarza, La Palma, Canary Islands, Neolithic
d) Carved stone from Gavr'inis passage grave, France (3000 B.P.)

about 2.5 cm in diameter, each of which contained dark-colored pebbles and fossil shells which may have been offerings to the Goddess. An undecorated rectangular screen projects into Room 18. Behind it was a cupboard niche, containing animal bones.[71]

When one climbs the staircase in Room 12 to the top of the walls, the labyrinthine configuration of the temple emerges clearly. Room 13, entered from Room 12, has a relief carving of a bull and also one of a bull and a sow with piglets (PLATE 35). We will discuss the interpretation and the importance of the bull avatar later.

Continuing to Tarxien East, the visitor passes the huge bowl found in Room 10 in front of an altar. This magnificent object, which has been restored, was no doubt used for ritual purposes (PLATE 36).

TARXIEN EAST

This smaller temple belongs to the early Tarxien phase. It has four apses, but the left side ones do not have the usual elliptical shapes, probably due to remodeling when the Tarxien Central was added. It does have the usual rope and bar holes found in the other temples. It also has an oracle hole in Room 24 which gives access to a small chamber — an oracle chamber — which worshippers could enter only through the temple's exterior wall.

EVALUATION OF THE TEMPLES

The temples provide valuable clues to the cohesiveness of the lives of their congregations. If we consider the range or cycle of activities mirrored in the remains of the structures, the figurines, altars and other artifacts and incised designs, we can begin to understand the many forces the religion of the Goddess involved and the many levels at which the faithful experienced them. The Ggantija temples clearly dominated daily life in Gozo. Even today legend and myth speak forcefully of a Great Goddess. (See page 14 for the legend of a female builder.) The central location of the temples, with their size and grandeur, makes them a continuing, unmistakably dominant force in the small island. Modern Malta has over 300 Catholic churches, some very large and imposing. Religion remains a powerful force.

On Malta itself, both Mnajdra and Hagar Qim give the same impression of grandeur. Yet, to the thoughtful observer, an additional factor is clear as she or he gazes toward the central entrance whose pillars and lintels once supported stonework rising almost thirty feet. The viewer must recognize the standpoint, i.e., the fact that outside the entrance but within the embrace of the curving facade there once lay an immense paved court. This was nothing less than an assembly area capable of holding hundreds of persons who, when assembled, would share the increased sense of common belief, common purpose and common duty that the physical awareness of community imposes. Concurrently, as we consider the increasing degree of finish and decoration within the main chambers of the temples, particularly at Tarxien, we must also remain aware of the growing complexity of floor plans in which a variety of smaller chambers were built. This complexity suggests an increasing degree of specialization in the rites and rituals, especially when we consider the oculi screens of Tarxien, separating different parts of the temple and blocking the access to many of the smaller chambers. The simplest conclusion is that a specialized group of people, distinctly separate from the people at large, was coming into being in the religious organization of the Maltese.

The Hypogeum, combining tomb and temple elements, reflected concern not only for death but also for regeneration or rebirth — as evidenced by the Tree of Life. The Sleeping Priestess of Malta demonstrates that the faithful sought and received dreams from the Goddess within the Hypogeum. The many altars, the presence of libation holes, the oracle chambers in Mnajdra and in Tarxien, the pubic triangles, *the phallic niches which appeared toward the end of the Tarxien temple building period,* and the still-frequent traces of red ochre all affirm that religion pervaded every aspect of daily life. Not least, the huge truncated statue of the Goddess at Tarxien with the nearby animal frieze and altars confirms the binding power of a living religion.

Perhaps the very size of the "great" statues of the Goddess is the central clue, particularly when we note the presence of the tiny human figures clustered within Her robe (see Fig. 19).[72] When considered together with the small but very obese figurines found at Hagar Qim, it becomes difficult to reject the belief that the entire temple civilization set amidst the stony soils of Malta centered on the powers of fertility and fecundity within the Great Goddess. Clearly, religion and the religious life of the community were dynamic forces.

Some prehistorians have suggested that the temples served a larger population than that of Malta and Gozo where the comparative poverty of agricultural land must have limited overall numbers.[73] They believe that the islands were a place of religious retreat, shrines where those with favors to ask of the Goddess or favors to thank Her for would congregate. This could well be, but, despite the fact that Mnajdra and Hagar Qim are dramatically visible from the sea, no natural harbor of any size lies below them. Of course, the visitor could have approached the islands from the other side and anchored in the natural harbor of what is now Valletta. More importantly, archaeologists have yet to find any troves of votive offerings or artifacts that suggest foreign visitors came to Malta in large numbers throughout a long period of time.

Only after the arrival of newcomers from the Aegean after 2500 B.P., and the collapse of the Tarxien temple-building culture do the fiddle-shaped idols of the Cyclades make any appearance in Malta (FIG. 32). Despite the almost certain contact with other burgeoning cultures, particularly those of Sicily

Fig. 32
Discoid figure from the Tarxien Cemetery culture (2500-1500 B.P.), 18 cm high

43

and Sardinia during the Tarxien temple-building period, there is minimal evidence of such contact in the archaeological record. In fact, the strongest artistic elements in the temples, the types of floral designs found in Tarxien, the temples themselves and the statues, are entirely indigenous to the islands. The double-axe symbol that was relatively common throughout the Aegean is very rare in Malta; to date archaeologists have found only a single example though the Hypogeum has yielded many small or miniature axe pendants, seemingly amulets to protect the dead.

To suggest, as the foregoing paragraphs have, that the megalithic temples of Malta somehow defy comprehension when considered in strictly ratio-nalistic terms is not intended to heighten or dress up the practical questions we have to consider. Rather, it is intended to emphasize the need to stand back, to leave aside the patterns of thought suited for contemporary needs and to attempt to enter the minds of the temple builders. Mircea Eliade, the distinguished historian of religion and myth, provides useful starting points. In his *Myth of the Eternal Return,* he notes that while modern people are concerned with the passage of time (which is merely interrupted by festivals and anniversaries), archaic peoples were concerned with the recurrence of the time cycle and the return of the seasons. In harmony with nature and accommodating themselves to the natural cycles, they sought to celebrate the great events of the year, particularly the winter solstice, which heralded the coming of the days of longer sunlight. Thus the place and the means of celebration were of great importance, with the temples as natural centers of communal life.

Eliade's comments on the "celestial archetype" are of value in any consid-eration of the number, size and constructional complexity of the temples. He notes that for archaic people, reality in many instances imitated a celestial archetype. Given the great power of symbols — in which the symbol of the sacred is in itself sacred — it becomes easier to understand the temple builders' motives. They were constructing more than sacred edifices. Their temples embodied the womb of the Great Goddess and, by so doing, ensured Her longevity and continued potency as a force infusing the production of new life. They enabled the community to focus, enter and share the Goddess' fecundating power. The temples represented — and thus assured — continuity of life and the abundance of domestic animals and harvests that supported it. The reliefs of goats, sheep, and pigs on the altars in the temples at Tarxien as well as the altar incised with the leafed plant bear witness to this belief.

MOTIFS AND DESIGNS: PLANTS AND SPIRALS

Plant motifs played an important part in the religion of the Goddess and provide primary evidence of the power ascribed to Her in ensuring fertility at seed time and at harvest. The representation of plants in the Tarxien temples runs the gamut from naturalistic forms to stylized curvilinear and abstract designs.

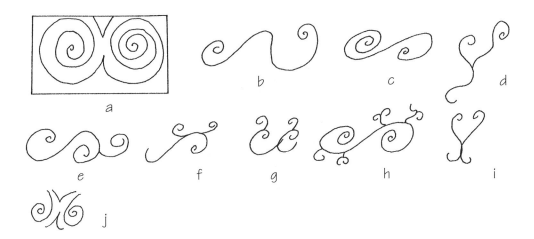

Fig. 33
Spiral motifs, Malta.

Basic spiral motifs (a-e) and
embellished spiral motifs (f-j).

a) oculi b) single spirals
c) S spirals d) looser spiral
e) a e o spiral f) horns
g) tails h) double horns
i) trunks j) wedges

The most striking naturalistic representation is provided by the Pillar Altar from Hagar Qim (see Fig. 16). Carved from a single block of globigerina limestone, this 73-cm high plinth-like altar bears the carving of a plant with symmetric leaves growing in parallel rows on each side of the stem. The plant, which grows out of a small bucket-shaped pot, occupies the whole front panel of the altar and is flanked on each side by a pitted column. The edges of the base and the plateau-like top of the altar are also pitted. Potsherds found at Hagar Qim and in other temples bear incised naturalistic plant designs, suggesting that the link between the Goddess and the concept of natural fertility was strong. This Pillar Altar suggests a possible plant or tree cult.[74] It was perhaps the forerunner of the tree cult that was to gain such prominence a millennium later in Crete and Mycenae.

Plant motifs can be basically divided into three groups: curvilinear abstractions derived from or consisting of spirals, both deasil and widdershins, and circles, naturalistic representations of plants, and abstract designs.[75] The most common motif and the one most characterisric of Malta is the curvilinear one.[76] The majority of examples in this group are at Tarxien although there are some at Ggantija, Hagar Qim, and in the Hypogeum. The basic component of these designs is the spiral in a number of forms. The circle is notable for its rarity[77] (FIG. 33).

According to La Ferla the spiral motif functions architecturally as a unifying theme.[78] Spiral motifs in the temples served not only a decorative and symbolic function but also an architectural one. Spirals generate a sense of motion because of their shape and because of their location and juxtaposition to one another in the temple. At Tarxien there is an exhilaration in the sense of movement and dynamism engendered by the curvilinear quality of the structure and the spiral motifs. The gently curving walls of the temples protectively surround the visitor yet prompt her or him to advance and explore. The spiral motifs reflect the elliptical sweep of the apse, and the viewer is drawn to the center of the temple. It is easy to see and feel how the faithful might have become transported in such biomorphic structures and how they might have achieved a spiritual state of ecstasy.

a

b

Fig. 34
Plant reliefs from Tarxien West temple (early 3rd millennium)

a) block 38 cm x 32 cm
b) 73 cm x 38 cm

Ridley offers a different interpretation. He sees spiral designs derived from plant forms and horned animals, both important in the daily life of the Maltese.[79] The accent on plant motifs emphasizes the importance of cultivation. On islands such as Malta and Crete, surrounded by water but themselves lacking springs and streams, water must have been a seductive substance, acting upon the inhabitants almost like an elixir. On small islands, both excessive rainfall and drought are terrifying and magnificent forces because they are inescapable, bringing into front-stage relief the cyclical nature of life. As we shall see in our later discussion of the Great Goddess in the Orkney and Shetland archipelagoes, islands held an unusually strong appeal for Neolithic peoples and temple builders. Perhaps the island environment, limited and limiting as it was, made for a heightened religious sensibility.

Stylized curvilinear plant reliefs reach their artistic height in the Tarxien temples where sculptors developed the basic form into exuberant tendrils and curlicues while maintaining an overall balance and symmetry. Room 2 in the West Temple provides well-preserved examples on a horizontal slab and on a small altar. A second horizontal slab features miniature espalier-style trees with upward reaching outer branches and inward-spiralling inner ones (FIG. 34). Equally compelling yet more restrained is the S-spiral relief altar from Tarxien Center. An obviously older block next to the S-spiral relief altar features curling plant tendrils above a narrow border of archaic pit marks.

A strong relationship exists between spiral motifs and naturalistic representations. This can be understood by comparing the "Tree of Life" fresco in the Hypogeum with the sculpted tendrils at Hagar Qim and Tarxien. In the fresco, three trunks are clearly visible, branching out into thick spirals and then smaller spirals. In this case, the spiral ". . . appears to represent the force and energy of nature, as represented by a vigorous tree which seems to be sending off shoots and branches in all directions."[80] As previously noted, the most sophisticated use of the spiral motif occurs on the Oculi Altar in Tarxien Center.

There are other abstract designs — pit marks, hobnail decoration, ovoid-and-bar motifs appear on pottery, sculpture and architecture — but they offer few clues to their derivation and development. Abstract hobnail decoration is often found on pottery with this convex version of the pit mark made by applying studs of clay on the surface of pots (FIG. 35).

ANIMAL AVATARS — THE BULL

The bull's[81] presence in Malta is both ancient and constant, and the engravings in the temples confirm that the bull was an important element in Maltese religion both symbolically as avatar of the Goddess and as a sacrificial animal.

Since Paleolithic times the bull has featured strongly within the religious beliefs of numerous peoples. The bull/cow appears in the cave paintings and rock engravings of the early gathering and hunting peoples and reappears in the art and in the religious rites of the more settled farming and city-dwelling groups that followed them in the Neolithic Age. Çatal Hüyük and Hacilar provide particularly rich examples with their many house rooms containing sculpted bulls' heads, often in vertical series, on the walls. These bulls' heads are clearly associated with fertility and rebirth. In Malta the horned facades of the temples and the bull images within suggest a bull cult.[82] The architectural motif is demonstrated at Ggantija, Mnajdra, and Hagar Qim, especially in the southern temples at these sites. At Tarxien the "horns" end in small pavilions, containing altars.

The connection between the bull and the Goddess is further strengthened by the curvature of the bull's horns which is reminiscent of the lunar crescent. "The bull's horns, emblems of the crescent and considered a

Fig. 35
Carinated bowl with hobnail decoration from Tarxien (early 3rd millennium). The upper portion has allover decoration of closely placed studs surrounded by a layer of white paste. The area in between the patterns is highly polished. Clay, 15.5 cm high, 22.5 cm diameter

Fig. 36
Bull and bird on Maltese pottery (early 3rd millennium). Pottery sherd from Tarxien showing horns and bird in relief. Bird is covered with pit marks. Horns each have three parallel lines cut across them near the base. 7.5 cm x 6 cm

source of life-giving fluid, account for the animal's powers of fertilization."[83] Farmers and healers have long claimed (and it's now becoming recognized) that certain plants grow better if planted by moonlight.[84] Bulls and their horns thus continued to be a symbol of the creative power of the Goddess; later, they became a symbol of Her male consort.

Images of bulls appear in the temples in several forms: they have been found as small clay models at Ta Hagrat, painted on ceilings and etched on terracotta bowls in the Hypogeum, and incised on potsherds and as relief carvings at Tarxien (FIG. 36).

On the Tarxien potsherds, the incised lines were filled with red ochre to highlight the bull images. The bull carved in low relief on a wall in the Center Temple, like the one outlined in black in the Hypogeum, is naturalistic and unmistakable.

The West Temple offers an altar of surprising interest. In Room 3, the left-hand altar of a pair connected by a frieze with a curvilinear design has a removable section in the front panel. Above and behind the altar is a trilithon with two flanking pillars and a porthole. The space behind the niche contained animal bones and a flint knife. This finding naturally suggests animal sacrifice. However, the evidence in Malta for animal sacrifice is not so strong as to suggest that this practice was central to religious observation throughout the temple period. No bone or ash pits have been found.[85] It is of compelling interest that this altar is in the chamber directly across from that containing the statue of the seated Goddess; the implicit sense of worship is greatly heightened.

With an effort of will the visitor moves back in time and blocks out the brilliant skies above and the warm familiarity of the roofless sunlit chambers. What we must envisage is this same West Temple at dusk. Unsteady flames light Rooms 2 and 3. The seated Great Goddess, serene and ubiquitous, watches over the ceremony. Throughout the temple complex, Her presence and Her power prevail. The Oculi Altar and the spiral-bearing screens guard the inner sanctums. Animal life — the goat, the pig and the ram — is in harmony with Her; plant life — the leaved shrub and the fruit-bearing tree — resonates within Her rhythm. Fire burns and ceremony is performed in Her honor. But only by looking beyond these traditional set pieces of religion and worship can we assess the full range of manifestation of the Goddess's power and pervasiveness. Other evidence, perhaps individually lacking in drama but forceful when accumulated, must be considered. It reflects what Neolithic Malta shared with and gave to the Mediterranean world throughout which the Goddess was worshipped. Though this worship involved many disparate elements, each reflecting the particularities of the local environment, all are basically linked in form and content, with the bull and its horns as a powerful underlying unifier.

Because the bull looms so large in the decorative and architectural patterns of Malta, a digression may be in order.

THE BULL, THE PIT MARK, AND PROCREATION

The bull plays an interesting role in the evolution of Maltese decorative style. Pit marks, a most typical and evocative Maltese decoration, might originally have been inspired by the bull's hide, which was represented in sculpture by short scratches or indentations. With time the meaning of these scratches faded or disappeared and through increasing stylization they became pit marks, a standard pattern of decoration for sacred areas. The practice of carving them may have continued, basically as an act of homage on the part of those who built the temples, noted by humankind but intended for the eye and mind of the deity. It is of interest to compare the slashes, probably representing a hide, on the Dancing Lady of Tarxien and on the bowl cover from the Hypogeum with the archaic and modern examples of pit marks, both of which are present in Room 5 of Tarxien West Temple.[86]

The pit marks are the single most common decorative motif in the temples. They are found on the trilithons and threshold slabs that form temple entrances, as at Ggantija and Mnajdra (see Plate 15); on altars such as the Plant and Flower Pot Altar and the Mushroom Altars at Hagar Qim; on lintels and upright limestone blocks in all the temples; and on the daïses supporting goddess figures of phalli, which will be discussed later. In addition to the mystery of purpose or significance, we have to add that of evolution, of change in form. In the early temples, such as Ggantija, the pit marks appear as close, shallow pock marks. In the later temples, including Mnajdra and Hal Tarxien, they are more widely spaced, deeper and more evenly patterned.

The seemingly commonsense explanation that the pit marks were no more or less than decoration, pure and simple, does not answer two basic questions: why is there significant variety in the depiction of pit marks in the major temples and their stonework; and why are pit marks often found in areas where they would not be visible to worshippers in their normal use of the temples? They do not seem likely to have been anchors for plasterwork, a suggestion that Ridley makes in his study of the megalithic art of the Maltese islands.[87]

The fact that pit marks decorate many of the important sacred spots in temples — including the sacred pillars and the daïses supporting deity figures or phalli — and that they often show traces of red ochre — indicates their religious and symbolic meaning to the Maltese. The use of pit marks in inaccessible areas confirms that their importance did not lie in their appearance as *decoration* but in their existence as *magical* decorations. Thus the act of decorating a stone with pit marks becomes a potent ritual act,

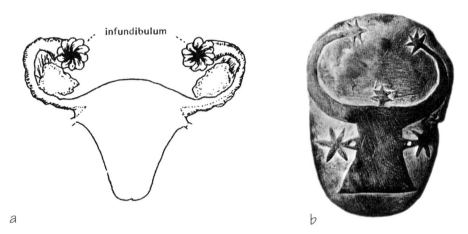

infundibulum

a   b

Fig. 37
The uterus and the bull's head

a) Diagrammatic illustration of the uterus with the flower-like ends of the fallopian tubes which, according to Cameron, could have been the source of inspiration for the rosette symbols b) Palette with bull's head from the Fayum el Gerzeh, Egypt. Pre-Dynastic period. Slate, 16 cm

and their very existence in hidden areas ensured their continued magical power. The importance of pit marks is further confirmed in their clear-cut stylistic evolution from the close, shallow pock marks found in the early temples (at Ggantija) to the deliberate two-stage holes found in the Central Temple at Tarxien.

Recent scholarship has much to say about the procreation-linked meaning of the bull motif. Dorothy Cameron asserts that the bull is a "supreme symbol of birth." Her supportive argument is fascinating and forceful. Cameron begins her analysis by returning to the bull head motifs of Çatal Hüyük. These, she claims, clearly reflect the configuration of the female reproductive organs and thus the bull, a male animal, comes to represent women's supreme power to give birth (FIG 37).

E. O. James provides a persuasive argument as to why the bull's role in procreation did not constitute any barrier to Neolithic peoples' concept of the bull as a birth symbol. He states that "Essential as the physiological fact of the conjunction of male and female is in the production of life, it would seem that at first there was some uncertainty about the significance of paternity. Therefore as the precise function of the male partner in relation to conception and birth was less obvious and probably less clearly under-stood, it is hardly surprising that he should be treated as supplementary rather than as a vital agent in the process. Consequently the mother and her maternal organs and attributes were the life-giving symbols *par excel-lence.*"[88]

In the simplest terms, Neolithic peoples did not *see* a specific outcome from the male's role. The visible processes of growth were entirely within the inner chamber of the woman. As intercourse can occur without pregnancy, and as a varied, even prolonged interval can occur between insemination and the cessation of menstruation, there is little reason to believe that an understanding of the physiology of pregnancy was among Neolithic people's earliest intellectual discoveries. In fact, many remote peoples even today have no understanding of the physiology of pregnancy. In *The Golden*

Bough,[89] Frazer comments that a number of primitive peoples did not accept the fact of paternity; they clung to their myths. It is possible that some people resembled their Paleolithic forebears in their lack of understanding of the procreative process.

We can question how Neolithic people acquired a knowledge of anatomy sufficiently accurate for them to determine the location and configuration of the ovaries, the Fallopian tubes and the uterus. Cameron notes that among early gatherer-hunters burial practices involved taking home the head of a dead person and collecting the skeleton later, after the flesh had been devoured by predators and insects, or had dissolved as a result of exposure to the weather.[90] We noted this practice at Jericho and at Çatal Hüyük.[91] Cameron suggests that the excarnation of corpses by vultures, as depicted in wall paintings at Çatal Hüyük, would provide impressive lessons in practical anatomy, so swift and complete are these birds in dismembering a corpse.[92] As the vulture is not native to Malta, we must assume that with the transmission of the ancient and potent symbol of the bull, and especially of the bull's head, there was also the transmission of the underlying knowledge and sacred belief.

Discussion of the bull motif and its meaning requires one further note. Bulls were also beasts of sacrifice in Malta; a ceremonial return to the Goddess of that which symbolized Her fertility and power. Of all animal remains found in the temple sites, those of the bull are the second most numerous,[93] with only the mixed bones of sheep and goats being more plentiful.

Goats, Sheep, and Rams

As noted in the description of Tarxien, goats, sheep and rams were depicted in a number of the friezes found in temple chambers. The remains of goats' horns have been found in many of the altar niches in the temples, which suggests that the animals depicted in the friezes were used for sacrificial purposes. In his account of the Tarxien temples, Evans notes that "Pigs modelled in relief appear on two sherds . . . and a sow with piglets is carved in relief alongside the humped cattle at the same site"[94] (see Plate 35). Pig, goat, and sheep bones found in the temples confirm that they too were used for sacrifice.

Michael Ridley has provided a challenging alternative interpretation of the sow-and-piglets relief at Tarxien. He considers that the animal represented is a cow, not a sow, and that the objects below her are phalli.[95] From my own examination, I think that the objects below the cow may be udders. The Artemis of Ephesus is depicted with a multitude of breasts to feed the world. Why not a cow with a multitude of udders?

Phallic Niches

One decorative feature of the Tarxien temple interiors that puzzles historians of religion are the phallic niches, also found at Skorba (FIG. 38). These

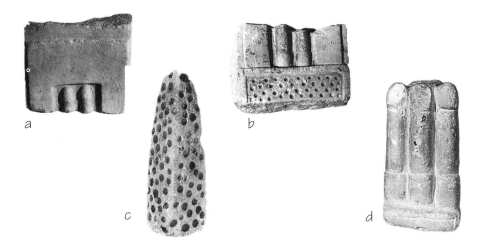

a

c

b

d

Fig. 38
Phallic niches and phalli (c. 2600 B.P.)

a) and b) Phalli in megalithic-like niches
b) resting on a pitted base. Both show traces of red ochre and are made of globigerina limestone. Tarxien Central. a) 14 cm high, b) 11 cm high
c) Pitted pyramid-obelisk-like stone with square section rising to a point; biconical hole just below the top. Found at Tarxien Central; globigerina limestone, 17 cm high
d) Group of three phalli standing on a triangular base, which is cut to resemble a carved slab in front. The stone projects at the back of the group to serve as a handle. There are traces of red ochre on the surface. Globigerina limestone

niches do not appear before the Tarxien period.[96] In most cases, they contain two phalli about 12 cm high, and carved in soft globigerina limestone. One niche at Tarxien, contains three phalli, and is more formalized and well-finished than other examples, as can be seen in the illustration. The phallic niches can take a variety of forms. Some have traces of red ochre and some have bases with pit marks.

Four factors provide clues to the specific meaning and function of these sculptures as ritual objects and their role in the religion of the Great Goddess: (1) location, (2) form, (3) use of stone, and (4) surface quality — the pitted decoration and the red ochre associated with them. As to their significance, von Cles-Reden suggests the following: "The mother-cults and legends of Ancient Greece contain indications of a primitive Mediterranean religion in which the phallus was an object of veneration. When we find Demeter sometimes surrounded by a strange swarm of small phallic beings, the so-called Dactyls or 'fingers,' this is surely a reflection of an age before the Greek imagination had humanized the gods, when the female principle still dominated . . . the worship of phallic pillars must have represented a stage in religious development before the war-like father-god appeared on the scene with his thunderbolts. . . . Archaic beliefs of this kind may have been well-adapted to the simple way of life of the original inhabitants of Malta, who apparently gave their goddess no anthropomorphic male partner, but an impersonal embodiment in stone of the forces of procreation."[97]

Kininmonth believes that the phallic niches made their appearance when man's role in procreation became intuitively understood.[98] In general, I agree with this view but consider that these enshrined phalli also represent the material evidence of a shift in the balance of power in Maltese religion. In an earlier work I stated, "The *de facto* or symbolic role of the male was also ascending in Maltese religion toward the end of the temple-building period. The phallic niches that appeared at this time perhaps suggest the appreciation and acknowledgment of the role of the male for his contribution towards the continuation of life and the cycles of nature. Yet the representation of the disembodied phallus in the pit-marked niches suggests that this talented member still belonged to the magic retinue of the Maltese Goddess, who was considered both male and female."[99]

OTHER OBJECTS OF IMPORTANCE

Two other types of objects from the Maltese assemblage must be mentioned here because they relate directly to the sparse but potent Scottish evidence we shall consider in a later chapter. These are a number of miniature axes and two spherical objects of undetermined use, both found in the Hypogeum (FIGS. 39 & 40). The miniature axes may have served as amulets to protect the deceased. The spherical objects are made of clay and consist of a number of rounded stems in a cluster. These may be objects of importance in a vegetation cult, perhaps representing some form of special fruit, and may be the precursors of the stone balls found at some of the Scottish sites.

a

b

Fig. 39
Maltese axe pendant and French menhir

a) Axe pendant from the Hypogeum, Malta (3500-2500 B.P.). Hard stone, approx. 50 cm
b) Drawing of statue menhir from L'Isle-sur-Sorge, Vaucluse, France. Neolithic period, stone, approx. 50 cm

Fig. 40
Rough clay object with protrusions found in the Hypogeum, Malta, 6 cm diameter

Chapter Eight

Malta: The Final Phase

The seemingly sudden beginning of the temple-building phase has intrigued historians but continues to defy full or convincing explanation. Trump states that "... about 3200 BC there is a marked change which signals the end of the first period of Maltese prehistory. Perhaps this is to be explained by the arrival of the new people from outside."[100] However, he is able to provide no convincing information as to who they were, where they came from, and how they organized their society, life, and the roots of their religious beliefs. It is tempting to assume that the newcomers (if indeed they were newcomers) came from Sicily or southern mainland Italy, where tomb and burial practices showed similarities in architectural forms.

Euan Mackie believes that the sudden appearance of temples was the result of some peaceful but vigorous intervention.[101] He indicates two particularly significant clues in determining foreign influence in Malta: (1) the appearance of collective burial, and (2) differences in skeletal remains from this period, reflecting societal stratification. "The appearance of the rite of collective burial on Malta may be the clue to the arrival of a new dominant group . . . no such graves are known from the earliest phases."[102] The examination of skeletal remains in these collective tombs has suggested that there was a priestly caste in charge of the temples. "A notable feature of the human bones found in the tombs was the absence of any grooves caused by the attachment of particularly strong muscles . . . it seems probable that they [the priestly caste as opposed to the farmers] did not engage in manual labor."[103] The teeth in the skulls showed a strikingly low incidence of wear, which would ". . . indicate a diet relatively free from fibrous and gritty particles . . . In other words the people buried in these tombs evidently ate a diet free of coarse, rough food — another indication perhaps of social status."[104] This is merely conjecture. The absence of bone grooves could merely indicate a difference in daily living practices.

Where did these newcomers who, in about 3500 B.P., inaugurated the temple culture come from? They could have arrived from Sicily as their predecessors had done. It might be helpful to examine the situation in Iberia which, in about 4000 B.P., saw the sudden appearance of collective burial in monumental tombs.[105] The evidence from physical anthropology also suggests that the Iberian chambered-tomb population might have been a blend of East Mediterranean and North African people that formed the more numerous group practicing collective burial.[106]

At this point we must move from the temples and their role in the religion and worship of the Goddess and take stock of our knowledge of the land and people that together form such a remarkable and forceful chapter in human history. Thereafter, we can consider the mysterious demise of the temple-building, Goddess-worshipping island civilization.

Though small in size, Malta and Gozo are large in mystery. Virtually every characteristic of the islands that prehistorians examine as likely to have explanatory power appears to posit a new mystery. The examples of this paradox are straightforward and many. Malta is blessed with a dry but benign climate yet offers only limestone-heavy soil of poor agricultural quality. The growing season is predictable and long, but Malta has no natural springs or underground water sources. Crops tend to be poor and the two islands show no signs of having had any substantial forest cover during the later Neolithic period.[107] However, indigenous forests probably covered much of Malta in the early Neolithic. Places like Rabat, Mtarfa and Tarxien contain soils rich in humus which indicate the presence of groves of trees. Regional names like Balluta (European oak), Weid el Luq (white poplar) and others may be a further indication that trees once flourished in Malta.[108] By the time of the Temple Culture, most of the trees were gone.

How then were the temples roofed? The models found at Ta Hagrat and the small temple relief in Mnajdra South Temple indicate timber beam roofs covering the span betweeen walls showing two or three courses of corbelling. Even though scant and occasional trees may have still existed, large timbers needed for roofing must have been scarce. Some historians have suggested that torba, used in floors, might have served to seal the roofs, an approach that would have lessened the need for planking.[109]

As the friezes in the Tarxien temples show — and as sacrificial remains confirm — the islands supported goats, sheep, pigs and cattle. With the exception of pigs, these animals are heavy and constant grazers.[110] The question naturally arises as to how a population large enough to build the temples over a thousand-year period was able to provide a varied and adequate diet generation by generation. Though animals and fish were available, we can only conjecture on how abundant fruits and berries were on arid Malta.

The only remains of habitation sites discovered so far are at Skorba. Some 7,000 skeletons were found within the Hal Saflieni Hypogeum, and other remains are being found in the new excavation at the Brochtorff Circle (see page 16) which may confirm von Cles-Reden's statement about an eighteenth-century antiquary who claimed to have discovered a Hypogeum near the Ggantija temples.

It is generally accepted that the Maltese emigrated from Sicily and southern Italy to Malta though it is possible that some settlers may have come from the Near East.[111] Pottery remains of the Stentinello culture, with the typical cleanly incised straight or angular lines, have been found at a number of Maltese sites, particularly the Hypogeum and Tarxien.[112] In addition, the

a

b

Fig. 41
Rock-cut tombs in Sicily and Malta

a) Rock-cut tomb at Cava Lavazzo,
Sicily (late 3rd millennium). Height
of pilasters, approx. 1.4 m; length of
inside chamber is approx. 5 m
b) Main hall in middle level of
Hypogeum in Malta. Height of
doorway is approx. 1.5 cm. Although
Cava Lavazzo is a smaller structure,
note the similarity of its carved
trilithon doorway to the Hypogeum's

peoples of Sicily used rock-cut tombs for multiple burials, a practice reflected in the Zebbug, Xemxija, and Hypogeum tombs (FIG. 41). Both the pottery and the burial characteristics are found in the earliest phases of the Maltese temple culture.

DECLINE AND FALL

What happened to the Maltese Temple civilization? "When one of the small rear chambers at Tarxien was excavated, a cemetery was found with cremated burials and numerous grave goods in a layer of black earth. These burials were totally unrelated to the products of the first island culture [the Tarxien Cemetery builders]. The level at which they were found was separated from the temple floor by a layer of fine, light earth nearly three feet deep. There had obviously been an interval long enough for the sea wind to have filled the desolate chambers of the shrines with dust and sand."[113]

From the above we can conclude that the Temple Civilization ended abruptly and that this termination was followed by a hiatus — a period about which archaeologists can provide but few details. The consensus among historians is that an entirely different type of people, who possessed and used metal tools, arrived at Malta sometime after 2500 B.P.[114] There are several theories about what led to the sudden ending of the temple civilization.

Zammit suggested that the islands were depopulated by a plague and later resettled by new people.[115] Evans thinks that the peaceful temple-folk were ruthlessly exterminated by metal-wielding invaders from across the sea.[116] Trump provides an interesting ecological explanation for the sudden and mysterious demise of the Maltese temple-building civilization. He argues that the intense temple building activity carried on continuously within a relatively short period of time led to deforestation, instability of climate, and crop failure. Famine followed, forcing the survivors to leave or die. Thus the island would have been subject to unopposed immigration by the Tarxien Cemetery people.[117] Renfrew suggests that the Tarxien Cemetery Culture that followed the temple-building period could have grown up in Malta itself, perhaps influenced by contacts with Sicily but without any full–scale invasion or massive immigration.[118] The possible explanations of the demise of the temple-building people and the radical changes in the make up of the Maltese population are varied; each reflects what the proponent has interpreted to be key environmental and human factors affecting Maltese culture.

Kininmonth suggests that the demise of the Maltese temple culture was a result of both interior and exterior forces. "Malta was a sanctuary for the old religion [Goddess] from which all taint of contemporary heresies was excluded. The heresies themselves were, of course, no more than the inevitable developments of the old philosophy becoming attuned to the social and psychological needs of a developing humanity. For all its fanaticism, though, Malta was influenced by its neighbours and in touch with the rest of the world. The invasion of the female religion by men — an inevitable if delayed result of the discovery of man's role in procreation — is witnessed by the male figures retrieved from the temples.[119] They wear skirts or kilts like the priestesses. These may represent a tacit admission that they had usurped duties formerly exclusively of women. They were possibly eunuchs; but they were men where once no man had officiated."[120] Ancient Malta, he goes on to say, was probably ruled by a priestess who took a consort for a period of time, after which he was ritually killed or deposed. Any power the consort had was derived from the Priestess Queen. Later, when newcomers arrived, it became necessary to enforce law and order. Thus the consort's office was extended and he was given military power. Meantime, the office of Priestess-Queen had become hereditary. Perhaps something of the kind happened in Malta, ". . . later when the bronze-wielding warlike peoples had settled there. The earlier, defenceless Maltese temple builders had adhered more strictly to the ways of the old female ascendancy than anywhere else in the Mediterranean world of their time."[121]

Kininmonth's thesis is persuasive if we accept that the "Priest Figure of Malta" was a *priest* and not a *priestess*. However, as I argued in an earlier work, the case for the figure being a priestess is powerful.[122]

Those adhering to the belief that the "Maltese Priest Figure" was indeed male might reconstruct events as follows. "The Maltese had a female-centered culture and worshipped a Great Goddess. A Priestess Queen guided the population in temporal as well as religious matters. But, contacts from abroad put the Maltese — especially a dissatisfied contingent dominated by men — in touch with new ideas. Men became more and more active in the religious matters; their temporal power also increased, as perhaps in trade. In the meantime, the economy of Malta was failing. Overpopulation and soil exhaustion caused disease and famine. A political crisis ensued and a large part of the population migrated to the mainland. The balance of power was upset, the Priestess Queen lost her credibility and the remaining Maltese were weakened, thus making it easy for the bronze-wielding people to come in and take over without much struggle."[123]

If the "Priest Figure" is considered to be a Priestess, then the scenario changes slightly: "The Maltese had a female-centered culture and worshipped a Goddess. Priestesses guided in temporal as well as religious matters. In time and with the increase in population and perhaps a move towards greater specialization, the influence of the priestesses increased; they became more specialized and perhaps less available to the general public. This may account for the depiction of larger yet not as refined priestess figures found in the secluded parts of Tarxien Center [the large 'Priest Figure.'"].[124] Belief that the Oracle Hole was designed for use by males would mean that men had become more active in religious practices. If, on the other hand, a school of trained female oracle singers or Bormlizas made their appearance, then the argument could be made that a high degree of specialization developed among the priestesses in service of the Goddess.[125] Despite evidence that the male became included in Maltese religious practices, his presence and influence was harmonious and not at odds within the egalitarian and matristic Goddess-worshipping cultures of the Late Tarxien Temple Period. The change from a female to a male identification appeared later in Malta and started with the bronze-wielding Tarxien Cemetery Folk who appeared about 2000 B.P.[126]

The fact that phallic niches did not appear until the Tarxien or last period (3000-2500 B.P.) does not significantly detract from the substance of the last interpretation as to what happened at the end of this period. Phallic niches probably appeared when the male's share in procreation was realized. This meant that men took a more central role in the rituals to the Goddess. However, the appearance of phallic niches does not necessarily mean that men became the leaders or priests of the religion of the Goddess. It is far more likely that the demise of the Maltese temple civilization was caused primarily by ecological and economic factors (as described above), which may have given rise to and precipitated a divergence and friction within the religious beliefs and ideology of the population.

Book Two

The Orkneys and Shetlands: Scotland's Islands of Challenge

INTRODUCTION

To transfer this investigation and analysis of tombs and temples from Malta to the Orkney and Shetlands means crossing oceans and continents. As noted in the introduction to Book One, megalithic structures abound in Sicily, Sardinia and along the French and Spanish Mediterranean littoral. They are found along the Atlantic coast of France and increase in number and impressiveness in Brittany and in Ireland and Western Scotland. In addition, surprisingly enough, we will find structures that reflect the archetypal Maltese lobed temples in the distant Shetland Islands. Western Europe also has many sites offering a multitude of different stone circles. In the Orkneys and Shetlands, there are tombs and temples that recall Maltese and Sicilian examples. There are also "humanoid houses," their survival helped by their remoteness and because the islanders, blessed with an abundance of easily available stone, did not have to tear down existing structures to provide materials for newer ones. Judging from the shape of the tombs, houses and temples in the islands, and the remains and inscriptions contained in them, we can argue convincingly for the presence of the Goddess. Nor was her presence limited to the islands. Incised symbols abound in the lands adjoining the western seaways, and examples of the spiral and eye-brow motifs associated with the Goddess are plentiful.

The literature on the megalithic tombs and structures of Western Europe is abundant. Those readers who wish to make stops along the route between Malta and the Orkney and Shetland islands should find the biblio-graphy helpful; it lists the well-illustrated, more accessible titles.

Chapter One

The Orkneys and Shetlands: The Challenge of Environment

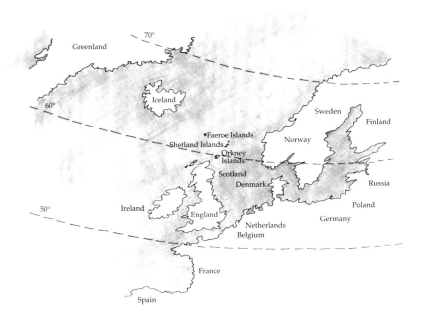

Fig. 42
The Northern Neolithic World

At first thought, the Orkneys and the Shetlands might seem unlikely sites for human settlements or for rich archaeological remains. The modern traveler generally finds these two northern archipelagoes to be dramatically stark and windswept, their natural beauty coupled with short summers and long, cold winters. Yet their human and religious history belies their location, climate and general lack of the natural resources associated with convenient or comfortable living. Tombs, temples, houses and other structures on the islands in the two island groups have long fascinated archaeologists and prehistorians. The origins of the island dwellers and their probable or possible communication and affinities with other Neolithic peoples are still hotly discussed and pose many unanswered questions.

The Orkneys lie closest to Scotland, with the nearest island being some 12 km northeast of the mainland (FIG. 42). Of the approximately 70 islands, many are too small or too barren to support settlement. In fact, fewer than 20 of the islands are inhabited. The surface area totals about 975 sq. km of which only a modest portion will support crops. Mainland, the largest island, about 32 km long, is irregular and indented in shape. With the exception of Hoy, all the islands are low-lying and have gently rolling land, largely devoid of trees, with large areas of moorland and heath. Hoy is predominantly hilly. Though northerly, the Orkneys enjoy a comparatively mild climate due to the Gulf Stream though constant wind, fog and generally poor soil make life demanding (FIG. 43).

1. Westray Cairn
2. Eday Manse
3. Traversoe Tuick
4. Blackhammer
5. Quanterness
6. Cuween Hill
7. Quoyness
8. Wideford Hill
9. Pickaquoy
10. Dwarfie Stane
11. Maes Howe
12. Ring of Brodgar
13. Unstan
14. Stones of Stenness
15. Skara Brae Village
16. Bookan
17. Knowe of Yarso
18. Midhowe
19. Bigland Round
20. Rinyo Village
21. Knap of Howar Houses

Fig. 43
Map of Orkney Islands

One early traveler, Dionise Settle (1557), left a rather harsh account of the inhabitants and their way of life:

"Their houses are very simply builded with Pibble stone, without any chimneis, the fire being made in the middest thereof. The good man, wife, children, and other of their family eate and sleepe on the one side of the house, and the cattell on the other, very beastlie and rudely in respect of civilitie. They are destitute of wood, their fire is turffes and Cowshards. They have corne, bigge, and oates, with which they pay the Kings rent, to the maintenance of his house. They take great quantitie of fish, which they dry in the wind and Sunne. They dresse their meat very filthily and eate it without salt. Their apparel is after the rudest sort of Scotland. Their money is all base . . . ."[1]

The Shetlands lie 80 km north of the Orkneys, and some 125 km north of the Scottish mainland (FIG. 44). Of the 100 or so islands, only 17 are inhabited. Mainland, the largest island, is 88 km long and 34 km wide. However, the long coastlines are deeply indented by inlets of the sea, and

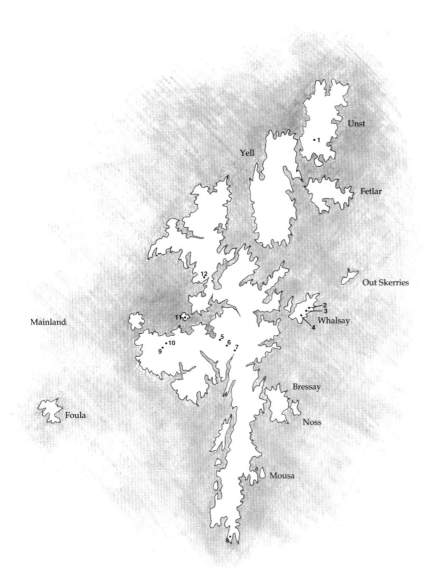

1. Scalloped Stone of Gunnister
2. Yoxie Temple
3. Benie Hoose
4. Gairdie House
5. Brouster House
6. Stanydale Temple
7. Gruting School House
8. Jarlshof Village
9. Gravlaba Cairn
10. Sulma Water Cairn
11. Vementry Cairn
12. Punds Water Cairn

Fig. 44
Map of Shetland Islands

no part of the island is more than 8 km distant from the ocean. Fragmented and eroded rock is one of the chief characteristics of the Shetlands, and besides the "voes" (inlets), there are many caves, chasms, skerries, and stacks. The Shetlands are hillier than the Orkneys; several hills pass the 305 m contour. In general, the Sheltands are more barren than the Orkneys, offering even less arable or good grazing land. Heather and coarse grass growing out of a peat layer predominate. Less than 5 percent of the land is arable. The Shetlands share the waning benefits of the Gulf Stream and though on the same parallel of latitude as the southern tip of Greenland (60 N) enjoy a relatively mild climate, though one character- ized by constant winds and winter gales.[2] Curiously enough, the Shetlands earned a substantially more encouraging report from William Lithgow, a 17th-century visitor, than the Orkneys had received from Dionise Settle.

Lithgow had this to say: "Those north-western islands, in summer, are neither hot nor cold, having a most wholesome and temperate air, and to yield abundance of corn, even more than sufficient for the inhabitants; which is transported to the firm land, and sold. They also have a great store of good cattle, and cheap; and the best fish that the whole ocean yieldeth is upon the coasts of Orkney and Zetland.

"In all these separated parts of earth, (which themselves, of old, made up a little kingdom), you shall find always strong March ale, surpassing fine aqua vitae, abundance of geese, hens, pigeons, partridges, muirfowl, mutton, beef, and termigants . . . ."[3]

THE NEOLITHIC RECORD

Throughout much of their more recent history, the two island groups have supported small populations that have taken their living as much from the sea as from the land. Most reports of the "distant Orcades" during the last century have suggested hard living at best: limited sun, grain and root crops, herbs, fruits and honey. What has proved to be of continuing interest to archaeologists and prehistorians is that these two Northern Atlantic archipelagoes are rich in Neolithic structures — houses, tombs, and temples. As the tombs and temples have affinities with those of Western and Mediterranean Europe, particularly Malta, it appeared logical to previous generations of archaeologists and prehistorians to assume that "the Neolithic way of life was brought to Britain by immigrants, since the principal domesticated plants and animals did not have wild prototypes in Northern Europe."[4] This assumption also means that most of the religious and cultural usages of the later population of the archipelagoes would have come in with their forebears.

These early assumptions were dramatically overthrown as radiocarbon and dendrochronology dating techniques gained ground in the 1970s. The revised chronology ruled out the derivation of the megalithic architecture of tombs and structures in Britain, Ireland and the northern Atlantic islands from eastern Mediterranean sources. The new dating techniques confirmed that "there were megalithic tombs in Britain a full millennium before their supposed Aegean prototypes, the round tombs of Crete."[5]

What then are the megalithic structures of major interest in the Orkneys and Shetlands? What does scholarly opinion conclude about them? Were some of these structures, whose architecture has some elements in common with that of the Maltese temples, in fact places of worship of the Great Goddess? These are the questions that we seek to answer. In so doing, passing reference must be made to other sites along the Atlantic seaboard — Spain, Portugal, Brittany and Ireland — where megalithic structures provide pertinent clues.

We can set the scene for our explorations with the help of some working

Suggested Calibrated Dates B.P.	Phases	Suggested Events	Tombs	Houses	Temples	Artifacts (Pottery)
4500	Mesolithic	Scattered bands hunters and gatherers (shell middens)				
4000-3000	Early Neo-lithic	First immigrant farmers (egalitarian society)	Small chambered tombs (collective burial) 3700 *Bigland*, 3500-3300, *Unstan, Taversoe Tuick, Quanterness, Wideford Hill*, 3000 B.P. *Dwarfie Stane, Holm of Papa Westray S., Mid Howe*	3800 B.P. *Knap of Howar* 3200 *Skara Brae*		Unstan Ware
3300-2800	Middle Neo-lithic					Orcadian Grooved Ware
2800-1800	Late Neo-lithic	(Centralized society begins)	2800 *Maes Howe* 2000-1600 (Shetland) Heel shaped cairns: *Vementry, Punds Water* (Orkney) single-cist graves	2000-1600 (Shetland) *Gruting School House, Stanydale House, Gairdie House*	2700 *Stones of Stenness, Ring of Brodgar* 2000-1600 (Shetland) *Stanydale, Benie Hoose, Yoxie*	2200 Beakers (Orkney and Shetland)
1800-1500	Early Bronze	Even more centralized society (Orkney)				

Fig. 45
Scottish Chronological Table

tools. These are maps of the two island groups, a chart indicating the accepted dating of the structures and line drawings of those we shall consider (FIG. 45).

A RICH LEGACY

We will not be able to discuss all of the listed structures or comment on every development in design and building techniques. But the temples I have selected provide dramatic evidence of an artistic and religious heritage that in many fascinating ways reflects the Maltese temple culture discussed in Book One.

The first tombs to be explored in this quest for the religion of the Great Goddess in the northern realms are the Orcadian ones of Taversoe Tuick,

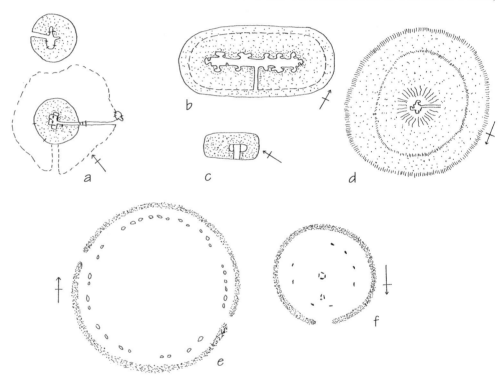

Fig. 46
Orcadian tombs and temples

a) Taversoe Tuick (c. 3500 B.P.)
b) Holm of Papa Westray South
(c. 3000 B.P.)
c) Dwarfie Stane (c. 3000 B.P.)
d) Maes Howe (c. 2800 B.P.)
e) Ring of Brodgar (c. 2700 B.P.)
f) Stones of Stenness (c. 2700 B.P.)

Holm of Papa Westray, Dwarfie Stane, and Maes Howe (FIG. 46). In discussing this last tomb, we shall touch upon the Stones of Stenness and the Ring of Brodgar, generally considered to have been temples. Thereafter the quest takes us to the Shetlands. Here we will first consider the heel-shaped cairns of Vementry and Punds Water and then the temples of Yoxie and Stanydale (FIGS. 47 & 48). We will also discuss houses in the Orkneys and Shetlands, as they help illuminate our quest. I will mention other structures which I consider important in demonstrating affinities with the artistic and architectural elements first encountered in Malta.

Though this treatment has been arranged with some degree of flexibility, the underlying question remains constant: to what extent can we assume

Plate 27. Spirals and pentagons in the Hypogeum. Room 17, middle level.

Plate 28. Facade of Holy of Holies, middle level, Hypogeum. Approx. 3.50 m x 2 m and 2.5 m high.

Plate 29. Libation holes in front of Holy of Holies, Hypogeum.
Diameter is 15 cm, 18 cm deep.

Plate 30. Cave-like hollow in Tarxien Far Eastern temple. Hollow is 3 m x 6 m.

Plate 31. Archaic shrine, Room 5, Tarxien West. Pillar on right approx. 1.20 m high.

Plate 32. Archaic pit marks in Room 5, Tarxien West

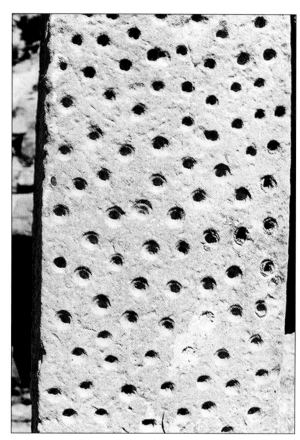

Plate 33. Modern pit marks in Room 5, Tarxien West. An area approx. 34 cm high and 15 cm wide is depicted.

Plate 34. Entrance to Room 9, Tarxien Center, with
Oculi Altar in back and hearth in front of it.
Hearth, 1.10 m diameter.

Plate 35. Bull, sow and piglets relief from Room 13, Tarxien Center.
Bull, 27 cm high; sow, 18 cm.

Plate 36. Huge ritual bowl, Room 6, Tarxien Center. Bowl 100 cm diameter.

Plate 37. View of Taversoe Tuick tomb, Rousay, Orkney. The small underground chamber appears on the bottom right.

Plate 38. Inscriptions on Southeast Wall, Main Chamber, Holm of Papa Westray.

a. Design approximately 1 m long.

b. E O approx. 10 c high.

Plate 39. Inscriptions on Southeast Wall, Main Chamber, Holm of Papa Westray.

Design approximately 1 m long.

that the Great Goddess was worshipped in the Orkneys and
Shetlands? We will focus on the
affinities between Maltese and
Scottish structures and their associations with the Goddess,
and make passing mention of
the complex sequence of tombs
and temples from the megalithic
civilizations of Sicily, Sardinia,
France, Spain and Portugal. We
will analyze the rich megalithic

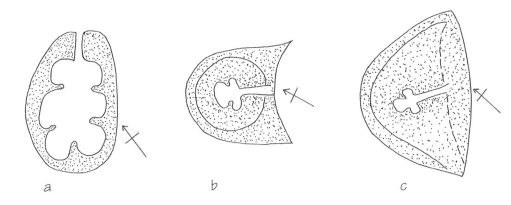

a   b   c

sites of Brittany, Ireland and mainland Scotland only if they relate directly
to our topic.

Fig. 47
*Heel-shaped tombs in Shetland
(c. 1800 B.P.)*

*a) Gravlaba
b) Vementry
c) Punds Water*

Before discussion of the Orcadian tombs, a brief note on the inhabitants of
the islands — their builders — will be of value. As noted, until the
discovery of carbon-14 and dendrochronological dating techniques, most
prehistorians dated the megaliths in the British Isles to the second millennium B.P. and considered their design to have been influenced by those of
the Aegean and Near East. The same historical thinking held that the
British Isles were colonized during the early Neolithic by European
peoples whose agricultural knowledge, customs and religious beliefs reflected Middle Eastern origins. These people
advanced slowly north, with the Danube, Rhine and Elbe
valleys forming one major group of routes and the Mediterranean and Atlantic littorals forming another. Prehistorians
explained the strange absence of metal tools, containers,
weapons or jewelry in the megalithic tombs and temples by
observing that the Neolithic period lasted longer in the
distant north of Europe and the acquisition and spread of
metal-working skills were delayed.[6]

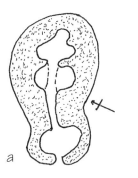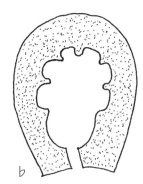

a   b

Fig. 48
*Temples in Shetland (2000-1600
B.P.)*

*a) Yoxie, Whalsay Island, Shetland
b) Stanydale, Mainland, Shetland*

During the 1970s, the new dating techniques led to far-reaching revisions
of the long-accepted chronology. Radiocarbon dates now indicate that
Neolithic farmers had settled many parts of the British Isles by about 4000
B.P.

"The Neolithic colonists spread rapidly over the British Isles, establishing
small settlements but not yet producing marked alterations in the natural
environment . . . In the latter half of the millennium . . . communities
started to transform the landscape by extensive forest clearance and by
building the first monuments of earth and stone."[7]

The earliest cairns on the Scottish mainland were built a little after 4000
B.P. and most of the megalithic tombs in the Orkneys were built between

3300 and 3000 B.P.[8] (FIG. 49). "The Shetland structures were built after 3000 B.C. by people who came from either England or from the Continent, . . . but in either case [were] ultimately of northeastern European origin."[9] These people, who were doliocephalic — long-headed, sinewy, gracile, Mediterranean types — built the chambered cairns, practiced collective burial, and lived in the Shetland communities we will be discussing. In about 2500 B.P., a new type of people began entering Britain from the Continent — a tall, robust, round-headed race (brachycephalic) who brought with them the earliest bronze tools. They buried their dead in individual graves. We know them as Beaker folk, a name that reflects the distinctive type of pottery they made.[10]

Fig. 49
Table of tomb types in Scotland

*O-C stands for Orkney-Cromarty. Cromarty is the northern region of the Scottish mainland.

Class	Group	Location	Examples	Number	Date	Art
Chambered Tombs	Clava	N.E. near Inverness	Dalcross Mains	12	3rd mill.	cup marks
	Clyde	Southern & Western seaboard	Mid Gleniron I	100	early 4th mill.	cup marks
	Bargrennan	S.W. Scotland	Bargrennan	12	early 4th mill.	
	O.C.*	North East Scotland Hebrides & Orkneys		300	4th mill.	cup marks
	types	Stalled 	Midhowe Blackhammer Unstan Ramsay Holm of Papa Westray Yarso			
		Camster Tripartite 	Bigland Round			
		Bookan 	Bookan Taversoe Tuick			
	Maes Howe	Orkney	Eday Manse Wideford Hill Cuween Hill Quanterness Quoyness Maes Howe	10	late 3rd mill.	cup marks
	Zetland	Shetland	Vementry Punds Water	57	late 3rd mill.	

CHAPTER TWO

CONSTRUCTION, DISTRIBUTION AND TYPES OF ORCADIAN TOMBS

Neolithic people used bone and stone tools to build their structures. They adopted drystone building and used large upright slabs easily squared and dressed because of the grain (FIG. 50). Cairn chambers were enclosed in

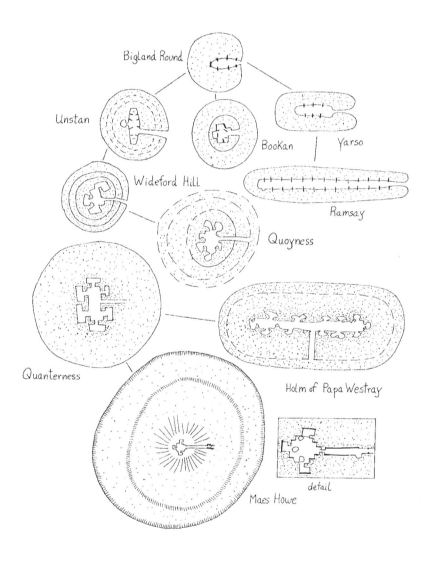

Fig. 50
Orcadian tomb types and suggested evolutionary sequence

circular, long or trapezoid-shaped mounds of stone.[11] Out of approximately 210 tombs in the Orkney Islands, two were partly rock-cut (The Calf of Eday NW and the small chamber in Taversoe Tuick), an operation which involved cutting through the natural clay and into the rock below. Tomb roofs were a combination of corbelled vaults and low lintels.[12] The floors were dirt or clay or, in the subterranean Taversoe Tuick chamber, of uneven rock. In some cases the clay floors seem to have been deliberately laid as if some ritual had been performed or intended.[13]

The method of construction was as follows: first a platform was levelled; the internal arrangement of the tomb was laid out, and the inside chambers were built to a height of about 1 m; then the outside wall was built and the space in between the two walls filled with rubble; finally a capstone was placed on top of the double walls and stones were piled on top so as to give the cairn a rounded appearance.[14]

Most of the tombs in the Orkneys are at the edge of agricultural land, not taking from the scarce commodity of cultivable soil yet not distant from the sea. In death as in life, the Neolithic inhabitants of Orkneys appear to have remained close to both soil and sea — the two poles of their existence. Other tombs are located on hillsides or rising grounds, giving the cairns a commanding view over land and water.

The tombs perhaps served in part as territorial markers, even as "social centers for the group within whose territory they lay and whose dead they received."[15] It is likely that Neolithic people lived their lives within defined territories, each with its place of worship and its tombs.[16] Those territories were essentially clan- or community-based units. As we saw from the map (see Fig. 1 in Book One), the locations of the Maltese temples support this idea. In considering the distribution of Neolithic tombs in the Orkneys particularly when their location and size make them dominant within a landscape, Renfrew suggests they may represent " . . . a cluster of cairns for each local territory, and one specific cairn for each subdivision of territory."[17]

Renfrew estimates that it took some 6,400 hours of labor to build an average tomb;[18] it is therefore reasonable to assume that their function was more than that of providing a resting place for the dead. The commanding position and bold rise of the Maes Howe tomb must have been intended to reflect the permanent importance it held for the community it served.

Audrey Henshall lists seven types of tombs found in Scotland, three of which are found in the Orkneys and Shetlands: (1) the Orkney-Cromarty, or O-C type, consisting of 200 tombs, (2) the Maes Howe type, consisting of 11 examples, and (3) the Zetland group, found in Sheltand and consisting of approximately 200 tombs (see Fig. 49). The O-C group range from round and oval cairns to long cairns, all with covering mounds. The internal chambers were built by combining drystone construction and large upright slabs. The chambers themselves were divided into compartments by slabs projecting from the sides, and the entrances to the chambers were between pairs of portal stones.[19]

All eleven Maes Howe-type tombs are on the Orkney Islands. The tombs are large square or rectangular chambers, dry-built without orthostats, under a round cairn. The entries to the cells consist of long passages, and the main chambers are centrally located under the cairn. In Maes Howe tombs ". . . there is little sign of later enlargment and elaboration: chamber and cairn are one magnificent conception and achievement."[20]

TAVERSOE TUICK

The Taversoe Tuick tomb (3500 B.P.) occupies a spectacular location on the island of Rousay (FIG. 51). The site, some 66 m above sea level, offers far-ranging views over the ocean and the nearby surrounding heather and hills and heather-clad moors. A home-owner accidentally discovered the tomb in 1898 when beginning work to make what appeared to be a four-foot high grass-covered knoll into a garden seat. The digging revealed a chamber.[21] Taversoe Tuick merits careful examination as it has some special features of type and construction. As other tombs do not reflect these features, the implication is that the Neolithic inhabitants of the islands were not members of a single culture living in total isolation in their distant archipelago, locked into one way of doing things or into a single style of tomb-building. When we later consider the human history of the Orkneys, this fact will be of importance (PLATE 37).

Taversoe Tuick, classified as an O-C type, is unique in being a two-storey tomb. The entrance to the upper chamber faces roughly west while the entrance to the miniature chamber faces the east. Both chambers are built of drystone, and the roofing slabs of the lower chamber form the floor of the upper one. The basically oval lower chamber has four cells in which a number of skeletons were found. The passageway leading to them contained fragments of cremated bone. Sherds of 26 Unstan Ware bowls were found in the upper chamber; a few pieces were found in the lower chamber.[22] This type of pottery, common in the Orkneys throughout the fourth millennium, is simple, linear, with considerable allowance for negative space in the pot design. The incised designs are confined to the collar, and motifs include "zones of upright or slanting lines, or hatched triangles, or variations on these themes."[23]

One particularly curious feature of the Taversoe Tuick tomb is a small egg-shaped drain that leads outward from the entrance passage to the tomb, running for almost 6 m before ending in a modest rock-cut chamber. The builders cut this chamber, which is only 1.5 m long, 0.93 m wide and 1 m high, out of the rock and then lined it with drystone masonry. The roof consists of three lintels and four upright slabs set radially from the wall and projecting slightly into the chamber. The entrance is through a vertical drop. Two complete Unstan bowls and fragments of a third were found in this chamber. No traces of any burials have been found, and the chamber's purpose remains in question. Did Taversoe Tuick have uses other than that of a tomb? Did the chamber with its own drain play a role in rituals of worship?

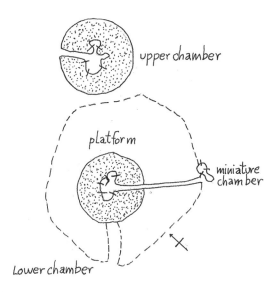

Fig. 51
Plan of Taversoe Tuick, Rousay Island, Orkney (c. 3500 B.P.)

Diameter of cairn, 9.15 m, height, 3 m; lower chamber 3.74 m x 1.6 m x 1.5 m high; upper chamber 5 m x 3 m x 1.6 m; miniature chamber, 1.52 m x 1.10 m x 86 cm

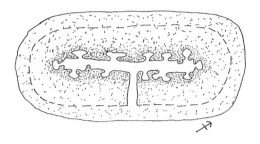

Fig. 52
Plan of the Holm of Papa Westray
South tomb, Holm of Papa Westray
Island, Orkney (c. 3000 B.P.).
External cairn, 35 m x 17 m;
chamber, 20 m long x 1.53 m wide
and 2 m high

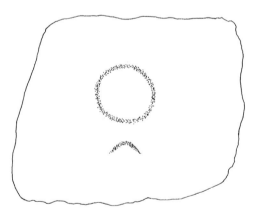

Fig. 53
Inscription in southeast wall of main
chamber of Holm of Papa Westray
South tomb. Circle with a hollow
under it. Circle is 10 cm diameter

The cairn and the two tomb chambers have yielded a number of finds, including an arrowhead and a number of small flint knives of no great distinction. The site has yielded a chipped star-shaped object, a slate cleaver, a pecked anvil stone, a pumice pendant, two whetstones and thirty-five disc beads of grey shale.[24] This meager haul is disappointing given the architectural interest of the tomb's upper chamber and unique detached cell. For the prehistorian, the tomb's primary interest lies in the rock-cut elements which reflect Mediterranean forms.

Taversoe Tuick's rock-cut features are rare among Scottish tombs. Though the Calf of Eday tomb is a second example of rock-cut elements, Taversoe Tuick calls to mind the *tombe a forno* (oven-shaped tombs) of Southern Italy and even the Hypogeum — but there are important differences. The drystone walling that lines the lower chamber of Taversoe Tuick seems to be an attempt either to suppress its rock-cut quality or to make it more magically effective by disguising it. In contrast, the builders of the Hypogeum seem to be striving for an effect of enhancement. Taversoe Tuick may thus represent structural elements from two separate traditions. Both Taversoe Tuick and the Dwarfie Stane tombs appear to have had their analogues in early Neolithic *tombe a forno* and in the Zebbug tombs of Malta.

HOLM OF PAPA WESTRAY
The Holm of Papa Westray tomb, 3000 B.P., is located on the highest point of the small islet of the same name (FIG. 52). The Holm, which is uninhabited, is separated from Papa Westray by a channel some 500 m wide. The long mound of the cairn is a conspicuous landmark easily visible from the water. The narrow, almost corridor-like interior of the tomb forms a strong contrast to the far more evenly proportioned interiors of Taversoe Tuick. The straight-line elements of Holm of Papa Westray tomb assign it to the Maes Howe group.

The tomb has been extensively restored. It has a concrete roof, and the cairn mound has been turfed to weatherproof and preserve it. The original entry passage was in the center of the southeast side and led to the elongated central chamber, but today entry is via a hatch in the roof. Fourteen small oval cells with corbelled ceilings — two of which are joined — open off this 20-meter long main chamber. The cells themselves are small, measuring about 1 m x 0.8 m x 1.10 m in height; the entrances are 0.5 m wide and 0.6 m high.

No grave goods or skeletons or other remains have been found in the Holm of Papa Westray tomb or in any of the cells. Like most other tombs, it did not escape the attention of looters centuries ago. The floor of the chamber, clay overlaid with white sand (now replaced by small pebbles), has yielded no artifacts. The few sheep and rabbit bones found in the cells

proved to be recent, though archaeologists excavating around the cairn
in the 1860s reported modest finds
of domestic animal bones and also
ashes. But material of great interest
remains.

Eight stones in the walls of the central chamber-corridor bear engravings. Two contain an eyebrow or
oculus motif, a number of small hollows and two symbols that look like
the capital E and O near the lintel of one of the southeast cells (PLATE 38).
Another inscription, on two stones on the opposite wall, consists of a
zigzag, double axe and dots (PLATE 39). Both inscriptions are about 1 m
from the floor and were pecked out with a pointed stone tool so the
outlines of the designs are rough — far different from the perfectly
designed and precisely executed spirals on the screens in the Tarxien
temples.

The other carvings, though faint, are on four carved stones — two in the
southwest and two in the southeast wall toward the central part of the
chamber. One design on a stone about 1.83 m from the floor is a circle
with a hollow beneath it (FIG. 53). On the two other stones are very faint
cup and ring markings with what appears to be a horizontal V and an
upside-down V next to it on the righthand side (FIG. 54). On the next
stone, alongside in the same course, are two conjoined circles with dots in
their centers (like a pair of eyeglasses), and to the right of this a triangular
shape has been carved with the apex facing downwards (FIG. 54). On
another stone close by is an arc flanked by two faint dots (FIG. 55).

I developed the following interpretations for the Holm of Papa Westray
carvings. On the southeast lintel, the O carving called to mind a stylized
bull's face with the two minuscule nubs on the upper part of the O
appearing to represent horns (see Plate 38). Though rough in comparison,
this bull's head is similar to one from the Ukraine, carved in bone and
dating back to the fourth millennium. On the left of this O is an E, which
for me recalls a schematic goddess giving birth to the bull on the right. The
"Goddess Giving Birth" was an archetypal visual symbol of great power —
one powerfully depicted at Çatal Hüyük (FIG. 56).

These two small, rough carvings have an importance that belies their size.
That they are small and not immediately or easily visible may mean they
were in a familiar shorthand code, like charms placed in tombs to ensure
that the passage of the dead back into the womb of the Goddess to be
reborn would occur without problems. The figure of the Goddess giving
birth at Çatal Hüyük is highly schematized but is nevertheless an elegant

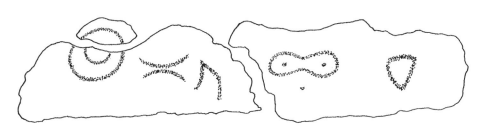

Fig. 54
*Inscription in southeast wall of main
chamber of Holm of Papa Westray
South tomb. Cup and ring, arcs,
chevrons, oculi, triangle. Approx. 50
cm long*

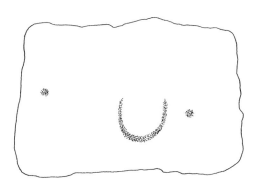

Fig. 55
*Inscription on south west wall of
main chamber of Holm of Papa
Westray tomb. An arc or U flanked by
two dots. U approx. 10 cm diameter*

73

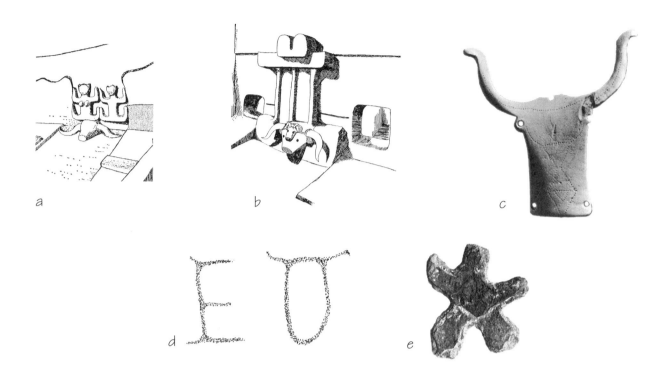

Fig. 56
Bull and Goddess images

a) Plaster relief of twin goddesses and bull's head from Çatal Hüyük VII (c. 6050 B.P.)
b) Schematic relief of twin goddesses from Çatal Hüyük VI (c. 5800 B.P.) 2.5 cm high
c) Bull-horned goddess in the shape of a bee rendered on a stylized bull's head of bone from Bilcze Zlote, Ukraine (4th millennium), 18 cm
d) Inscriptions of southeast wall, main chamber of Holm of Papa Westray South tomb, Orkney (3000 B.P.) 20 cm long
e) Star-shaped object from Skara Brae (3200 B.P.), 11 cm

image (FIG. 56b). The E inscription of the Holm of Papa Westray tomb (FIG. 56c) is very crude in comparison, but I believe the message of rebirth through the agency of the Goddess is there. It is even possible that *knowledge* of the specific derivation and meaning of the triune columnar symbol was lost while it retained its propitiatory power. The two carvings are important because they help to confirm the essential unity of the Neolithic world. As in the Paleolithic Age, when we find similar figurines or symbols in areas as distant as Malta, Siberia, and France, the explanations for this unity have given rise to much argument. But, for the peoples of the northern fringes, like their neighbors to the south and in the southeastern Mediterranean, the processes of birth and death would have been equally mysterious, and the need for intercession by the dead on behalf of the living must have seemed just as necessary. We find ourselves accepting the roughly incised E and O as no more than shorthand glyphs, hurriedly executed codes of confirmation that the return of the dead to the Goddess will occur smoothly.

On the opposite wall from the E and O in the Holm of Papa Westray tomb are a zigzag, a double O, and a series of dots (see Plate 39). Both inscriptions are about 1 m from the floor and have been executed with a pecking technique so that the outline of the design is rough. The dots have an ancient ancestry that harks back to the sacred Paleolithic cave paintings. The double O could be the Goddess as butterfly, Her symbol of rebirth which later became a double axe. The zigzag next to it may represent a snake, the chthonic manifestation of the Goddess — an apt symbol of regeneration.

Fig. 57
Oculi motifs

a) Eyes and beak of Bird Goddess
from the neck of a vase from
Ruginosa, Romania, Cucuteni
culture (late 5th millennium, B.P.),
terracotta, 11.4 cm
b) Chalk drum found in a child's
grave at Folkton, Yorkshire, England
(c. 2000 B.P.) 13.2 cm height
c) Oculi in Holm of Papa Westray
tomb, Orkney (c. 3000 B.P.) approx.
12 cm long
d) Eye Goddess from Brak temple,
Syria, (3,000 B.P.) clay, 100 cm

The four other carved stones on the southeast and southwest wall in the central part of the chamber are also significant. The "eyeglasses" (see Fig. 54) are, of course, the oculi motif — the Eye Goddess common throughout European iconography (FIG. 57). The cup marks interspersed throughout the design could be interpreted as vulvas (FIG. 58).[25] The shield shape, the inverted V to its left, and a horizontal V again to its left could represent schematized vulvas that first appeared with cup marks in the Upper Paleolithic. The wide U flanked by two cup marks could perhaps be a pair of horns[26] and two vulvas (see Fig. 55).

Part of the importance of these inscriptions lies in the fact that to date prehistorians have found nothing else like them in the British Isles. That these carvings are located in relatively inaccessible areas suggests their function as powerful magical symbols, their meaning passed down

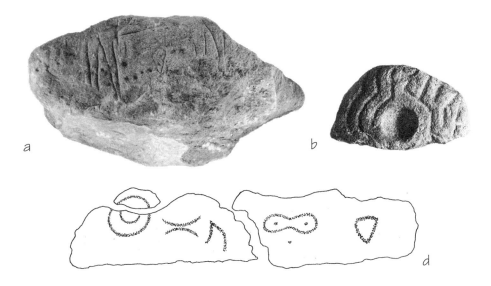

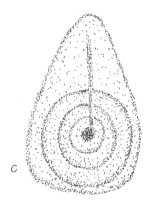

Fig. 58
Vulvas, dots and cupmarks in the Paleolithic and Neolithic

a) Engraved vulvas and dots from the Paleolithic. La Ferrassie, Dordogne, France, Aurignacian period (34,000-30,000 B.P.), 6.75 cm long
b) Vulva altar from Lepenski Vir, Yugoslavia (6000-5800 B.P.) 27 cm x 16.2 cm
c) Greywacke slab from Bardristane, Scotland (Late Neolithic), 30 cm x 20 cm
d) Inscriptions from Holm of Papa Westray South tomb

through the ages. Compared with the three other Orkney carvings discussed below (see Fig. 60), which have a decorative quality as if their original meaning had been distilled by aesthetic considerations, I consider the Holm of Papa Westray carvings to be inscriptions meant to convey a message to the chthonic deity — just as urgent as the messages to Ptah, Osiris or to Isis found in Egyptian tombs.

Fig. 59
Neolithic plaques from Shetland,
Iberia and Cyprus

a) Bone plaque from Jarlshof,
Shetland (early 1st millennium) 19
cm long
b) and c) Stone plaques from Anta do
Olive da Pega, Portugal (late 3rd
millennium B.P.),13 cm long
d) Stone plaque from Idanha-a-Nova,
Portugal (late 3rd millennium
B.P.),15 cm long
e) Stone plaque from Cyprus (3rd
millennium B.P.), 18 cm

Sibylle von Cles-Reden adds further threads of connection by noting that "The Goddess from Almeria [Portugal] appears in a tomb in Papa Westray in the form of eyebrow and eye symbols of the Portuguese kind. That Her sway extended to the even more distant Shetlands is shown by the finding of a bone amulet on which the holy triangle motif and zigzag lines of the Iberian slate idols is scratched"[27] (FIG. 59).

The tomb is *one of only three among the nearly two hundred tombs* in the Orkneys and Shetlands in which islanders engraved symbols on the stonework. What makes this paucity of engraving in tombs the more puzzling is the rich array of carved, incised and engraved rocks and rock faces in other parts of Scotland. The other three tombs that contain engravings are Eday Manse, in the island of Eday, Pickaquoy and Westray in Mainland island (FIG. 60).

These inscriptions in the Holm of Papa Westray tomb suggest belief in a chthonic deity. The tomb is unique. These carvings, their characteristics and their location—sometimes 1.8 m off the ground and consequently relatively inaccessible—indicate their function as magical symbols, carved to place the tomb under the protection of the Goddess of death and fertility.

DWARFIE STANE
The Dwarfie Stane (c. 3000 B.P.), the third Orkney tomb we shall examine, differs distinctively from Maes Howe and Taversoe Tuick (FIG. 61). It is situated in a small valley on the east side of the island of Hoy — the hilliest of the Orkneys. The landscape is bleak but majestic. Stark and inhospitable, the boggy moorlands are punctuated by high sheer cliffs. Two of the tallest hills on the island flank the Dwarfie Stane tomb, yet the sea is visible at both ends of the valley. The tomb was carved from a red sandstone block that projects above the level of the valley floor. The entrance on the west gives access to a short passage with a cell on either side (PLATES 40 & 41). A large block of sandstone, probably used to close off the tomb, stands in front of the entrance. The cells that open off

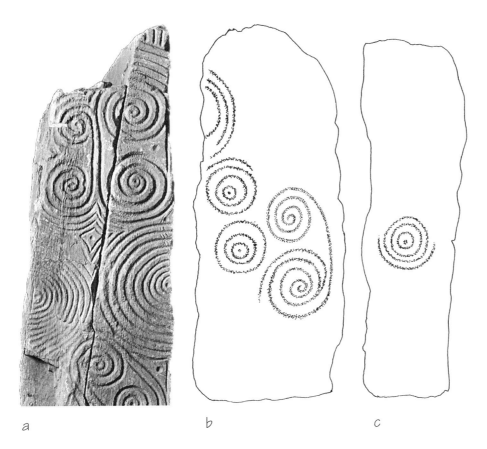

a   b   c

Fig. 60
Three tomb engravings from Orkney

a) Stone found in Westray (late 4th or early 3rd millennium B.P.), 1 m long
b) Eday Manse in Eday Island, Orkney (early 3rd millennium, B.P.), approx 1.20 m long
c) Pickaquoy in Mainland, Orkney (early 3rd millennium B.P.), approx. 1.1 m long

the passage are rectangular with rounded corners. A low kerb separates them from the passage itself and gives the sense of a frame. At the east end of the south cell is a low ridge of rock that looks like a pillow (PLATE 42). The peck marks made by the masons' tools as they carved out the interior of the chamber can still be seen on its ceiling. One striking feature about the Dwarfie Stane is that the lintel above the entrance is convex while the jambs are concave.

No artifacts, skeletons or other human remains have been found at the Dwarfie Stane. Like the Maes Howe tomb, it was looted many centuries ago of whatever it had once contained. The inscriptions found at the entrance and inside the tomb are from the last two centuries. Many are recent and are of the facetious "Kilroy was here" type.

A second large sandstone block, almost as big as the Dwarfie Stane, stands some 0.5 km higher up the southeast slope of the adjoining hill. Because this second rock is sunk in the turf and half-obscured by heather, it does not seem as big as it is, nor does it attract immediate attention. Two markings, perhaps cup marks, can be faintly discerned on this rock.

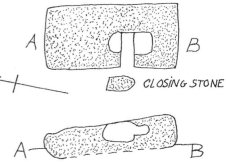

Fig. 61
Plan of the Dwarfie Stane (3000 B.P.). Sandstone, 8.5 m x 4.5 m x 2 m high

The Dwarfie Stane is the *only* rock-cut tomb in Scotland. Some archaeologists consider that an intruding people of a nonlocal cultural background made the tomb. The spectacular location of the Dwarfie Stane and the lack of any other tombs on the island may indicate the settlement on Hoy of a small, forceful group possessed of strongly held beliefs that they were determined to keep. The group may have died out or been absorbed by the indigenous population.

The similarity between the miniature rock-cut chamber of Taversoe Tuick and the Dwarfie Stane is superficial — they are both rock-cut. The differences are more substantial. The Dwarfie Stane's interior chambers are square with rounded corners, but the miniature chamber is egg-shaped with slabs applied to the ceiling and projecting from the walls in imitation of a built tomb. As noted, in the Dwarfie Stane, the sides of the entrance are concave, the lintel is convex and there are rounded kerbs between the cells separating them from the entrance corridor. But the Taversoe Tuick miniature chamber has straight doorway lintels, straight walls and ceiling slabs. Overall the Dwarfie Stane has a curvilinear quality; the only curvilinear aspect in the miniature chamber is its oval shape.

Consideration and comparison of both Taversoe Tuick and the Dwarfie Stane make it clear that the latter is linked to Mediterranean prototypes. The fact that it is not "cut into the living rock" but in a huge standing rock does not necessarily bring it closer in form and intent to the built cairns. There are few clearly suitable, accessible sites in the Orkneys in which to carve tombs from the "living rock." The makers of the Dwarfie Stane tomb had to make do when they carved this tomb. It was the only dramatically sited rock on which they could make a permanent statement of their beliefs and customs. The Dwarfie Stane might represent a very early cultural element from the Mediterranean that fertilized Britain and subsequently either disappeared or was incorporated into the existing cultures. The element may have surfaced at a later date and inspired the Taversoe Tuick rock-cut tomb and the Calf of Eday tomb, with its rock-cut element.

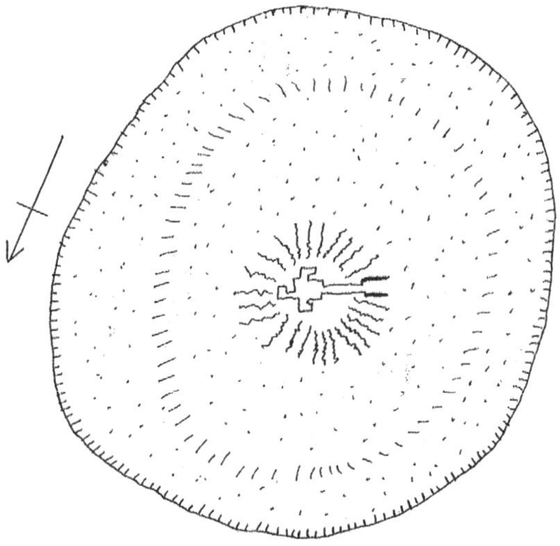

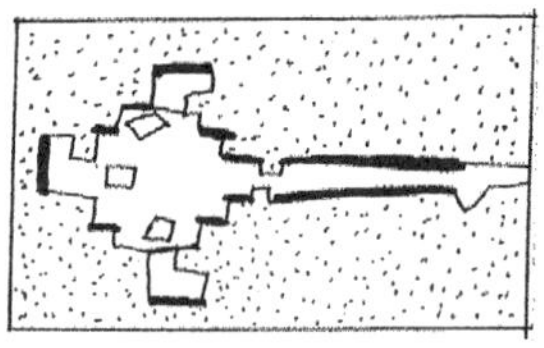

Fig. 62
Plan of Maes Howe (2800 B.P.).
Cairn is 35 m in diameter, 73 m high

Examination of the Dwarfie Stane tomb gives rise to several questions. What type of society, driven by what impulses, built the tombs? How did these people live? From where did they come? Where did they go? Technical questions also abound. Why do the tombs differ so much in configuration, architecture and degree of finish? Is this in part answered by the time sequence in which the tombs were built?

MAES HOWE

It is fitting to discuss Maes Howe last (FIG. 62 & PLATE 43). As I noted in the overview, this spectacularly fine structure on Mainland, Orkney, gives its name to eleven other tombs of the same type and style, all in the Orkneys. The type, in contrast to Taversoe Tuick and Dwarfie Stane, has large square or rectangular chambers built from mortarless courses of stone under a circular or rounded cairn.[28] It is of passing interest that now, in their final development, the Orcadian tombs have evolved into large multichambered structures with differently shaped mounds, quite different from their supposed ancestor with its segmented single chamber (see Fig. 50).

The Maes Howe tomb itself (c. 2800 B.P.) is the culminating effort of the tomb builders and is the link between tombs and henges. No other tomb is in so fine a state of preservation or exhibits so wide a range of architectural and constructional features. I believe that the proximity of the Stones of Stenness points to the fact that Maes Howe was not only a tomb but adjoined a place of worship and rituals.

Maes Howe represents the finest flowering and the most grandiose of the varied tomb-building traditions of the Orkneys. It appears complete and finished, the result of a clear-cut visualization. More than any other tomb, it presents a focus and an aspect of grandeur as though built for the interment of a leader or powerful personage who enjoyed the privileges of a newly established hierarchical state. The projecting stalls or visible niches noted in other chambered cairns are not present at Maes Howe; the economy and starkness of the single chamber are designed to create a powerful impact on the viewer.

In commenting on the Maes Howe type of tomb, Audrey Henshall, the pre-eminent authority on Scottish tombs, notes that: "The entries to the cells are minimized so as not to detract from the splendor of the main chamber. The chambers have long passages from the exterior of the large cairns which are of complex construction . . . ."[29] Nowhere is this observation more dramatically confirmed than at Maes Howe. This is in sharp contrast with the gentler and embracing approaches and continually evolving architectural forms that marked the construction of the Hypogeum and the later Maltese temples. But then, the fact that the Hypogeum was *excavated* as opposed to *built* may be in large part responsible for this quality.

The construction of Maes Howe is masterful. The visitor does not wonder that the structure has remained entirely intact for millennia but immediately feels that it will outlast time itself. The entrance to the tomb faces southwest and consists of a lintelled megalithic drystone passage. The tomb chamber is square with a projecting stone buttress in each corner. In addition to their practical function of strengthening the corbelled vault of the chamber, these buttresses have an aesthetic function. Their vertical thrust contrasts with the horizontal courses of stone, giving a feeling of added height and immense strength to the chamber. The chamber walls rise up vertically for 1.35 m and then converge gradually, rising to a total height of 3.8 m. Three small cells open from this impressive central chamber; the roofs and backs of each are contructed of single slabs of rock, while the side walls are built of drystone masonry. Large rectangular stones, now lying in front of the entrances, closed off the cells. No artifacts or remains have been found in the cells or in the central chamber. The site — highly visible because of the prominence of the cairn — was looted by the Vikings centuries ago. These sea-raiders or even later visitors made the few inscriptions found in Maes Howe.

The lack of any grave goods or remains in the Maes Howe tomb is a disappointment in part made up for by the state of preservation of the tomb. Unlike the Ggantija, Hagar Qim and Mnajdra temples whose surfaces have been exposed to wind and weather, this turf-clad tomb has known no deterioration through wind, rain, heat or cold. Like the Hypogeum, it is a fully finished work of creative energy, but differing from the Maltese structure in two important ways. Unlike the Hypogeum, built in an organic manner over a protracted period of time as the need for more space arose, Maes Howe was built over a relatively short period. The Hypogeum is, of course, an excavated structure. Maes Howe is a built one. The first involved a subtractive technique and the second an additive one. Both, however, share a high level of basic structural integrity.

The four great orthostats in the central chamber of Maes Howe, powerful vertical lines contrasting with the long clean horizontal courses of drystone, seem to be a distant echo of the "long-short" construction reflected in the finish given to the Great Hall, the Oracle Chamber, and the Holy of Holies of the Hypogeum. In actual construction, the "long-short" technique uses megalithic blocks horizontally or vertically to create a very strong structure. In the Hypogeum, the look of "long - short" construction is created by the contrast between the voids of the doorways and the alternating jutting pillars which frame them.

Maes Howe offers a wealth of information about construction techniques. Archaeologists have confirmed that bone and stone tools were used to trim the flagstones and the drystone used in its construction. As the four corner orthostats had to be brought to the site with at least some of the drystone, the need for endless hours of labor from a relatively small island population becomes easily acceptable. Renfrew estimates that the islands' population was about 11,000 during the Neolithic period. Clearly the construction of a tomb such as Maes Howe would require thousands of hours of labor — perhaps 100,000 — from the community.[30] Fortunately sandstone usually splits easily and cleanly into long slabs ideal for building purposes, but cubical blocks required for the ends of courses or for building up corners require a lot of hand-working. Unlike Malta, the Orkneys offer no soft globigerina or coralline limestone. Rather, the rock is sedimentary and subordinate volcanic rock and sandstone. Though more easily workable than the granite of the Shetlands, Orkney rock must have posed a challenge to the worker who had neither bronze nor iron tools.

The size and weight of slabs and flagstones and even of cut rock are substantial. The buttresses at Maes Howe weigh four tons or more, yet so precise is their alignment to abutting stone work that there is not room to insert a knife blade.

Who was buried in the tombs? Did the majestic Maes Howe tomb serve the same sort of community members as the Holm of Papa Westray tomb is assumed to have served? Archaeologists who have considered the whole corpus of evidence from throughout the islands disagree as to whether the tombs served as repositories for the excarnated skeletons of all members of a community or for the select few who led in religious and secular matters or possessed the wealth of the community. Citing the length of time the tombs remained in use and the ". . . relatively small number of interments—only twenty-five in Mid Howe and only two in Rousay . . ." Calder concluded that only a select group was buried in the tombs.[31] Mackie shares this belief, but Renfrew argues that the Scottish tombs were the chief monuments of basically egalitarian tribal societies and that they functioned primarily as territorial markers.[32]

THE STONES OF STENNESS AND THE RING OF BRODGAR

About 1.5 km to the northeast of Maes Howe are the Stones of Stenness, a henge monument that when complete consisted of two rings of stones (FIG. 63). Today only four great outside stones and three smaller inside stones remain. Two, more or less trapezoidally shaped, are set on end close together. Through the gap between them the third can be seen lying horizontally a few meters away (PLATE 44). In addition, two outlying standing stones may be associated with the Stones of Stenness. About 1.5 km northwest of the Stones of Stenness is the Ring of Brodgar, another henge monument. In the Ring of Brodgar and the Stones of Stenness many of the stones are wider at the top than at the bottom, giving these uprights the distinctive shape of an inverted trapezoid. Though these two circles are at a distance from the Maes Howe tomb, I believe that the trapezoidal standing stones, like the Pubic Triangle stones of the Ggantija and Mnajdra temples in Malta, serve as symbolic reminders of the Goddess' procreative power.

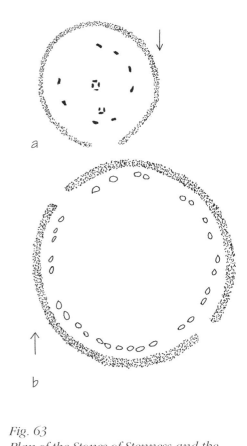

Fig. 63
Plan of the Stones of Stenness and the Ring of Brodgar

a) The Stones of Stenness, Mainland, Orkney (2700 B.P.), diameter, 61m
b) The Ring of Brodgar, Mainland, Orkney (2700 B.P.), diameter, 113 m

The stone circles of the Orkneys can also be considered temples, open-air places of worship. The most logical explanation for the Ring of Brodgar and the Stones of Stenness is that they were places for assembly and ritual, serving the Maes Howe tomb. However, the circles are not contemporaneous with the tomb; they belong to a *later* period and were probably built by a different people. Since controversy still surrounds many aspects of them, and as they are not central to our quest, we will not analyze them here but will merely touch upon them. An increasing body of opinion considers the circles to have been built with significant astronomical and calendrical purposes and to have served from early in their history as places of assembly and ritual as well. This does not preclude affinity with the power of the Great Goddess over the seasonal and agricultural aspects of life. Even though the openness of the stone circles beneath the windy skies contrasts with the concerns of burial, it could act as a complement to the tomb within the dark womb of the earth.

Maes Howe may represent a connecting link between an earlier more chthonic earth-oriented religion (c. 4000 - 2800 B.P.) and the subsequent sky religion of the henge builders (after c. 2550 B.P.). The earlier tombs have no consistent compass orientation, and their location appears to have been influenced by agriculture. Many are at the edge of belts or stretches of arable land overlooking water. In contrast, the builders of Maes Howe surely selected its spectacular location to cause a visual impact on the viewer. Maes Howe seems to impose itself on the landscape rather than to blend with it. The magnitude of the Stones of Stenness and the Ring of Brodgar may have indicated a new interest in a sky deity and in astronomy. Yet this change was not absolute. The greater emphasis on a sky deity did not mean the abandonment of the long-established orientation to the Goddess. The standing stones of the two great rings seem to imply a continuation of belief in the powers of an earth-generated chthonic deity. The inverted trapezoid shape[33] that many stones share might indicate that certain aspects of these old religious beliefs persisted, perhaps because they enshrined deeply held observances which were considered crucial for the spiritual survival of the community.

What perhaps most surprises the visitor to Maes Howe is the extent to which the tomb differs from the earlier one of Taversoe Tuick. Both share the basic external features of being turf-clad stone cairns, rising above the landscape; both have tunnel entrances; both have small cells opening off the central chamber. But beyond these basic configural similarities, the two tombs differ distinctively in most aspects.

As noted, Maes Howe has a finely finished central chamber, dressed in well-cut drystone, with corner orthostats. By contrast, Taversoe Tuick's central chamber is oval and the drystone interior walling is less well finished. The second storey is a unique feature. The upward sweep of the chamber is abruptly cut off, providing for a different physical effect and a much greater sense of enclosure than in the Maes Howe tomb.

With this consideration of the Maes Howe tomb, the Stones of Stenness and the Ring of Brodgar, perhaps the most spectacular grouping of megalithic structures in northern Europe, we end our examination of the religious structures of the Orkneys. However, an unrivalled site — the Neolithic village of Skara Brae — offers dramatic insights into the daily life and the religious concerns of the people who built the tombs. Before describing Skara Brae in the detail it deserves, I should touch briefly upon other Neolithic houses to provide a context and developmental sequence for these dwelling places.

Chapter Three

Orcadian Houses and Artifacts

The oldest stone structures in the Orkney Islands are houses. They may well be the oldest houses in Europe discovered to date. Among the best known and best preserved are those at the Knap of Howar on Papa Westray, at Skara Brae on Mainland and those at Rinyo on Rousay. They are not properly megalithic structures; the builders generally used moderate-sized roughly dressed drystone blocks and not large slabs such as those used at Maes Howe. However, as Skara Brae clearly demonstrates, the builders used modest-sized slabs as shelves, recess dividers and container walls. These Neolithic dwellings have a twofold importance: they provide detailed and fascinating insights into the lives and domestic economy of their Neolithic inhabitants, and they shed light on the architectural evolution of the islands' tombs and temples to which they have structural relationships. The illustration (FIG. 64) clearly confirms that the shapes of the Orkney habitations recall some of the interior features characteristic of the Maltese tombs and temples. Each of these dwellings also has individual features or has yielded artifacts worthy of comment.

The Knap of Howar site has two oval-shaped drystone buildings. Like almost all the Orkney and Shetland structures they are now roofless (PLATE 45). The two connecting buildings are divided internally into

Fig. 64
Plans of houses in the Orkney Islands

a) Knap of Howar (3800 B.P.), 9.5 m x 4.8 m and 7.8 m x 3.4 m
b) Plan of Skara Brae, Mainland, Orkney (3200 B.P.); Hut 8 (on right) 11.7 m x 8.8 m; other huts from 6.1 m x 6.4 m to 3 m x 4.3 m

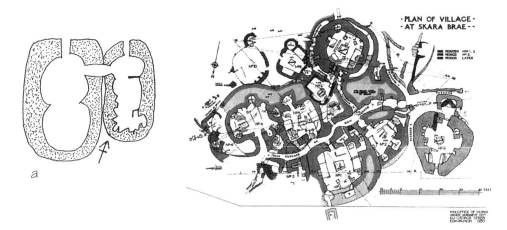

compartments by projecting stone slabs which probably also provided support for a timber and turf roof. Both houses have a series of stone cupboards and recesses. These two features — slab dividers and recesses — occur in the Orcadian cairns.[34] Maes Howe clearly shows the construction of recesses set into and projecting outward beyond the drystone inner walls of the chamber. Bigland Round, Unstan and Yarso, three cairns we did not examine, are further fine examples of tombs in which the central chamber is partitioned off into stalls by a series of vertical slabs projecting inward from the exterior wall.

Skara Brae

Skara Brae is the best known of all the Neolithic dwelling sites because of the spectacular range of houses excavated, their fine state of preservation and the richness of the finds (FIG. 64b). The settlement, dating back to 3200 B.P., is situated along the shore on the Bay of Skaill in North Mainland. It consists of 11 drystone houses linked by covered passageways. The houses are roughly rectangular in plan and have rounded corners; the walls, built of rectangular flagstone, tend to corbel in at the corners. The floors were made of dirt and sand, and the roofs probably consisted of turf or skins stretched over rafters of wood or whalebone. Although the Skara Brae houses show substantial advances in interior arrangement and use of space, they are similar to those of the Knap of Howar site in terms of their drystone construction and in their use of niches and a central hearth. The appearance of the site today — one of sunken cells through which a subterranean labyrinth had been cut — reflects the growth of middens outside and between the houses and the piling-up of wind-driven sand and soil. The surviving walls and the middens with their piles of shells, peat, broken bones, and refuse mixed with sand which has hardened to the consistency of clay, are now covered by a carefully kept lawn which effectively preserves them.

In the center of each house the builders constructed a rectangular hearth framed by four pieces of slate. This can be seen in the illustrations of Huts 4 and 8 (PLATES 46 & 47). There are two or more cells built in the thickness of the wall of each hut. Some of these cells are supplied with shallow stone-lined drains roofed with flagstones; in a number, beads and elaborately carved implements were found. A few incised designs have been found on stones in hut walls, generally low down, suggesting that they were not meant to be visible.

Hut 7 contained a fallen pillar, a whalebone dish full of red pigment, incised designs, and the bodies of two old women buried at the base of the wall of the hut.[35] Hut 8 is totally different from the other huts in shape and in internal configuration. It is humanoid instead of square and, unlike the other huts, it contains no beds, limpet boxes or dressers. An inscribed pillar was found inside plus a number of incised designs, including a design of hatched lozenges, and a number of ox bones.[36]

The special features at Skara Brae raise a number of questions that need to be explored. The "hidden" locations of the incised designs and their configuration might indicate their possible magical function. The small cells in the houses may have been repositories for valuables, but if so, why do they contain drains? The cell in Hut 8 contained none of the artifacts that would warrant calling it a repository for valuables. Could the cells have functioned as shrines or places of ritual and meditation? What is the function of the pillars found near the hearths, some of which bear incised designs? Why was red ochre, usually associated with death rituals, the only pigment found in the houses?[37] Is it mere coincidence that the only human remains found at Skara Brae were those of women? Could their remains have been considered more desirable — more potent in a magical sense than those of men — in helping ward off danger and safeguarding house structures?

Three possibilities emerge: the houses at Skara Brae were dwellings with special areas reserved for ritual; they were homes of a particular group with special beliefs; or their function was a combination of the above.

The humanoid shape of Hut 8, the fact that it was built at a little distance from the others, its incised designs and its internal configuration all suggest that this structure was not a dwelling but had a specialized function. Because of the finds, some archaeologists have called it a flint-knapper's workshop. The flint-knapper, a creator of tools, must have been as important in a Neolithic village as the cave painter had been in Paleolithic society. The flint-knapper's status may have had an element of sacredness. Perhaps she or he was on par with the village priestess, priest or shaman or was also the priestess or shaman. Even to the casual eye, Hut 8 is obviously a special, sacred space. Although the finds support the theory that Hut 8 was a flint-knapper's working place, its separateness, shape and incised designs, and particularly the seven ox phalanges found within it, all imply that the hut functioned as a religious building, a place of rites. It is not inconceivable that the functions of workshop and shrine co-existed. Recently, a Philistine city (Ekron,1000 B.P.) revealed a similar combination between the sacred and the profane. A series of four horned altars was found in the same room as equipment used to produce olive oil.[38] In ritual, many sacred and common objects are used jointly.

Perhaps the inhabitants of Skara Brae represented a later group of people that coexisted with the original inhabitants and merged with them in time. That the pottery found at Skara Brae was Grooved Ware lends support to the theory that an incoming group settled in the area in the Late Neolithic Age and that Skara Brae was one of the villages they founded. Renfrew's suggestion that this later group brought about a more centralized society.[39] does not rule out the possibility that its members may have had a cult of the dead and may have worshipped a goddess of death and rebirth. The possible religious functions of Hut 8 suggest that the Neolithic inhabitants of the Orkneys may have performed some, if not many, of their religious ceremonies within the village, within a building having many of the physical characteristics of a home. Employing a part of their living space to perform religious ceremonies does not exclude the possibility that certain religious activities may have occurred in the open air with the cairns as a backdrop or focal point.

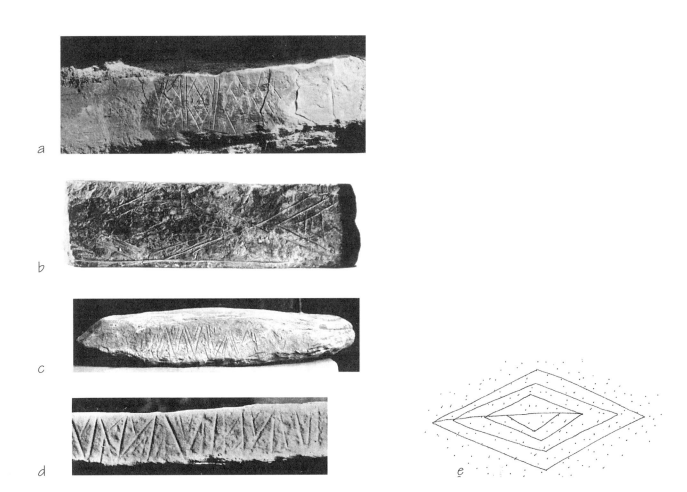

a

b

c

d

e

CARVINGS

The carvings at Skara Brae range from large compositions on stone slabs to a finely engraved ornament on a small polished stone plaque (possibly a knife), and the motifs employed are based on zigzags, triangles, chevrons and lozenges, with cross-hatching and 'shading' on occasion (FIG. 65). Most of these engravings are situated toward the base of walls; *some are located in inaccessible positions.* In addition, simple chevrons and some checkerwork patterns were found on the edges of stone shelves, higher in the walls and more easily visible than the other carvings just cited. *One series was found in Hut 7 on a wall at the base of which the remains of the two old women were found* (FIG. 66).

At Skara Brae there are no eyebrow motifs, no spirals, circles or arcs; all the carvings have a geometric, design-like quality. Conversely, we noted that at Papa Westray there are no lozenges or checker patterns, and the carvings have an ideogram-like quality. What further distinguishes the Skara Brae carvings from those of the Holm of Papa Westray tomb is that the makers employed three techniques in producing them. Some they scratched onto the drystone surface with a sharp-edged flint or instrument that left a single thin line; others they engraved, producing a deeper incision; still others they pecked out, producing a wide, uneven line. Some

Fig. 65
Skara Brae carvings (3200 B.P.)

a) stone on east of Hut 8. Hatched lozenges, 27 cm long
b) row of horizontal lozenges between parallel lines found on edge of a block, 23 cm
c) stone on wall of passage C. Triangles between chevrons, 28 cm long
d) frontal slab on right-hand bed in hut 7, 18 cm
e) lozenge pattern on stone from Skara Brae

87

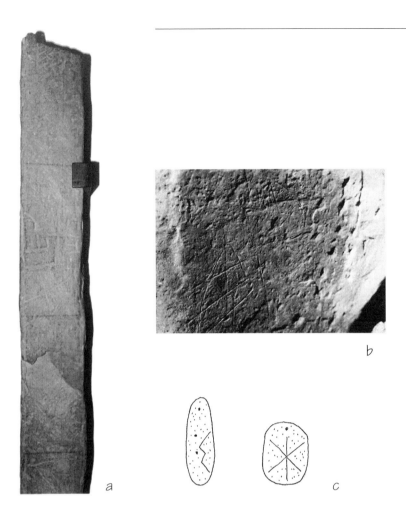

of the Skara Brae carvings cover an entire stone. Others are concentrated on a small portion of a stone. The Holm of Papa Westray carvers seem to have treated the surfaces of stones as two-dimensional spatial boundaries on which to confine their designs. At Skara Brae there is a geometric quality; at the Holm of Papa Westray the inscriptions are like ideograms. The lozenge patterns such as those found at Skara Brae appear in Mesolithic engravings, and zigzag forms have been interpreted as stylized snakes for at least as long.[40]

The carved motifs found at Papa Westray and at Skara Brae belong to an ancient tradition common throughout Europe and the Mediterranean, that of worship of and belief in a chthonic deity that had its roots in the Paleolithic period. This tradition was based on the cult of the dead and, as we have seen throughout this period, cosmic fertility embodied in a female deity. This we have traced in a number of ways including the numerous female figurines, the use of red ochre and the inclusion of grave goods with the bodies of the dead. As the Neolithic Age advanced, this chthonic tradition is traceable through the complex burial rites of Çatal Hüyük, Hacilar, Jericho and Malta. With the development of agriculture, the cult of the dead became combined with the fertility cult of the Neolithic: the goddess of death and resurrection became also a goddess of growth. The symbols used by Paleolithic artists over so wide an area of Eurasia continued to be used by their descendants, altered according to their geographical location and by the passage of time. And, in keeping with a universal reality, the shift in style seems to be from the representational toward the abstract and finally back to the representational.

A second possibility is that the Holm of Papa Westray reflected an earlier group of people whose iconography was still semi-representational. Skara Brae represented a related, but later, group whose iconography had become more abstract. The fact that the engravings and incisions at Skara Brae were concentrated in certain parts of the houses — in passageways and on ritual objects and pillars — confirms that the designs were considered important as symbolic images or were thought of as having prophylactic power.

Fig. 66
Skara Brae carvings

a) Engraved pillar from Hut 8, flagstone, 1.8 cm high
b) Stone from one of the house cells showing triangle, 20 cm
c) pendants from Skara Brae. Right pendant is 3.5 cm high

a

b

c

d

e

The pillar, together with the stone and tree (both of which can be pillar-like in configuration), had ancient associations with the Goddess as Her non-animal avatars. This concept of divinity, already broad, becomes even broader as "The pillar may represent either a male or a female aspect of divinity, or both, being hermaphroditic."[41] At Çatal Hüyük the relationship between Goddess and pillar is manifest. Sometimes the Goddess stands in a pillar-like stance between two animals, sometimes She is represented by a pillar, as at the Lion Gate at Mycenae.

Fig. 67
Stone balls from Scotland and engraved motifs on tombs

a) Carinated sphere from Skara Brae (c. 3200 B.P.), 6 cm diameter
b) Smooth sphere with inscriptions found in Hut 2 Skara Brae, 5 cm diameter
c) Sphere carved with knobs from Skara Brae found in Hut 7, 4 cm diameter
d) Sphere from Towie, Aberdeenshire, with carved spiral designs (c. 3rd millennium B.P.), 10 cm diameter
e) Carved stone from New Grange, Ireland (3200 B.P.), 3.2 m long

The pillar, together with the stone and tree (both of which can be pillar-like in configuration), had ancient associations with the Goddess as Her non-animal avatars. This concept of divinity, already broad, becomes even broader as "The pillar may represent either a male or a female aspect of divinity, or both, being hermaphroditic."[41] At Çatal Hüyük the relationship between Goddess and pillar is manifest. Sometimes the Goddess stands in a pillar-like stance between two animals, sometimes She is represented by a pillar, as at the Lion Gate at Mycenae.

We can never, of course, be sure that any one interpretation is the right one: absolute certainty is beyond our scope. However, two theories seem to be broad enough to accommodate most if not all of the evidence. First, the Skara Brae carvings represent the continuity of spiritual values at a time of change; secondly, they reflect a measure of religious syncretism. The settlement's position close to the open beach, the defensive potential provided by the trench-like passage ways connecting the houses suggest that the inhabitants lived in a time of threatening change, possibly at risk of attack or invasion, with the associated need to have a means of escape. The Skara Brae folk may have represented a last wave of settlers who worshipped the Great Goddess in their home shrines, standing at the periphery of a rapidly changing society, desperately clinging to their ancient beliefs.

The element of syncretism — the combination of two symbols that are similar but come from different cultural traditions and finally become interchangeable — may explain in part why the prehistorian can make so few definite pronouncements about the Skara Brae and Holm of Papa Westray carvings.

STONE BALLS

Some 380 stone balls have been found in Scotland. Most of them are about 70 mm in diameter though 12 are distinctly larger, measuring between 90 and 144 mm in diameter. Fifteen balls were found in the Orkneys, six at Skara Brae (FIG. 67). Some are decorated with spirals, some with concentric circles, others with a variety of incised designs. Some have been very deeply incised in a way that leaves bosses of stone projecting either in patterns not unlike those of the surface of a pineapple or in other consistent designs. Stone tools were used in finishing most; some were carved with metal tools. The balls were carved from a variety of stones of different degrees of hardness.

The theories about the meaning or use of the balls are wide ranging: they were used as ceremonial maceheads,[42] as primitive weights,[43] as oracles,[44] in a sort of game[45] or at a conference, ". . . the chief handling [the ball] as he considered a judgement, or perhaps [it was] handed around, the one holding it having the right to speak."[46] So few balls have been found in graves that Marshall feels ". . . they must have been family or clan possessions rather than personal ones. The balls must have been prestige objects."[47] In addition to the fifteen stone balls found at sites in the Orkney Islands, two have been found at the Ness of Gruting house site in Shetland.[48]

Despite the initial mystery the carved stone balls pose, careful examination provides some lines of explanation of their purpose and use. They were durable; they could be moved by hand and in the hand; some show signs of wear but have not lost their spherical shape — and thus still present the concept of unbrokenness, of continuity. If we compare the heavily incised stone ball from Towie, Aberdeenshire, with the stone slab carvings of Pickaquoy and Holm of Papa Westray, we see the oculus motif clear-cut in both. It is equally clear-cut in the New Grange and Gavr'inis passage tombs (FIG. 67e). It is possible that the same motifs were used because they were thought to possess the same magical power. The fact that some of the balls belong to a later date does not exclude this. Although the original significance of the design appearing on them may have been lost or forgotten, they still evoked an emotional response. This fact can be considered in conjunction with another one: of 385 stone balls found in the British Isles, all but five were found in Scotland. There is good reason to assume that the carved stone ball may have been the preferred type of artistic expression in Neolithic Scotland and that it served the same purpose in the Orkney and Shetland Islands that the carved megaliths served in Brittany and in Ireland. Both balls and megaliths were associated with the propitiation of and contact with the dead.

STAR-SHAPED OBJECTS

Archaeologists have found a number of star-shaped carved stone objects in both the archipelagoes, with four coming from the Orkneys (two from Skara Brae, one from Taversoe Tuick, one from Quoyness), and one from the Benie Hoose site in Shetland (FIG. 68a). The immediate interpretation would be that these carvings represent human beings. However, Childe sounds a note of warning in saying that the carvings ". . . may be interpreted as human figures with outstretched limbs . . . At the same time it must be admitted that [the object]. . . bears no significant likeness to any

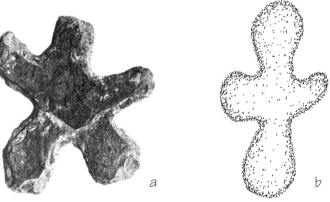

known group of prehistoric figurines though a comparison with a schist figurine from the late Neolithic tomb at La Pernera in Almeria would be legitimate"[49] (FIG. 68b). The La Pernera pendant Childe is referring to may be a derivation from a pregnant Goddess-type image. The frescos at Çatal Hüyük, which date from the 7th millennium, depict several such figures, some of which are very crudely executed.

Fig. 68
Star-shaped objects from Scotland and Iberia
a) Skara Brae object (3200 B.P.), 9 cm
b) Object from La Pernera, Almeria, Spain (3rd millennium B.P.), 10 cm long

Although the sparse number of these star-shaped objects and their limitation to three Neolithic villages in the Orkneys makes any attempt at definitive interpretation risky, their very singleness and their scarcity may be helpful toward determining their significance. Despite their somewhat rough appearance, that they were carved out of stone may indicate that lasting importance was attached to them. To date, no fully representational three-dimensional images of deities have been found in the Neolithic settlements of the Orkneys and Shetlands. It is possible that the prehistoric Scots did not usually portray their deity in a representative manner. When they did, in response to incoming cross-cultural influences, the result was crude and perhaps not as magically effective as finer, more representational figures were thought to be. If the star-shaped figures are indeed images of a deity, it may well be that they reflected an intrusive foreign element, the expression of a subculture.

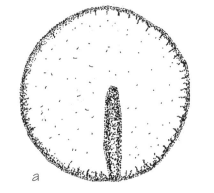
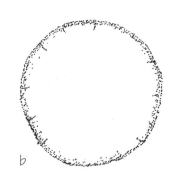
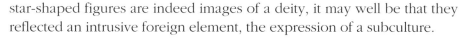

Fig. 69
Disks from Central Europe and Shetland

a) Disk from Brno, Czechoslovakia, Upper Paleolithic, Gravettian (28,000-22,000 B.P.), mammoth tooth, 7 cm diameter
b) Bone disk from Gruting House site, Shetland (c. 1800 B.P.), 8 cm diameter

DISKS

Stone disks, some 6 cm in diameter and with shaped edges, have been recovered from Skara Brae (FIG. 69). Burl thinks that these disks may have been associated with death because they are usually found in chambered tombs, round barrows or stone circles.[50] The most striking fact about the disks is their close resemblance to those found in Paleolithic burial sites. The Brno disk with its slot-shaped incision from rim to center has been held to be an abstract image of the vulva. Though the disk from the Gruting School House lacks this incision, it bears the same type of small, carefully spaced marks along the circumference. Close comparison compels the belief that the two disks have the same religious significance, one that is surely tied to the cycle of life and the concept of rebirth.

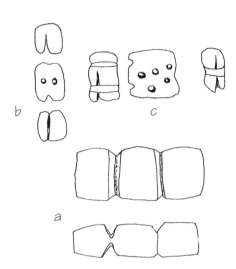

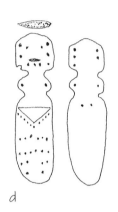

OTHER OBJECTS

Other items of interest are quartz pebbles, ivory dice and miniature axes. The ivory dice have an uncanny resemblance to stylized bone figurines from Ruse, Bulgaria, from the 5th millennium (FIG. 70). Neolithic tomb builders appear to have been heavy users of quartz; perhaps because of its special surface brilliance and transparent properties, it was considered magical.[51]

Fig. 70
Ivory dice and bone figurines

a-c) "dice" from Skara Brae (c. 3200 B.P.), 1.5-7 cm
d) schematized figure from Ruse, Bulgaria (4000 B.P.), 8 cm high

Small axes have been found in Orcadian tombs. We know from the excavations at Çatal Hüyük that the double-axe symbol, derived from the butterfly avatar of the Great Goddess, is an ancient and widespread symbol of the Goddess throughout the Mediterranean and Near East, except in Malta where only one example has been found (see Fig. 90a).

Burl emphasizes the connection of axes with death and rebirth in the Neolithic Age: "In Brittany miniature perforated versions of axes in rare stones were hung as pendants around the neck. Chalk axes were buried at Woodhenge and Stonehenge. Shapes of axes were sometimes carved on slabs covering the dead."[52] Certainly these axe motifs can be accepted as within the wider tradition, common throughout the Mediterranean, in which the double axe symbolized the Goddess.

Unlike the carved stone balls and the star-shaped figures, miniature axes and bone pendants with what appear to be stylized axes engraved on them have been found in tombs, houses and temples in both the Orkney and the Shetland Islands. That they were found in all the sites strengthens the hypothesis that religious rites may have been performed in houses as well as in front of the tombs and inside the temples. Given the belief expressed and illustrated by Cameron that the double axe of Çatal Hüyük was a stylized image of the butterfly avatar of the Goddess, it is well within the bounds of possibility that the much modified single-axe image still referred symbolically to the Goddess.

POTTERY

Orkney sites have yielded a substantial harvest of pottery and sherds. Unstan Ware from the early Neolithic is generally shallow, with the design

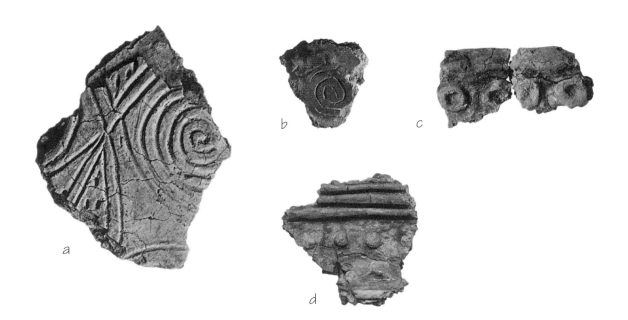

Fig. 71
Pottery from Skara Brae (c. 3200
B.P.)

a) Sherd showing incised spirals, 14
cm x 10 cm
b) Sherd with incised spiral, 6.6 cm
long
c) Sherd with Oculi motif, 14.5 cm
long
d) Sherd with applied hobnail-like
decoration, 9 cm x 9.2 cm

limited to the collar. Motifs incude " . . . zones of upright or slanting lines,
or hatched triangles, or variations on these themes. . . . The great majority
of Unstan bowls have been found in Orcadian tombs."[53] Grooved Ware
from the late Neolithic is flat-based and profusely decorated (FIG. 71). It
has been found ". . . in quantity in southern and southeastern England,
but elsewhere it is very scattered and generally in small quantity, except
at the two Orcadian habitation sites of Rinyo and Skara Brae."[54]

The Grooved Ware pottery of Skara Brae employs the usual patterns:
triangles, simple parallel lines, hatched bands, trapezes, chevrons, bi-
sected chevrons, wavy lines, lozenges, applied dots[55] and oculi motifs. In
addition, two potsherds with incised spiral ornaments were found. One
shows what is almost certainly a double spiral between two lozenges, the
only example of this Goddess symbol on pottery found in the British
Isles[56] though spirals have been found at New Grange and on stone balls.
But "The lozenge-and-spiral design on a potsherd from Skara Brae, closely
resembling the design on a kerbstone at New Grange, is a definite link
with Ireland and nowhere else."[57] Other links between the Orkneys and
southern Europe may have existed. Piggott states that pottery similar to
that of Skara Brae has been found in Portugal at Serra Das Equas,
Carenque, Gruta da Furadeiro, and Roca Forte Serra do Monto Junto.[58]

Most of the Shetland pottery comes from house and temple sites. It seems
to be related to the Hebridean Neolithic and to Beaker pottery.[59] The most
common motif ". . . is a profuse decoration by incision or channelling of

herring bone, chevrons and diamonds, in general in the same tradition as the pottery of the chambered tomb builders of the Hebrides."[60] One vessel from Stanydale temple was decorated with impressed circles, and a rim sherd from the Benie Hoose was decorated with a series of small impressed dots.[61] Though the pottery of both island groups hints strongly at external influences, we lack the evidence needed to make definite pronouncements on migration, contact and trade.

CHAPTER FOUR

ORIGINS OF ORCADIAN TOMB DESIGNS

Where did the designs of the Scottish tombs originate? What is their derivation? The earliest known passage graves (c. 4500 B.P.) are those of Brittany, but the rite of collective burial in megalithic chambers within cairns was established even earlier — in Portugal before 4500 B.P.[62]

Henshall proposes four phases of tomb development in Scotland. The first phase (4th millennium) sees the appearance of rectangular megalithic chambers under small cairns, which seem to be versions of a widespread indigenous type found on the Irish sea coasts but resembling small cairns found in other parts of Western Europe, such as in the Pyrenees and Scandinavia.[63] The second phase, before 3000 B.P., saw two developments: the evolution of the square chambers into segmented chambers and the arrival of a new people — the passage grave builders — from northwestern France or Iberia.[64] The amalgamation of the rectangular chambers and the polygonal passage graves gave rise to the early Orkney-Cromarty (O-C) group.[65] The third phase, about 3000 B.P., is marked by the addition of long cairns to chambered tombs.[66] The tombs in Orkney were built during this time. Tombs developed into larger, more elaborate structures with deep crescentic forecourts.[67] Heel-shaped cairns (in Shetland) appeared at this point.[68] During phase four, from 2500 B.P. to about 1700 B.P., all the large tombs were built. "The Maes Howe group of tomb builders arrived from Ireland probably soon after 2500 BC . . . *[sic]* At this time Bookan-type and Tripartite stalled chambers were being built, and the larger stalled chambers were developing."[69]

Comparison of the Knap of Howar habitation site and the Holm of Papa Westray tomb suggests that Papa Westray may have been the first settlement of the Orkney farmers. The soil is unusually rich there.[70]

Mackie's approach to the origin of the Scottish megaliths is more sociological. He states that many Scottish long cairns show evidence of cremation in contrast with English megalithic tombs where inhumation burial in collective tombs seems to have been the usual rite.[71] Either the builders of passage graves found a well established local funerary tradition in Scotland when they arrived or ". . . it may reflect the influence of the universal Irish tradition of cremation in collective tombs."[72] Mackie believes that the rite of collective burial and the passage grave megalithic temple-tombs were Iberian Neolithic developments.[73] There is a possibility that they came from further east and spread across Europe and along the seaways toward the north through the efforts of a small group of priests and wise men ". . . who settled among, and came to dominate, the Neolithic peasant population of Atlantic Europe."[74] The first farmers arrived in Britain a few centuries before the practice of building collective tombs began. "At about 4200 . . . an entirely new people practicing collective burial — using wooden mortuary structures and burying these under long [mounds] arrived. . . ."[75] Other Neolithic graves found in Britain are relatively humble burials in causeway camps that probably represent the funerary habits of the ordinary rural population.[76] There is some Scottish evidence of the remains of an ordinary rural population which would ". . . test the caste theory properly. . . ."[77] The material culture of early Britain is remarkably uniform, and the people buried in the unchambered long barrows in England and Scotland are racially almost undistinguishable, notes Mackie.[78] However, the inhabitants of Skara Brae were non-farming specialists supplied with food by others. They were ". . . not peasants at all but some kind of elite group which was supported by gifts and tributes of food from the local rural population."[79] Mackie believes that this view is supported by the connection between the pottery of Skara Brae and that found at the ceremonial centers of southern England; by links with Irish passage graves and with Chalcolithic Portugal; and by the complete disappearance of mutton and beef remains after the storm (which overtook Skara Brae and caused the inhabitants to flee), suggesting the sudden cessation of tribute.[80]

Gordon Childe believes that the Orcadian tombs were developed from houses.[81] Hadingham considers that, in the Orkneys and in Malta, the central megalithic ideas may have been borrowed from outside but that the Orcadian tombs underwent an independent development.[82] Renfrew surmises that the *idea* was brought to the Orkneys by the first settlers but the *development* was purely a local process which evolved according to the needs and materials of the inhabitants.[83] The megalithic tombs reflect the interaction between Neolithic farmers and the existing local Mesolithic population.[84]

I think that two ethnically divergent groups could have coexisted peacefully for some time. I further surmise that the disappearance of mutton and beef from Skara Brae could have been due to the severity of the storm and not from the cessation of willingness to provide tribute.

Book Three

The Shetland Islands: The Northernmost Home of the Goddess

INTRODUCTION

Our quest now takes us north to the Shetland Islands. We could well expect that the Shetlands with a climate and physical environment similar to that of the Orkneys would reflect similar types of religious structures. What is surprising is the range and extent of differences, particularly in the architectural configuration of the tombs, temples and houses we shall examine. Among the most striking of the distinctively different features are the crescentic facades of the heel-shaped cairns and the lobed interiors of the temple buildings.

Scholars have advanced many hypotheses to explain these differences. We will touch upon them in this chapter and will note two major facts. First, the Shetland structures we will examine are later than those of the

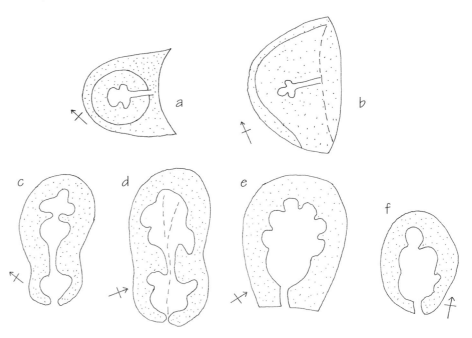

Fig. 72
Tombs, temples, and houses in Shetland (2000-1600 B.P.)

a) Vementry, Mainland
b) Punds Water, Mainland
c) Yoxie Temple, Whalsay Island
d) Benie Hoose, Whalsay Island
e) Stanydale Temple, Mainland
f) Gruting School House, Mainland

Orkneys, dating from between 2000 and 1600 B.P. compared with the period 3300 to about 2800 B.P. for the Orkney structures. Second, the abundance of Beaker-type pottery found in the Shetlands and associated with many of the sites reflects the arrival of a new immigrant group, the Beaker Folk, a tall, large-skulled (brachycephalic), robust people from northeastern Europe. Because the crescentic facades of the heel-shaped cairns and the lobed interiors of the temples reflect commonalities with other architectural forms, including the Maltese, we will face a puzzling question. Were the incoming Beaker Folk the medium for the transmission of these distinctive forms and, if so, in what way or through what linkages?

In the Shetlands, as in the Orkneys, I will limit my analysis of tombs, temples and other structures to those I personally visited. These are Vementry, Punds Water, Yoxie, Stanydale, the Benie Hoose and the

Plate 40. The Dwarfie Stane, Hoy, Orkney. Sandstone, 8.5 m x 4.5 m x 2 m high.

Plate 41. Entrance as seen from inside of Dwarfie Stane. The doorway stone appears on the outside. Note the convex lintel above the entrance.

Plate 42. Pillow in the south cell of Dwarfie Stane.

Plate 43. The Maes Howe tomb, facing northwest, Orkney. Mound 7.3 m high, 34.5 m diameter.

Plate 44. Three stones inside the Stones of Stenness, Orkney. Stones are 1 m high.

Plate 45. Knap of Howar house on Papa Westray, Orkney.
Inside measurements: 9.7 m x 4.8 m and 8 m x 3 m.

Plate 46. Inside Hut No. 8 at Skara Brae, Orkney. Note the dresser in the top center and the beds on the left and right.

Plate 47. View of Hut No. 8, Skara Brae. Note the humanoid shape — the "head" is on the right. Interior, 6 m x 4.8 m; exterior, 11.7 m x 8.8 m.

Plate 48. View of Vementry tomb, Mainland, Shetland, north side.
Tomb diameter 7.93 m, height, 1.80 m.

Plate 49. Southeast facade of Vementry tomb.
Length 10.98 m, height 1.22 m.

Plate 50. Triangular stone in Vementry facade. Stone is 1 m high.

Plate 51. Yoxie temple, Shetland, facing west.

Plate 52. General view of Stanydale temple, Shetland, facing east.

Plate 53. Stanydale temple facing southeast.

Gruting House (FIG. 72). I will mention or briefly discuss other structures when necessary. Though few in number, each is representative of a substantially larger corpus of sites.

In total, some 70 Neolithic houses[1] and 57 tombs[2] have been found in the Shetland archipelago. (Audrey Henshall claims that the total number of tombs is probably much greater; many still await discovery.[3]) Also, in Shetland, archaeologists have found the remains of temples or places of worship at Yoxie, the Benie Hoose and Stanydale.

Chapter One

Origin, Construction, Distribution and Tomb Types

As Audrey Henshall emphasizes, the question of tomb origins is complex. She discusses three possibilities: that the heel-shaped cairns were built by a new group of people from England or from Northern Europe; that they developed from Orcadian tomb types; that they originated from some tomb types that had existed in Shetland earlier.[4]

Shetland tombs, like Orkney tombs, were constructed from the inside out with more finished interior stone work having substantial exterior strength contributed by rougher stone courses. The chambers were roofed at a height of about 1.8 m, and the cairns were not very much bigger. The appearance of a tomb from the outside must have been that of a shallow dome built of stones.[5] The distribution of Shetland tombs, like that in the Orkneys, seems to have a maritime orientation[6] while reflecting agricultural land and settlement patterns.[7] This results in a visible relationship between tombs and house sites. The Shetland cairns are small in size but conspicuously placed in the harsh dramatic landscape. The facades and doorways of tombs and temples both face the southeast. Temples are located near houses and tomb sites.[8]

Most Shetland tombs are heel-shaped although a few are round, oval or square. The cairns tend to be small; the largest has a diameter of 17 m and the smallest 4.25 m. Most of the chambers are either trefoil-shaped or rectangular in plan, but some have five or six rounded recesses or apses. In building the chambers, the masons used massive blocks of stone, some of which measured 1.25 m or 1.50 m long and 0.61 m or more deep. They occasionally used orthostats in the form of tall slender stones as portal stones at the entrance. The length and width of chambers were about the same. Sometimes both chambers and passage were paved. The concave facades were carefully built with two or three courses of irregular vertical blocks and two tall uprights at either end to contain the vertical courses. The cairn entrance was through the facade or through a drop entry behind, leaving the facade unbroken.[9]

The Tombs — Vementry

The first site I visited was the Vementry tomb, a heel-shaped cairn, taking its name from the small uninhabited island on which it is located (FIG. 73). Visiting this tomb was an extremely exhilarating experience. The island of Vementry is inhabited only by sheep, seals and sea gulls. On the way back from the tomb, I went swimming in one of the many lochs on the island and suddenly found myself surrounded by seals who were curious about my presence in their domain. Vementry is separated from Mainland, the

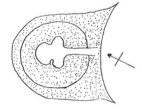

Fig. 73
Plan of Vementry tomb (c. 1800 B.P.). Diameter of cairn, 7.93 m; height, 1.80 m; facade 10.98 m x 1.22 m; chamber 2.74 x 3.2 m

largest of the Shetlands, by a narrow channel no more than 200 meters wide at its narrowest point. The cairn is situated on top of the highest hill, the Muckle Ward, 90 m high, at the north end of the island. It was built directly across the uppermost ridge of the hill with the ground falling away sharply in front and behind. The view is spectacular: an endless succession of deserted islets, inlets, and lochs.

The Vementry tomb is as dramatic as its setting (PLATE 48). The structure consists of a heel-shaped platform from which rises a circular cairn that encloses the chamber. An impressive and well-preserved facade faces the southeast (PLATE 49). It is slightly concave but, unlike the crescentic facades of the Maltese temples, it is not breached by an entrance. The wall forming the facade is constructed of massive, roughly square blocks of pink granite, carefully dressed and positioned so that their edges are in close alignment. The east end of the facade terminates in an upright triangular stone, 1 m high, placed with the longest side and the hypotenuse aligned against the two-course continuation of the wall (PLATE 50). So carefully fitted are the blocks that the triangular end-stone is essentially "locking in" its neighbours, preventing any slippage or movement.

The back wall of the facade has a number of dislodged and tumbled blocks, and it is not easy to discern where the platform ends and the cairn begins. The entrance to the cairn, behind the facade, faces southeast. The entrance passage consists of two courses of irregular granite blocks. The chamber itself is basically trefoil with a recess on each side of the entrance and a larger recess at the back of the chamber. A number of stones fell into the chamber with the collapse of the roof, and it is difficult to be sure of the details of its shape or to work out its exact size, which is within the 2.5 to 3.5 m range from cell back to cell back and from the entry point to the rear wall.

The chamber walls consist of five courses of long rectangular drystone except where stones of greater thickness occupy two courses. In many cases the stones are megaliths big enough to serve as an entire cell wall. There is very little corbelling in the two side cells and practically none in the back recess. The northeast part of the chamber still retains part of its roofing. Two beams extend across it and slant down toward the back, but the rest of the roof has collapsed into the chamber. Archaeologists have found no remains of any kind at Vementry, either inside the tomb or close to it.

The facades of Shetland cairns are their most imposing feature and indicate their function both as places of burial and ritual. The placement of triangular upright stones at the horns of the facades suggests an architectural as well as a symbolic purpose. One important aspect of the Vementry tomb lies in the extent to which its principal architectural features — the crescentic facade with retaining "horns" at either end and the trefoil or

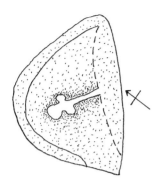

Fig. 74
Plan of Punds Water Tomb (c. 1800 B.P.). Diameter of cairn, 9.76 m; height 2 m; facade, 15.25 m x 1.3 m; chamber, 2 m x 1.76 m

lobed chamber — echo characteristic Maltese forms. Since the Shetland heel-shaped cairns belong to a later date (2000 B.P.), *it is not inconceivable that the idea for certain structural elements had come from the south.* The heel-shaped cairns of Shetland represent a variety of chamber tombs developed independently in Shetland by people from the south and west. Though many Shetland cairns have spectacular locations, they are not intrusive but blend with the landscape the way natural rock outcrops do.

PUNDS WATER

The second tomb I visited was Punds Water, a heel-shaped cairn on Mainland (FIG. 74). It is in a valley on a small knoll between two lakes and faces a large hill. The surrounding countryside is wild moorland studded with hillocks covered with heath and sometimes crowned by outcrops of rock. As is the case with many of the more remote cairns, Punds Water is not protected or maintained by the Bureau of Antiquities. As a result, there are no signs or markings to help the visitor find the cairn. I searched for Punds Water for three hours and finally, after climbing four hills, I saw it — a pile of rock in the distance.

Punds Water is larger than Vementry. Its concave facade is some 15 m in length and faces east. Just as at Vementry, large triangular stones act as end-supports for the facade wall. However, the tomb differs markedly from Vementry in that the center of the facade is pierced by the entrance passage to the tomb. Punds Water is roofless, and its facade has several badly deteriorated sections. However, the entrance is impressively intact at the entry point through the facade. The tomb chamber is basically a trefoil, not a distinctive chamber, giving onto three separate cells. The walls of the trefoil section stand about 1.5 m high.

In 1930, archaeologists cleared and partly excavated the trefoil chamber finding steatite sherds and tools, both of which seem to be typologically related to other such finds at Yoxie, the Benie Hoose, Stanydale and the Ness of Gruting house sites. The excavation of Punds Water showed that ". . . the floor consisted of clay in which were embedded red water-rolled pebbles which must have been brought from a distance."[10] That these pebbles were round, red and had been brought from a *long* distance is clearly significant. As we know from the evidence of the Paleolithic period, red is associated with death and resurrection, hence the importance of red ochre. That Neolithic Shetlanders went to the trouble of providing a red floor at Punds Water indicates the universality of this belief.

Though obvious questions arise from the tombs, we will better serve our immediate purpose in considering the temples of the Shetland Islands. Then, with two broad streams of architectural evidence observed, we can consider what we can deduce about the tomb and temple builders, their religion, and the extent to which it embraced the Great Goddess.

CHAPTER TWO

THE SHETLAND TEMPLES

A number of structures in the Shetlands are generally considered to be temples. They meet two basic criteria. They offer formal assembly space, and they allow for ritual and ceremonial functions. The structures I visited — Yoxie, the Benie Hoose and Stanydale — differ absolutely from the Stones of Stenness and the Ring of Brodgar. Though we can consider these two Orkney stone circles to be temples, this characterization reflects their likely use as assembly places for religious ceremonies. As large-scale, open-air arenas, they do not meet the traditional criteria of being roofed buildings dedicated to religious purposes. The Shetland structures were roofed buildings. My interpretation of the evidence leads me to believe that they were used for religious purposes. Some archaeologists oppose this interpretation, conceding only that Yoxie and Stanydale had some as yet undefined 'religious' or 'ceremonial' use and maintaining that the Benie Hoose was a non-religious structure.

YOXIE

Yoxie temple (2000-1600 B.P.) is located on Whalsay Island in an area known as Pettigarth Field, about 30 m from the sea, on the lower slopes of Gamla Vord Hill (FIG. 75). The hill ends in the cliff of Yoxie Geo. Higher up on the hill, about 91 m west of Yoxie, is the Benie Hoose. Like Vementry, Punds Water, Benie Hoose and many other sites, Yoxie has not come into the custodianship of the Bureau of Antiquities so despite its importance it is neither marked, fenced, nor in anyway protected. Deterioration of the limited remains has been extensive, and the inexperienced viewer might well consider the site to be no more than a ragged area of rock and rubble (PLATE 51).

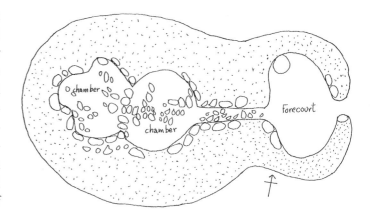

Fig. 75
Plan of Yoxie Temple, Whalsay Island, Shetland (c. 2000-1600 B.P.). Exterior, 18.75 m x 10.98 m; interior, 15 m x 4.4 m

Yoxie temple is a chambered structure with the upright stones set in drystone walls. The entrance is on the seaward side and the temple's 18 m longitudinal axis is in line with the Benie Hoose. As the illustration shows, once within the site, the visitor can clearly see the basic two-chamber configuration. The ground plan resembles a figure-of-eight with a large heel-shaped main section to the west and a central chamber from which a passageway leads into a horned forecourt. The tips of the horns almost meet. The degree of concavity is far greater than in the Vementry or Punds Water tomb sites or in any of the Maltese temple facades. Charles Calder, the archaeologist who excavated Yoxie, postulated in his article that the internal configuration of Yoxie and the Benie Hoose bear striking resemblance to Tarxien Far East.[11] This is now very hard to see because of

103

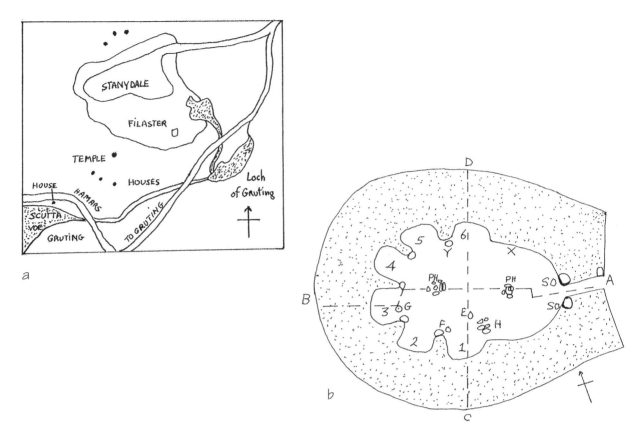

Fig. 76
Plan of Stanydale Temple, Mainland,
Shetland

a) Location map of Stanydale
b) Plan of Stanydale Temple (c. 1600
B.P.). Exterior, 24.4 m x 13.23 m x
3.66 m high; chamber, 11.98 m x
6.71 m; apses, 2.44 m x 1.22 m

the deteriorated state of Yoxie. However, resemblance becomes even more significant when two other factors are considered. The Shetland structures are later in time (c. 2000 to 1600 B.P.) and fall within the period of the Beaker people immigration from northeastern Europe. But our sequence of possible linkages is incomplete at present. Prehistorians can only speculate about possible links between the newcomers who overthrew the Maltese temple culture or the possible transmission of the island's architectural forms. In the census of tombs and megalithic monuments in western Europe, there is a tantalizing yet tenuous suggestion of intermediate forms in southern France and Italy. This will be considered in due course.

The walls of the Yoxie temple chambers were built of stones set upright in drystone courses. Calder states that, "The passage was lined with boulders, was paved, and showed a sill-stone on edge, but no door checks were found, this part of the side walls having been destroyed."[12] The main chamber appears to be circular and ". . . is mainly lined with slabs which, no doubt, originally carried rubble-faced walling above."[13] The inner of the two chambers is trefoil in plan, and is entered from the outer one " . . . through a doorway flanked on each side by a large upright portal stone, the taller of which is 4 ft 6 in. high. [sic]."[14] As was usual for Scottish tombs, houses and temples, the wall consisted of an inner and an outer row of boulders, the space in between being filled with rubble and peat. I was unable to find the south horn of the forecourt, intact when Calder excavated the temple. The floor is now one of grass though Calder reported it to have been of peat ash when he excavated the temple.[15] However, it is possible that this ash resulted from fires made by visitors over the centuries.

In sharp contrast to the other sites I have discussed, Yoxie has produced a large number of artifacts. The finds consist of ". . . between 120 and 130 rude stone implements including hammer and anvil stones, two rubbing stones, a socket stone and many of unusual but indefinite shape but none of precise datable value."[16]

STANYDALE

Stanydale (c.1600 B.P.), the second temple I visited, is in the center of Mainland, near the modern towns of Stanydale and Filaster (FIG. 76). Its site is flanked by Scutta Voe and the Loch of Gruting (PLATES 52 & 53). To the southwest is the high rocky ridge known as The Hamars. To the south of the temple are six standing stones, the nearest 12 m away, the farthest 35 m away. These stones appear to be related to the temple. They are probably the remains of an oval of standing stones (which Calder surmises were added during the Bronze Age[17] and which completely surrounded the temple.) There are also the remains of seven Neolithic dwellings close to the temple.

The temple is heel-shaped with the two ends of the heel forming the concave facade that shows clearly in the plan. The entry to the temple is through the center of the facade. The entrance passage leads into a single large oval chamber, almost 12 by 7 m (PLATE 54). The furthermost two-thirds of the chamber extend into six contiguous apses, three on each side of an imaginary center line. These apses are clearly separated from each other by radial partitions that end in rough orthostats placed in proper alignment with each other and the curving wall of the chambers. They appear to be entirely intrinsic to the original plan. As they project outward beyond the wall of the chamber, they do not lessen the area of the chamber to be spanned in roofing.

The temple walls are of the usual double-wall and rubble-fill type (PLATE 55). Massive sandstone blocks were used, either lengthwise or on edge, but positioned to fit closely and cleanly. The largest and best stones were reserved for the inner wall, which in some places is still two or three courses high.[18] Each end of the passage has a kerb stone and gives onto a small paved area with rocks at the edge. These small rocks may have been part of a device to secure the door or prevent entry to the temple or to the chambers.[19] The floors of the chambers are now grass-covered but originally were probably packed earth. Two post holes have been found along

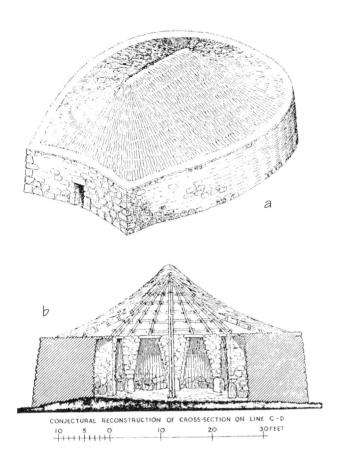

the longitudinal axis of the floor (see Plate 54 and Fig. 77). These were 61 cm deep and contained the remains of spruce poles about 25 cm in diameter. Without doubt these poles helped support a ridge pole and roofing timbers. In addition, ash from pine wood was found in the floor soil of the temple. Calder records the surprise occasioned when experts declared that the spruce and pine must have been imported since neither tree was native to the Shetlands during the Neolithic period. "The presence of these timbers implies that they reached Shetland from a source of origin either in Scandinavia or America or else, for the pine only, from Scotland, either as driftwood or by direct importation."[20] In all, some 700 meters of timber would have been required to make a roof strong enough to withstand the winter weather of the Shetlands.[21]

Fig. 77
Conjectural reconstruction of Stanydale temple

a) reconstruction on isometric projection
b) cross section

Stanydale has provided a modest haul of fragments from small and large pots, some probably related to potsherds in Whalsay though no primary source or type has been established. Some Beaker sherds were found,[22] suggesting that the temple remained in use for a prolonged period of time. Quartz cores and a perforated adze-shaped pendant made from pumice stone were also found.[23] This latter item is very much like one found in the Unival chambered tomb on North Uist by Sir Lindsay Scott, "who traces their distribution from the Mediterranean."[24]

A brief basic examination of Stanydale indicates that its purpose probably was to serve as a temple. The internal configuration has nothing in common with any chambered tomb. Stanydale's size (about 19 m long), the unique arrangments of the cells in the western half of the chamber, and the lack of evidence of any burials or cremations all suggest that it was a place of assembly. Since it is much larger than the average Shetland house, it is also conceivable that it could have also served as a habitation for communal living. The special efforts involved in roofing this structure indicate that it played an important central role in community life. There are similarities between Stanydale and Yoxie and the tombs: the curved facades, the long-short building techniques, the heel shape, and the entrances facing southeast.

But the differences are meaningful. Stanydale and Yoxie are twice as large as the tombs. Even though the facades of temples are important, the builders seem to have concentrated more on articulating the interior space. In the tombs, the emphasis is on the exterior, on the facade — and on creating a dramatic or even spectacular setting.

EVALUATION OF TEMPLES

To determine what links might exist between the Shetland tombs and those of Malta and whether Yoxie and Stanydale are likely to have been places in which the Goddess was worshipped, we must ask: What are the accepted beliefs about findings on the similarities and differences between these Shetland tombs and temples and those of Malta? What do the artifacts tell us? Why do only two structures appear to have temple-like characteristics?

Calder notes one leading researcher as stating that the heel-shaped cairns have certain structural details which suggest a link between them and the Mediterranean tradition, and also that the heel-shaped cairn "is not simply a degenerate Orkney or Caithness monument but is a variety of tomb developed independently by people with traditions of their own who perhaps reached the islands, not by way of North Scotland but directly from the south and west."[25] But again, prehistorians are reluctant to enlarge upon the theory and indicate the channels through which Maltese architectural forms may have traveled so far north after the demise of the island's temple culture.

The siting of structures provides interesting parallels between the two island groups. There is an observable similarity between the environment and location of Yoxie and that of Mnajdra in Malta. The Benie Hoose and Yoxie are about as close to the sea as Hagar Qim and Mnajdra; in both cases the distance between the two structures is much the same. Both Yoxie and Mnajdra are located in somewhat bleak and deserted parts of their respective islands, each approximately 50 m from the sea and 100 m from the associated structure.

In addition to Stanydale's Maltese-style configuration, the construction of the temple uses a long-short building technique, not as obvious and systematic as at Ggantija, but definitely present. This was particularly prevalent on the inside walls. The apses were built with horizontally laid courses of stone alternating with the vertical orthostats that form the edges of the alcoves.

We lack direct evidence from statues or incised signs and symbols of Shetland-Maltese Links, and one of the two Shetland temples, Yoxie, is in so poor a state of preservation as to make comparisons with Maltese temples very difficult. If we want to understand the Shetland temples' religious significance, it is crucial to examine the problem from every angle, paying attention to every clue that might establish a creative line of questioning. Prehistorians have advanced several possible reasons to account for the presence of only two temples: others exist but remain to be discovered; the temple builders were an incursive and possibly heretical group that either died out, moved on, or were subsumed into the native population. That there are only two such temple structures in all the British Isles and that they are similar to Maltese temples may support a connection between Scotland and the western Mediterranean. The artifacts that have been found (such as the fragments of big pots at Stanydale, suggesting a ceremonial function), the careful siting of the temples within their environment, the emphasis on interior space all indicate the worship of a chthonic deity. The temples share some important characteristics with the tombs, particularly in shape and in the long-short construction technique. This emphasizes an intended functional and symbolic relationship between the structures realized through burial rites and customs.

In the foregoing descriptions of tombs and temples, I have taken into account recent evaluations of major remains and artifacts considered to provide clues about their builders and allow for deductions about the type of lives they and their communities lived. But in contrast with my account of the Maltese tombs and temples, my discussion of the Orkney and Shetland island structures touches upon only a small part of a much larger census of cairns, stone circles, and other structures. Many of these have not been excavated; some that have been did not provide any new evidence supporting the worship of the Great Goddess. However, other structures discussed in the next chapter offer further clues.

CHAPTER THREE

SHETLAND HOUSES

My examination of house sites in Shetland, chronologically later than those in the Orkneys, served the same two purposes that governed my site visits in the Orkneys. It enabled me to develop beliefs and ideas about how the inhabitants lived and provided some light on the evolution of the temples and the extent to which they share in the Maltese architectural tradition that grew up around the worship of the Great Goddess.

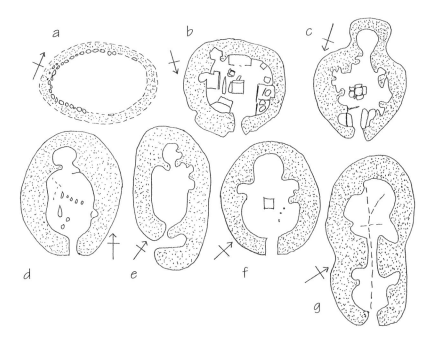

Fig. 78
Plans of Maltese and Scottish houses

a) Ghar Dalam, Malta (c. 4500 B.P.)
b) Hut 7
c) Hut 8, Skara Brae (3200 B.P.)
d) Gruting School House, Mainland, Shetland
e) Stanydale School House, Mainland, Shetland
f) Gairdie House, Mainland, Shetland
g) Benie Hoose, Whalsay Island, Shetland*

(d-g) c. 2000-1600 B.P.)

*The Benie Hoose appears with houses on this page for purposes of comparison.

The Shetland houses differ significantly in shape, size, construction and environment from those I examined in the Orkneys. They are oval and tend to be larger than the Orcadian houses. The walls consist of an outer and inner facade of large round boulders with a core of earth and rubble. While most Orcadian houses are clustered together and connect, as at Skara Brae, those on the Shetlands generally stand apart from each other. However, houses excavated in the Shetlands present very similar interiors to those of the Orkneys with recesses, bed alcoves, central hearths, stone benches, and — in some cases — a small chamber almost closed off from the house proper. As with the dwelling places in the Orkneys, the roofs were probably made of skins stretched over timber or whalebone rafters.

Many Shetland houses are actually humanoid in internal configuration (FIG. 78). Their interiors reflect, with a measure of restraint, the human icon more exuberantly encompassed in Maltese temples such as Ggantija and Mnajdra. There, Goddess and shrine were one. The Benie Hoose, the Gruting School House, the Gairdie, and the house or houses at Ness of

Gruting, Stanydale and at Jarlshof all reflect this configuration, though with a substantial degree of individual variation.

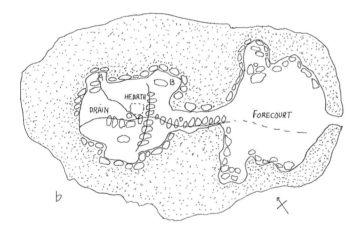

Fig. 79
Plan and location of Benie Hoose, Whalsay, Shetland (mid-2nd millennium B.P.)

a) Map of the Benie Hoose and Yoxie sites
b) Plan of the Benie Hoose. External, 24.40 m x 12.81 m; internal, 18 m x 7 m

THE BENIE HOOSE

The Benie Hoose has special significance and interest because of its size and its proximity to Yoxie temple on Whalsay island (FIG. 79). As noted earlier, the Benie Hoose is aligned on the same axis as the temple but is sited some 90 m higher up on the hill, about 200 m from the sea. The house, carefully excavated by Calder in 1954, is now in a poor state of preservation and difficult to locate. In my frantic two-hour search over hill and dale, I nearly had my eyes pecked out by a giant skua who was protecting her nest. On the way back from these monuments, I rescued a sheep that had become trapped in a bog, and then nearly missed the last ferry of the day.

Today, at first glance, the site gives the appearance of a pile of stones. On closer inspection, I could discern the shape of a chamber with recesses (PLATE 56) and a horned forecourt. The house has a figure-of-eight plan and a curved facade inside a horn-enclosed courtyard. With exterior measurements of 24 m x 12 m x 3 and interior measurements of 18 m x 7 m x 2.5 m, the structure is larger than " . . . any known habitation belonging to this phase of Shetland culture . . . as none of the ordinary houses is either heel-shaped or provided with a forecourt."[26] The western end of the interior chamber has been scooped out to make the floor level. The walling is of drystone construction with numerous large boulders on end or edge and incorporated in the lower courses. As usual, the filling between outside and inside walls is earth, rocks and peat. The forecourt, more or less circular in plan, was entered through a gap left between the ends of the horns. These were constructed from large boulders scarcely distinguishable among the general mass of rubble on the east side (PLATE 57). A drain ran along the axis of the structure, ending beyond the entrance to the forecourt. In the middle of the back recess is a small upright stone whose purpose remains obscure.[27] A hearth was probably situated in the center of the inner chamber. Whether people used it for domestic or for religious purposes is a matter of conjecture as prehistorians can make no final determination on the role the Benie Hoose played in community life. Other structures in the vicinity include a chambered tomb, a cisted cairn and a house.

The large Benie Hoose with its complex interior is obviously related in plan and construction to Yoxie. The similarities are basic, extensive and striking. They share a common axis; both face east. The Benie Hoose is bigger and its interior plan more complicated than any other of the Shetland houses I visited. Henshall states that there is a difference in type between pottery found in house sites and the Benie Hoose finds.[28] The contrast might indicate a difference in function. Perhaps the Benie Hoose pottery was ceremonial rather than utilitarian. Certainly Benie Hoose was no mere house. More probably it was another temple, a twin to Yoxie, whose function was to house the votive offerings of local residents, farmers who came to dedicate their precious tools to the goddess of death and fertility in order to ensure a good harvest. It may have served several functions, including a communal living area.

OTHER HOUSE SITES

Other house sites I visited in the Shetlands included the Gruting School House on Mainland, in the vicinity of Stanydale temple (FIG. 80). This house, which Calder excavated in 1951,[29] has a very humanoid shape. As there has been no attempt to protect this structure from the ravages of weather, the stonework has deteriorated, and its shape is no longer discernible. In fact, after searching for this site for one hour, I finally decided that I had been looking at it all along: it was an oval mound consisting of rocks and debris.

The historian Michael Dames, well known for his analysis of the purpose of Silbury Hill, suggests that the humanoid shapes of the Gruting School House and Shetland houses in general represent the Goddess. He noted that "Sometimes, as at Gruting School and Stanydale, she [the Goddess] is seen in profile, with the entrance corresponding to the vulva; the occupants of these houses lived out their lives within the protective body . . . At Gairdie, the house goddess is seen frontally, rather than in profile, and a setting of stones in the head may indicate, eyes, nose, and mouth"[30] (FIG. 81).

The plan of Gairdie seems to be closely related to the larger Yoxie temple. "For love of the same goddess," Dames relates, "the temple/house/figurine [sic] amalgam was probably created in both places."[31]

EVALUATION OF SHETLAND STRUCTURES

The impressive array of structures and related material, particularly pottery and household objects, we have examined sheds little direct light on the religious beliefs of the Neolithic islanders. Though many features of the tombs and temples, especially the horned forecourts at Vementry and

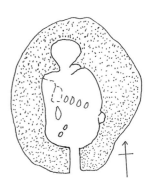

Fig. 80
Plan of Gruting School House, Mainland, Shetland (mid-2nd millennium B.P.). Exterior 18 m x 14 m; interior, 14 m x 10 m

Fig. 81
Plan of Gairdie House, Mainland, Shetland (mid-2nd millennium B.P.). External, 14.6 m x 12 m x 2.5 m; interior, 10 m x 8 m x 2 m

at Punds Water, the concave door jambs at Dwarfie Stane and the trilithon framing of burial cells at Holm of Papa Westray, recall the forms of the Maltese temples, we still lack needed direct evidence of the deities on the Neolithic islanders. To provide the strongest possible case in favor of the Goddess' power of life and death having been recognized by the tomb builders and Her worship maintained in the temples, we must draw upon anthropology and art in conjunction with architecture. The clues offered by parietal art, by carvings on stones in drystone walls and rocks and by artifacts, sculpture and pottery will be helpful in advancing our quest.

The fact that the tombs are the chief material evidence of the religious beliefs of their builders indicates the primacy of a religion rooted in a cult of the dead and a life after death, a religion whose deity held power over death and rebirth. Audrey Henshall notes that "The large number of tomb and their frequently astonishing size and elaboration indicate a powerful belief in a life after death . . . The 'Mother Goddess' associated with the tombs, particularly in Iberia and France, is also found depicted apart from the tombs, and even in areas where no tombs occur."[32] Goddess associations are found among the symbols and designs engraved on rock faces at a number of sites, some not connected with or close to tombs. Cairnbaan (near Lochgilhead) in Argyll is one such site. But New Grange, in Ireland, is perhaps the most famous of the tomb sites where carved rock faces within the tombs bear the spiral symbols and eye-motifs associated with the Great Goddess.

Gertrude Levy proposes that the mound-like outward appearance of the tombs, their crescentic forecourts, like horns, and the use of upright megalithic slabs — the pillar — are the symbolic manifestations of the Goddess.[33] Michael Dames shares this concept and demonstrates its validity through the Gruting School House, the Gairdie House, Hut 8 in Skara Brae, and Stanydale temple.[34] The illustrations in his text strongly support his theme. Dames adds that "Recent excavation carried out in Shetland enables one to say that the goddess is also found in the design of over 60 Neolithic houses belonging to the British Isles."[35]

The northern islands are rich in the remains of Neolithic dwellings places, often in suprisingly good states of preservation. Two factors account for this. The stone-built dwellings were not destroyed and recycled to the extent that occurred in settled areas — such as the Mesopotamian, Aegean, and Italian regions — where populations increased and people saw older structures as sources of building materials for newer ones. Secondly, the comparative isolation of the island groups and the harshness of life offered little attraction to outsiders. The original Neolithic inhabitants appear to have dwindled in numbers and either died out or moved away, probably to the Scottish mainland.[36] Other than Beaker folk and the Vikings, the Orkneys and Shetlands seldom saw invaders or permanent settlers from the outside.

CARVINGS IN TOMBS, TEMPLES AND HOUSES

As a class, carvings are the most numerous type of Neolithic artistic endeavor. Scattered throughout the British Isles and much of Europe are thousands of prehistoric carvings. They are found on natural rock faces and free-standing boulders overlooking wide-ranging views, in chambered tombs, on standing stones and in stone circles. In tombs, carvings can be found on adjacent stones or inside the tomb itself. The latter may be at the entrance, deep within or even hidden on the undersides of ledges or in narrow corridors, unlikely to be seen at all.

Fig. 82
Carved motifs in the Boyne Valley, Ireland

a) circle, b) spiral, c) arcs, d) serpentiforms, e) dot in circle, f) zigzag, g) lozenge, h) radials, i) parallel lines, j) offset

Claire O'Kelly illustrates the ten common motifs she had examined in the Boyne Valley in Ireland (FIG. 82). These motifs may well be termed archetypal as they occur — sometimes in modified forms — in almost all parts of ancient Europe and the British Isles. Most of the ten — circles, spiral, arcs, serpentiforms, dots-in-circles, zigzags, lozenges, radials, parallel lines, and offsets[37] — we commented on earlier as examples of engravings or carvings in the stonework of the Maltese temples.

Most tomb carvings are found in the south of Scotland. In the Orkneys, only four tomb sites (The Holm of Papa Westray, Eday Manse, Pickaquoy, Westray) and one habitation site (Skara Brae) contain carvings. In Shetland, only one carved stone has been found — the Scalloped Stone of Gunnister, from the island of Unst (FIG. 83).

The other three Orkney tomb sites that contain carvings are not among those we will examine from an architectural and structural viewpoint; however, the engravings merit discussion. The sites are at Eday Manse on Eday, on Westray, and at Pickaquoy on Mainland (see Fig. 60 and Plates 38 and 39). The carvings are very different from the inscriptions in the Holm of Papa Westray tomb. The Eday Manse carving consists of a double spiral, two sets of concentric circles and three arcs on a stone slab at the entrance of the tomb. The Pickaquoy carving consists of a series of concentric circles on *an upright stone* in one of the two cells of this tomb. The spirals and concentric circles of all of these carvings recall Maltese designs.

I cannot go so far as to suggest that the Neolithic cultures of Malta and the

Orkneys and Shetlands were in direct contact. There is no hard evidence of major sea voyages from the sheltered Mediterranean to the northern Atlantic. However, the unlikeliness of open sea voyages does not preclude local coastal traffic. It is possible that ideas were transmitted from the Mediterranean over land or by means of short coastal sea journeys, through trade, through casual intermediaries or by any combination of these channels.

The single example of carving found in Shetland is the Scalloped Stone of Gunnister. It is roughly oval in shape with a flat surface with a series of human-made depressions evenly spaced around its outer edge, ". . . rather as though a giant thumb had been at work on a huge pie crust."[38]

The Scalloped Stone has a counterpart at Mallia in Crete.[39] "There the stone is round, an offering table serving the same purpose as the *kernos,* used in the cult of the goddess from Mycenaean to Classical times, ringed with the same type of cup marks gouged out along its rim."[40]

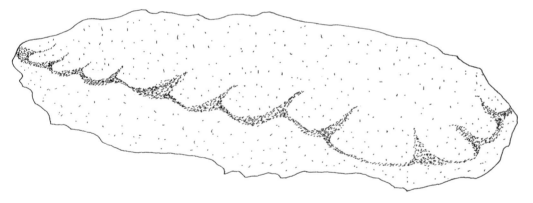

Fig. 83
The Scalloped Stone of Gunnister in
Unst, Shetland.
Limestone, 1.8 m x 92 cm

CHAPTER FOUR

CARVINGS: DESIGN, DERIVATION AND THE SEARCH FOR MEANING

The search for the meaning of cup and ring marks has given rise to a greater range of answers, suggestions and speculations than any other type of incised or engraved mark found in the Paleolithic and Neolithic ages. Scholars have considered these marks (which vary greatly in size, shape, depth, and configuration) to be anything from receptacles for liquids used in sacrifices or rituals[41] to signs of sun worship,[42] trade marks of prospectors for metals,[43] representations of the stars,[44] signs connected with ancestor worship,[45] much modified symbols representing woman,[46] and much modified symbolic representations of realistic portrayals of the goddess of death.[47]

Some prehistorians have suggested that ring and cup marks might represent the patterns in tapestries that had hung on the walls of dwellings.[48] Others have argued against this possible interpretation, noting that there is no ornamental or rhythmical scheme in the distribution of cup and ring marks on the stones on which they are carved. Others have suggested that the repetition of design elements (even though irregular) might represent movement. Thus cup marks might represent a deity looking first left then right, with the sweep of the eyes shown by the placement of cup marks while the head of the deity (which might be the rock upon which the cup-marks were incised) remains a single image, the face centered. Several cupmarks might therefore symbolize the omniscience of the Goddess.[49]

Macalister suggests a mutuality between visual art conventions and transmitted folklore.[50] Because ancient peoples made no formal separation between religion and ritual before the Hellenistic age, I believe it is plausible that some carvings were made as part of the rituals involving performance, or perhaps as visual manifestations of myths. Herberger notes that mythopoetic thinking was normal among "primitive" peoples;[51] there is no separation in the "primitive" mind between art and religion. Both are integrated aspects of life.

Dames provides a strong argument in support of the Goddess-with-moving-eyes hypothesis: "The eye motif played an orthodox and vital part in Great Goddess worship, wherever Neolithic culture developed; certainly it was important in Spain, France, and the British Isles . . . the oculi designs were integrated so thoroughly as to become wholly characteristic, appearing on pots, portable idols, such as the chalk Folkton Drums . . . and engraved on the walls of tombs."[52] If seen in isolation as they sometimes are, the eyes should be considered as a ". . . formalized iconography of a goddess figure and . . . they 'assume the visual role of the complete figure elsewhere'."[53]

Other prehistorians have noted that spiral motifs have a multitude of meanings, many associated with the Great Goddess. These include the flow of energy, the transition from death to life; they may symbolize ". . . the belly and navel of [the Goddess]. . . the navel of the earth — the omphalos."[54] Levy mentions that ". . . milk was still poured in recent times upon the cup-holes."[55]

The French archaeologist and art scholar Déchelette believes that the

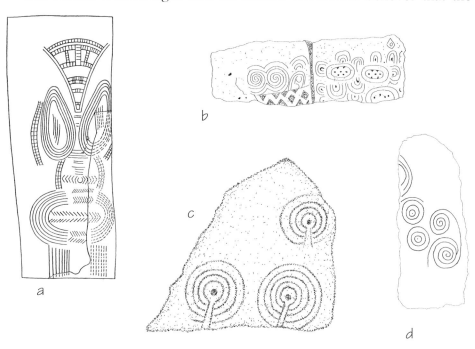

Fig. 84
The Eyes of the Goddess

a) Abstract female figure engraved on a mammoth tusk from Předmosti, Czechoslovakia, Upper Paleolithic, Gravettian Period, 28,000-22,000 B.P., 15.5 cm high
b) Carved stone from New Grange (3200 B.P.), 3.4 m long
c) Carved stone found in Kirkdale Burn, Galloway, Scotland (late Neolithic), 50 cm x 50 cm
d) Stone carving found at Eday Manse tomb in Eday Island, Orkney (early 3rd millennium B.P.), 1.20 m long

carvings may be symbolic, deriving their forms as a result of religious syncretism. They might be ". . . the progressive degeneration of a small number of traditional images, which were originally perfectly understandable, and which were perpetuated, in spite of their distortions, thanks to the conservatism of funerary rites and customs."[56]

Spiral motifs could have had a multitude of meanings, some or many associated with the Goddess. They could have symbolized the pathway between two worlds or from one state of being to the other, the flow of energy[57] or a regenerative connection between earth and sky. In New Grange, a few minutes after dawn at the winter solstice, a beam of light travels 21 m into this tomb and shines for a few moments on the basin within, where cremated bodies must have lain, overlooked by a triple spiral carving — the eyes of the Goddess.[58]

Hadingham reflects that similar designs appear not only in Europe but all over the world.[59] Piggott thinks that the Orcadian carvings are related to Irish passage grave art from the Boyne culture which in turn originated in

Iberia.[60] Hadingham indicates that many of the examples from Spain are accompanied by representational elements that are stylized and are therefore probably later.[61] Also the record shows that these motifs first appeared in the Paleolithic as far back as the Mousterian period (35,000 B.P.).[62] In fact, there seems to be a similarity in style and concept between French and Irish Neolithic carvings and certain images from the Upper Paleolithic (FIG. 84).

At first reading, this list of suggested interpretations of cup and ring marks may seem fanciful and contradictory. However, each interpretation has been based upon the careful study of specific sites and the location of the site and its markings in the context of other archaeological clues such as the types of dwelling places, tombs, and temples and other remains found in the vicinity. In his discussion of cupmarks, Aubrey Burl says: "The carvings on many cist-slabs in the British Isles show just how much variation there was, and perhaps no other facet of prehistoric life shows how important symbolism was to those people."[63] He notes that at several sites, including Baluacraig and Achnabreck in Argyll, Scotland, and at Burgatia, County Cork, and Ardmore, County Donegal, none of the groups of numerous cupmarks presents a self-explanatory pattern.[64]

We appear to have prehistorians who interpret the possible meaning of these carvings according to four viewpoints: practical, aesthetic, ritualistic and symbolic. Those who believe the primary function of the carvings was aesthetic see them as decorative or representative of tapestry. Some claim that, although the symbolic element may originally have been more important, aesthetic consideration subsequently influenced and modified designs. Others ascribe a ritualistic function to the carvings: Neolithic people used them for divination, as offerings of appeasement or, in ceremonies of ancestor worship they fulfilled a ceremonial, spiritual, or symbolic purpose.

What we have, then, is the presence of cupmarks in their many variants found on the dressed stones of cairns, on the surfaces of moorland rocks,

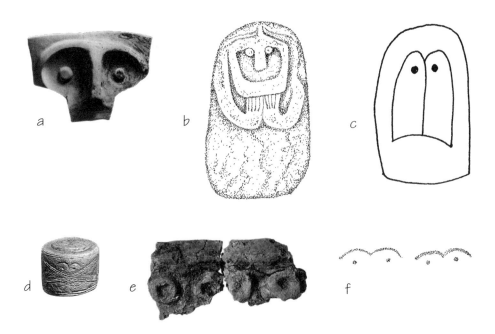

Fig. 87
The Eye Goddess in Europe

a) Ruginosa vase (late 5th millennium B.P.; 60 cm x 38 cm
b) Stele from Benezet, France (Neolithic)
c) Statue-menhir from L'Isle-sur-Gorge, Vaucluse, France (Neolithic)
d) Folkton Chalk Drum (2000 B.P.)
e) Eye motif on Skara Brae pot (3200 B.P.)
f) Eye motif in the Holm of Papa Westray South tomb (3000 B.P.)

on standing stones and on the walls of dwelling places. It is possible that these shallow depressions, when on horizontal surfaces, were meant to contain liquids — as part of a ritual or sacrifice — or that they were no more than random decoration. Several interpretations may be valid and acceptable in part or in full. However, while the cupmarks of the British Isles and of the Orkneys and Shetlands are within the far wider tradition of such markings throughout western Europe, they do not of themselves provide irrefutable or compelling evidence of worship of the Great Goddess. Nevertheless, given the frequent proximity of cupmarks to other symbols of the Great Goddess in Malta, in Iberia and in Portugal (for example, at Almeria), it is difficult to dismiss the strong suggestiveness of the cupmarks of the Orkney and Shetland islands.

SCULPTURE

When we assess the very few pieces of Neolithic sculpture that have been found in Great Britain, we are likely to associate them with the religion of the Great Goddess. Unfortunately, "very few pieces" must be read literally. The Folkton Drums (three linked items) and the Chalk Goddess of Grimes Grave represent virtually the whole trove of somewhat representationally depicted images found to date (FIGS. 85 & 86).

It is of interest that while the Folkton Drums were found in Yorkshire, the Chalk Goddess was found some three hundred miles south in Norfolk. Both are east coast sites. The three Folkton drums were found together in the grave of a five-year-old child. They are solid chalk, presumably taken from the sea cliffs nearby, and they are elaborately and beautifully carved, grooved circles incised on the tops and lozenges, triangles and chevrons carved on the sides.[65] Prominent on each side is a panel with a carefully carved eyebrow and eye motif. We can see early similarities of these oculi designs in the eyes of a bird goddess found on a vase from Ruginosa, Romania, dating from the fifth millennium and from statue menhirs from Neolithic France such as the ones from Benezet and L'Isle-sur-Gorge (FIG. 87).

The symbols engraved on the Folkton Drums suggest a recognition of the Great Goddess as the goddess of death and regeneration. However, this instance of Her symbols being interred in a grave may be unique. It is possible that this particular child was thought to have some special intercessory power and therefore should be buried with some additional marks of respect.

The English archaeologist O.G.S. Crawford suggests that the Folkton Drums are of Iberian inspiration, and Déchelette considers that they represent an important link in the simplification process whereby the goddess image shifted from Iberian and Portuguese owl-faced representations to the abstract conceptions found at Gavr'inis and New Grange, in which spiral forms are exuberantly expansive (see Fig. 31).

The Chalk Goddess of Grimes Grave was found on a chalk pedestal at the bottom of a flint mining pit and dates from c. 2460 to 1720 B.P.[66] "In front of her lay a triangular heap of blocks of mined flint, with a chalk lamp opposite. The seven red deer antlers which lay on this heap, presumably as offerings, were a possible indication of the number of those working in this pit. This assemblage strongly suggests the propitiation of an 'Earth Goddess' combined with the appeal for more abundant or better quality flint in the next pit."[67] The Goddess displays the classic features that characterize the figurines of the Paleolithic period, the same overall obesity, the same large breasts. The arms, truncated, are positioned in a way that would have allowed for the hands to be clasped together low on the abdomen. Typically, the Goddess is sculpted with a massive pubic region. The upper thighs also are massive, but nothing is present below the midpoint.

Though the Folkton Drums and the Grimes Grave Chalk Goddess are virtually the only sculptured representations or figurines of a female deity to be found in Neolithic Britain, this should not obscure their significance. As noted, the Folkton Drums were found with an interred child's skeleton in a grave that was part of a larger burial site; the place of transition to the world of the dead. The association and its meaning cannot be more direct. Similarly, flint miners carefully placed the Chalk Goddess in a site whose product, the high-quality flint, was an essential working and domestic tool in the Neolithic world. Given the poor quality of the pit and the careful placement of the figurines, it stands to reason that some propitiatory rite or pleas for assistance led the miners to their action. Both the Grimes Grave

Goddess and the Folkton Drums strongly reflect the iconographic characteristics of the Great Goddess. If not proof that She was worshipped in at least some areas of Britain, the goddess and the drums remain very convincing clues. Other sculptured artifacts found at Neolithic sites in the British Isles suggest that in some parts of the country Neolithic Britons worshipped the Goddess (see Fig. 67). As noted in the discussion of the Maltese temples, two stone spheres with grooves and protrusions were discovered in Tarxien and the Hypogeum (see Fig. 40). As these spheres do not seem to have any practical purpose, it is possible that they had symbolic importance in some part of the rituals of worship, which may also be the case with the Scottish stone balls.

In keeping with the Paleolithic custom of burying jewelry, pendants, and other decorative objects with the dead — a custom that carried on into a number of Neolithic cultures including Malta — we could expect to find grave goods recovered from British Neolithic tombs and burial sites. Both in the Orkneys and in the Shetlands such items have been found in houses and in tombs. Archaeologists have found some 1800 implements at the Benie Hoose;[68] Taversoe Tuick revealed Unstan Ware, disk beads, and a star-shaped object; Punds Water yielded steatite sherds and tools. There are other such finds at Yoxie, the Benie Hoose, Stanydale and the Ness of Gruting house site. Skara Brae has yielded beads of the most common type made from a variety of materials — boars' tusks, killer whales' teeth, and cows' teeth.

Archaeologists found miniature adze-shaped pendants in Stanydale temple, at Unival in North Uist and in other Shetland temples sites. As noted on page 106, Sir Lindsay Scott traced their distribution to the Central Mediterranean.[69] Miniature axes used as pendants have been found in Shetland House sites and in Orcadian tombs.

Scholars have analyzed the Orkney and Shetland carvings intensively and have argued over their beliefs. The bulk of published findings confirm that the symbols and motifs fall well within the major traditions represented throughout Europe. Of greater importance is the extent to which these findings confirm that the Orkney and Shetland islanders were in continued contact with Neolithic peoples from the western European seaboard and that some of the island dwellers — if not all — had originally migrated from that seaboard.

The oculi forms found at the Holm of Papa Westray and Pickaquoy call to mind the screens of the Tarxien temple (FIG. 88) and their forerunners — the oculi motifs and bird goddesses of Danubian Europe — e.g., the Bird Goddess of the Ruginosa Vase. The triangles incised at Skara Brae may seem to be poorly executed, pale reflections of those in the shrines of Çatal Hüyük — yet the fact that they were executed at all suggests their

a   b

Fig. 88
Spirals in Orkney and Malta

a) Pottery sherd from Skara Brae
(3200 B.P.)
b) Spiral on stone screen, Tarxien
Center, Malta (mid-3rd millennium
B.P.). Globigerina limestone, area
approx. 1 m x 50 cm

importance as magical images. Also significant is the commonality of forms between the Westray stone and the Pickaquoy Stone's paired spirals and those of Gavr'inis and New Grange — where spirals have been carved with exuberant energy. These spirals have their antecedents in the Paleolithic Age; the Prědmosti figurines (a female figure engraved on a mammoth tusk) bears the same type of concentric circles (see Fig. 84).

One further engraved symbol found both in Malta and Orkney needs to be mentioned here as it may have some hidden significance hitherto fathomable: a three-pronged engraving (FIG. 89). In Malta it appears on a pebble, on a potsherd and on a bead while in Orkney it is part of the magical engraved symbols of the Holm of Papa Westray tomb. Maybe it is an extreme abbreviation of the Goddess giving birth as first seen in the Çatal Hüyük sanctuary. The double-axe motif is also found both in Malta and in Orkney (FIG. 90).

The Orkney and Shetland carvings may seem to provide, at best, scant evidence of the worship of the Great Goddess in the archipelagoes in Neolithic times, and that scant evidence may seem indirect when compared to the forcefulness and richness of the evidence that the Maltese carvings provided. Yet, when examined in the broader context of representations of the Great Goddess in Paleolithic times, this evidence confirms that the Orkney and Shetland findings clearly reflect the continuing forms and patterns of which the Maltese carvings were only one development.

CONCLUSION

Our survey of tombs, temples, carvings, sculptures and other artifacts is as complete as space will allow. Throughout, I have kept a single aim in sight: to determine to what extent physical evidence suggests that the religion of the Great Goddess was present in the Orkney and Shetland Islands. The megalithic tombs (Maes Howe, Taversoe Tuick, Dwarfie Stane, Holm of Papa Westray, Vementry) that I visited and examined, and the temples I studied (Yoxie and Stanydale) in and of themselves present

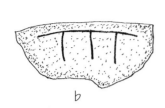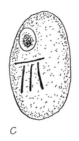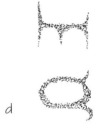

a   b   c   d   e

Fig. 89
Three-pronged engraved symbols

a) Maltese cylindrical bead of hard greenstone; the engraved pattern is inlaid with gold and precious stones (3000-2500 B.P.), 2.5 cm
b) Maltese potsherd (3000-2500 B.P.), 4.5 cm
c) Maltese pebble pendant (3000-2500 B.P.), 4 cm
d) Triple Goddess giving birth to a bull motif, from Holm of Papa Westray tomb, Orkney (3000 B.P.); approx. 150 cm
e) Schematic relief of Twin Goddesses giving birth to two bulls, from Çatal Hüyük (5800 B.P.), 2.2 m high

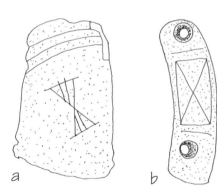

a   b

Fig. 90
Double-axe motifs in Malta and Scotland

a) Maltese potsherd with scratched decoration including double axe motif (3000-2500 B.P.), 5 cm x 3 cm
b) Engraved boar's tusk pendant from Skara Brae (3200 B.P.) showing double axe motif, 5 cm x 3 cm

122

particular affinities and analogies with the tombs and temples of Malta. The artifactual evidence is less substantial; carvings, sculpture and beads and pendants are fairly sparse. However, all the examples seem to fit easily within the broad range of symbols, designs and images that depicted or reflected the Great Goddess in the Neolithic Mediterranean world. Some of these designs and depictions, particularly the cup and ring marks, date back to the Paleolithic; others, such as the double axe, were clearly expressed at Çatal Hüyük; others, including the spiral and pit marks, reached a high stage of development in Malta; others such as the oculi designs found on the Folkton Drums, have their origins in southeastern Europe; finally others like the Grimes Grave Goddess, hark back to the Paleolithic.

The task now is to compare directly the tombs and temples of the Orkney and Shetland Islands with those of Malta in an effort to determine to what extent the megalithic architecture of Malta influenced the tomb and temple builders of the distant northern islands. A number of prehistorians have addressed this question; some in passing, others with intense concern. Most, however, have restricted themselves to comments based on a personal commitment to either the diffusionist theory or the independent invention theory as being the valid means of accounting for the occurrence of similar structures in widely separated places.

Both theories are straightforward. Diffusionists, for example, would hold that the architecture of the tombs and temples of the Orkneys and Shetlands reflect design and construction ideas that were consciously brought, by whatever means, from the Mediterranean littoral and the Neolithic settlements of the Atlantic seaboard by peoples able to apply them in a new setting. Prehistorians supporting the independent invention theory emphasize that these architectural and constructional forms could have been developed independently with little or no knowledge of similar forms elsewhere. As expressed here, the two theories appear simple, clear-cut, and opposed. In reality, seldom is either offered as an absolute. Generally the arguments among historians focus on the extent to which independent invention can be supported versus the degree of likelihood of ideas or forms being transmitted by the trader, the traveller and the teacher. The literature of argument is copious. It addresses not only the problems of prehistory but also those of contemporary scientific progress in archaeology and in analysis of ancient artifacts.

Of the prehistorians who have addressed the question of similarities between the Scottish and Maltese temples, few have chosen to bring a close analysis of all the relevant factors — sites, design, construction, carvings, sculpture, grave goods, and other artifacts — when discussing the possible and probable links between the Maltese tombs and temples and those of the Orkney and Shetland Islands.

This chapter has attempted to show that a certain unity existed between various megalith-building groups in Scotland, perhaps due to comparable religious practices involving a similar chthonic deity. The present enquiry will, we hope, spur further investigatory work.

Book Four

Comparison: The Architectural Legacies of Malta and Scotland

CHAPTER ONE

TOMBS: ABODES FOR THE SACRED DEAD

A glance at the chronology of the Maltese, Orcadian and Shetland tombs is a necessary prelude to any comparison of the structures and their commonalities. Widely accepted radiocarbon dates for the Maltese and Scottish tombs are listed (FIG. 91), and comparative line drawings of the structures are presented (FIG. 92).

The evolution of form and function is straightforward in the case of the Maltese structures. The Xemxija tombs clearly evolved from the earlier Zebbug tombs and these probably from even earlier Italian examples such

Fig. 91
Radiocarbon dates for Maltese and Scottish tombs

(The scale reflects the radiocarbon dates for the construction of tombs and temples; it is therefore not a series of equal divisions.)

Date B.P.	Malta	Orkney	Shetland
Before 4,000	Zebbug tombs	– – –	– – –
after 4,000	Xemxija tombs	– – –	– – –
3,800	Hypogeum	– – –	– – –
3500-3000	Hypogeum	Taversoe Tuick Dwarfie Stane	– – –
3000-2800	Hypogeum	Holm of Papa Westray	– – –
2,800		Maes Howe	– – –
2,000-1800			Vementry (1800) Punds Water

as the tomb at Pizzone near Taranto or the one at Serra d'Alto.[1] The multipurpose Hypogeum is an advance. It encompasses both tombs (in the upper and lower levels) and temple chambers (middle level).

The sequence of form and function in the Scottish structures is less clear. Buildings on these distant, isolated islands reflect a surprising range of designs, approaches and construction techniques.[2] An explanation that may well accord with the physical evidence is that the population groups arriving from the mainland, from Ireland and later from Scandinavia, each brought somewhat differing tomb and temple traditions reflecting locally evolved burial and worship practices. Given the great distance of these northern archipelagoes from the Mediterranean birthplace of megalithic architecture and its long migration north — both in time and through differing local environments — we can expect temples and tombs to have evolved significantly from the earliest Italian and Maltese archetypes. The Holm of Papa Westray, Taversoe Tuick and Maes Howe tombs derive from the small tripartite type of chambered tomb found both on the Scottish mainland and in Ireland.[3] Taversoe Tuick, in addition, is one of only three cairns out of 50 that have rock-cut elements.[4]

Maes Howe has given rise to more wide-ranging comment. Henshall believes that this superb tomb was the prototype for a series of tombs (the Maes Howe Group which includes the Holm of Papa Westray and Quanterness tombs)[5] while Renfrew[6] thinks it is the last of the Maes Howe series and was a link between tombs and henge monuments of which the nearby Ring of Brodgar and the Stones of Stenness are dramatic and stirring examples. (We should note that Henshall published her findings in 1963, while Renfrew published his in 1979, thus having additional archaeological research to draw upon.)

The Dwarfie Stane might be derived from Sardinian examples (3rd millennium) or from southern Italian *tombe a forno* (oven-type tombs) going back to the 5th millennium.[7] Vementry and Punds Water, the two Shetland tombs, originate either from forms found in north central Europe[8] via early Shetland heel-shaped cairns (such as Crooksetter SE and NW, near Delting in Shetland[9]) or from structures found in southwest Europe and on the northern Mediterranean littoral.[10] What is compelling about these two tombs (and other heel-shaped cairns) is that their forecourts and curved facades reflect — in somewhat crude miniature — a graceful and distinctive characteristic of the Maltese temples. A comparison of the Vementry and the Mnajdra facades illustrates this.

The burial practices of the Orkney and Shetland islanders appear to have differed from those prevalent in Malta. The Xemxija tombs and the Hypogeum were both repositories for human bones. These were few at Xemxija, but the Hypogeum can better be described as an ossuary as it contained the bones of some 7,000 persons. Prehistorians have qualified this impressive total by noting that the bones date from about 3800 B.P. to 3000 B.P. and probably represent in part the transferring of bones from other tombs and burial sites.[11] No ancient remains were discovered at the Holm of Papa Westray, the Dwarfie Stane, Maes Howe and Vementry. Taversoe Tuick

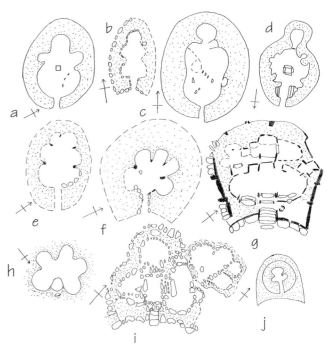

Fig. 92
Plans of various Maltese and Scottish structures

a) Gairdie House, Shetland
b) Tarxien Far East Temple, Malta
c) Gruting School House, Shetland
d) Hut 8, Skara Brae, Orkney
e) Brouster House, Shetland
f) Sulma Water Cairn, Shetland
g) Mnajdra South Temple, Malta
h) Xemxija Tomb 5, Malta
i) Ta Hagrat South and North temples, Malta
j) Vementry Tomb, Mainland, Shetland

revealed Unstan Ware disk beads, and a star-shaped object was found in the small chamber, as well as cremated human bones discovered in the upper and lower chambers. Punds Water yielded a steatite sherd and tools. These latter seem to be typologically related to other such finds at Yoxie, the Benie Hoose, Stanydale and the Ness of Gruting house site.[12]

Even a summary comparison between the Orkney and Shetland tombs and those of Malta clearly demonstrates a variety of links in design, construction and siting. It also demonstrates the substantial differences between the Orkney tombs and those of Shetland, with the latter having strong similarities to the Maltese temples. Looting in ancient times and the effects of wind and weather over the centuries have left little on which we can anchor any substantial case about the people who built and used the tombs or about the rituals their religion called for. But the little that has survived strongly suggests that at least the Orcadian society was an egalitarian one.[13] The engravings and artifacts that have been found lend support for, but cannot prove, the worship of the Goddess. The comparison of the Yoxie temple with Tarxien Far East and of Stanydale with Mnajdra South temples (see pp 133-137) may furnish stronger and more direct evidence. However, our first step is to compare the Scottish tombs with those of Malta.

SIMILARITIES AND DIFFERENCES IN MALTESE AND SCOTTISH TOMBS

A comparison of Maes Howe, Taversoe Tuick, Dwarfie Stane, and Holm of Papa Westray (Orkneys) and Vementry and Punds Water (Shetlands) with the Xemxija tombs and the Hypogeum will establish the extent to which specific commonalities of form and function suggest links between these far distant structures (FIG. 93).

FORM

In size and proportion, the Xemxija and the Hypogeum tombs are similar to those at Vementry and Punds Water (Shetlands); there is also a similarity in shape between the tomb chambers at Vementry and Punds Water and those of Xemxija and the Hypogeum (see Appendix A-1). However, we cannot record this similarity between the Maltese structures and the Orkney tombs. Rectangular slabs vertically slice the interior space of the Taversoe Tuick chambers; the Dwarfie Stane bears no resemblance beyond having a tripartite chamber; Maes Howe and Holm of Papa Westray are characterized by a high level of conscious design and fully finished construction; both have almost symmetrical plans. Though the side chambers of the Holm of Papa Westray are lobed and irregular, they seem orderly and calculated in contrast with those of the other tombs we have discussed.

Although the Dwarfie Stane is a single structure fully above ground and small and primitive in comparison to the Hypogeum, it inspires in the visitor a sensation somewhat similar to that experienced in this Maltese

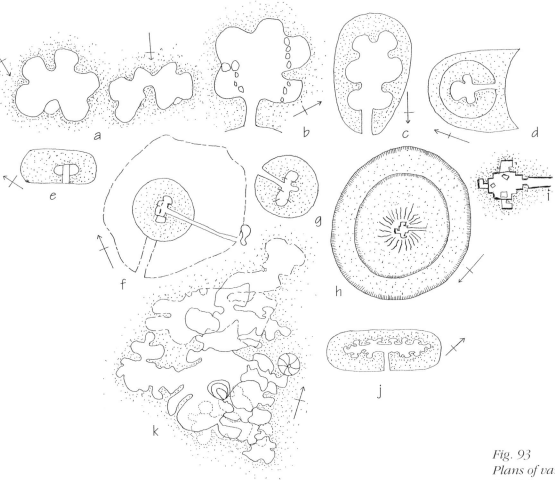

Fig. 93
Plans of various Maltese and
Scottish tombs

a) Xemxija tombs, 1, 2, 5, Malta
b) Punds Water tomb, Shetland
c) Gravlaba tomb, Mainland,
Shetland
d) Vementry, Mainland, Shetland
e) Dwarfie Stane, Hoy, Orkney
f) Taversoe Tuick, Rousay, Orkney
g) Taversoe Tuick, upper chamber
h) Maes Howe tomb, Mainland,
Orkney
i) Maes Howe chamber
j) Holm of Papa Westray South
tomb, Orkney
k) Hypogeum, Malta

subterranean site. One reason for this is the awareness of being within a hewn-out space with solid walls as opposed to a constructed space with built masonry walls. The Dwarfie Stane's two side chambers, almost cubical, with rounded corners and entered through thresholds that have low stone kerbs, concave jambs and slightly convex lintels, reflect — in a less refined version — similar features in the chambers of the Hypogeum's middle level (PLATES 58 & 59).

In an interesting contrast, the lower chamber of Taversoe Tuick, though cut out of the surrounding rock, is lined with drystone walling that seems either an attempt to suppress its rock-cut reality or, by disguising it, make it more magically effective. It is as if Taversoe Tuick represented structural elements from two separate traditions.

From most points of view, however, Maes Howe seems to stand outside the basic form found in Maltese tombs and, although it represents the culmination of Orcadian tomb architecture, it possesses a number of finely developed features that make it unique among these tombs. Maes Howe is symmetrical, finished and grandiose while the other tombs (both Maltese and Orcadian) have an organic, asymmetrical quality stressing process as opposed to finished product. For instance, Taversoe Tuick shares with

Maes Howe a round cairn with centralized chamber and side cells. But, while the tomb chambers of Taversoe Tuick are curvilinear and asymmetrical, the Maes Howe chamber is square, and its side chambers, all the same size, are symmetrically disposed around it. At Taversoe Tuick, the vertical slabs divide the space. At Maes Howe, the orthostats have a structural and an aesthetic function. They help support the high, weighty roof, and they create vertical accents that constrast with the finely finished and even courses of horizontal stones with which the chamber is built. In contrast with Maes Howe's symmetrical balance, Taversoe Tuick is organic and asymmetrical. Its unusual combination of structural elements creates the feeling of evolution over time. On the other hand, Maes Howe is complete and impressive, the result of a single architectural conception.

The contrast between Maltese tombs and Maes Howe is even more pronounced. Maes Howe seems to be an absolute structure in stylistic terms while the Hypogeum reflects an organic architecture, a feeling of having developed over the centuries. In fact, from its overall plan, the Hypogeum looks like an accretion of Xemxija tombs, a likeness which reveals its origin.

In general, excavated spaces are more frequently rounded and less often angular than built structures are. The former use tunnel forms and rounded corners; the latter frequently use angular and straight line forms, adopted for ease of construction or for purposes of strength and stability. Thus it is not surprising that the tomb chambers of Vementry and Punds Water are more angular than the lobe-shaped tombs at Xemxija.

One further observation should be made. Perhaps the most substantial difference between the architecture of the Orkney and Shetland tombs is that the latter have paved forecourts with crescentic facades or retaining walls. These end in a triangular stone that locks-in the drystone courses. This feature is a clear reflection of a major and constant characteristic of the Maltese temples (PLATES 60 & 61).

SPACE

Space includes exterior space, the orientation of a structure and its environment as well as interior space, the space enclosed by the interior mass of a structure.

The interior space of the Xemxija tombs and of the Hypogeum is the most important structural characteristic. Because of their small size and scooped-out quality, the Xemxija tombs made me feel enclosed, as in a womb. The interior space of Tomb 5 creates the sensation of one moment in time; the interior space of the Hypogeum evokes the sensation of the passage of time, a time that is forever recreating itself. The Dwarfie Stane is a container; the space is too limited to do much else than enclose. Unlike

Plate 54. Inside chamber of Stanydale, facing south. Note the posthole in the center towards the right.

Plate 55. Stanydale, detail of outer wall. 1.2 m high, 3.6 m thick.

Plate 56. Inside chamber of Benie Hoose, Shetland, facing east.

Plate 57. Facade of Benie Hoose, north side of forecourt, facing west; left upright stone, 1 m high.

A comparison between the doorways of the Hypogeum and the Dwarfie Stane.

Plate 58. Doorway lintel and jamb in Hypogeum, Malta.

Plate 59. Doorway lintel and jambs inside the Dwarfie Stane, Hoy, Orkney, facing west.

The end stones of Maltese and Scottish structures.

Plate 60. Detail of southeast facade of Vementry tomb, Mainland, Shetland.

Plate 61. Ggantija South Temple, west outside wall.

Comparison between Stanydale and Mnajdra temples from the back.

Plate 62. Back of Stanydale temple, Shetland, facing southeast.

Plate 63. Back of Mnajdra Central and South temples, facing southeast.

Inside chambers of Stanydale and Mnajdra East temples.

Plate 64. Stanydale, facing northwest.

Plate 65. Mnajdra East, facing southwest.

Facades of the Benie Hoose and Mnajdra temples.

Plate 66. TheEsat facade of the Benie Hoose temple, Whalsay, Shetland.

Plate 67. the east facade of the Mnajdra South temple.

Overview of the Benie Hoose and Ggantija South chambers.

Plate 68. Ggantija south temple.

Plate 69. The Benie Hoose temple.

the Xemxija tombs whose internal space is radial, the Dwarfie Stane's space is segmented in three parts. In contrast to the internal space of the Hypogeum which creates a feeling of movement and evolution with the multidirectional space it encompasses, in the Dwarfie Stane the space creates a feeling of segmentation because it occurs sequentially on only one level.

Unlike Taversoe Tuick and the Xemxija tombs whose focus is the internal space created by the structure, at Maes Howe, the articulated internal structure is dominant and the space it creates is subordinate. The interior space of both Vementry and Punds Water is radial and mimics the exterior structure to which it is subordinate. The long, narrow, high, rectangular space of the Holm of Papa Westray chamber is axial and reflects the shape of its cairn.

Little can be said about the location of the Maltese, Orcadian and Shetland tombs in relation to the total land area theoretically available — which was, of course, far greater in the Orkneys and Shetlands than in Malta. However, the Xemxija, Orkney and Shetland tombs all occupy dramatic natural sites without any evidence (to date) of major settlements close by. All the sites are reasonably close to the sea. The Hypogeum is more centrally located, under the modern village of Pawla and near the Tarxien temples. With the exception of Maes Howe, whose orientation is precise, the orientation of Maltese and Scottish structures seems to have been of less concern.

MATERIALS AND TECHNIQUE

The materials used to construct both the Orkney and Shetland tombs and the Maltese tombs were those indigenous to the sites: rock, either excavated as at the Dwarfie Stane and at the lower level of Taversoe Tuick, or drystone used as untrimmed megaliths or as trimmed rectangular blocks of differing sizes. Both in Malta and in the Orkneys and Shetlands only bone and stone tools were available. The Xemxija tombs, the Hypogeum and Dwarfie Stane were laboriously excavated; Holm of Papa Westray and Taversoe Tuick were built of undressed slabs of stone of different sizes; Maes Howe reflects a high degree of finished stonework with true megalithic orthostats, not just vertically placed slabs, used decoratively at the corners of the central chamber. Vementry and Punds Water were built of the granite boulders typical of the Shetland land surface. Since both the Maltese and the Scottish tombs were built of the natural materials at hand, little in the way of analytical comment can be made. Where stone-finishing and building techniques can be observed, those of the Shetlands and Orkneys are similar to those of Malta, but they also have their analogues in contemporary structures in Crete, Sardinia, Iberia, Ireland and the Scottish mainland. Thus we have to limit comment to stating that building techniques noted in the Orkneys and Shetlands, in general, fall within a

Mediterranean and western Atlantic megalithic tradition and are not strictly Maltese or restricted to the traditions of that island.

Both Mnajdra and Stanydale have double-wall construction that uses a drystone technique combined with megalithic blocks of dressed and undressed stone. The two wall faces are each one stone thick, and the space between them is filled with earth and rubble (Malta), and earth, peat and heather (Scotland). In Malta, the space between the two walls was sometimes left unfilled to allow for the construction of subsidiary chambers within the wall thickness. Doorways and passageways in both the Maltese and Scottish structures used the trilithon principle. Porthole doorways are found at Mnajdra but not at Stanydale. At Mnajdra, corbelled vaults rose to a certain level and were then completed with a flat roof of beams, brushwood and clay. At Stanydale, the roof, made of straw or heather laid over spruce or pine rafters, was further supported by two vertical spruce beams whose socket holes are still visible in the soil.

Chapter Two

Temples: Ritual Spaces For the Living

Before comparing the Stanydale and Yoxie temples with Mnajdra and Tarxien Far East, the two Maltese temples with which they seem most markedly to share common features, it will be useful to refer to the figures that follow and note the floorplans and the radiocarbon dates for the structures (FIGS. 94 & 95).

Date B.P.	Malta	Scotland
3600-3300	Tarxien FE	– – –
3000-2500	Mnajdra S	– – –
2000-1500	– – –	Stanydale
2000-1500	– – –	Yoxie

Fig. 94
Radiocarbon dates for Maltese and Scottish temples

In comparing Yoxie and Stanydale with Mnajdra South and Tarxien Far East, we will also refer to Mnajdra East, Ta Hagrat North and South, Hagar Qim, Korbin II and Ggantija South when one or more provide information on substantive points. To date, no undoubted temples have been found or excavated in the Orkneys though these islands can be considered somewhat more fertile and of a slightly more moderate climate than the more northerly Shetlands.

FORM

Stanydale and Mnajdra South compare favorably in size and ratio of length to width in their external plan (see Appendix A-2). Both are heel-shaped. Mnajdra has six uneven apses, Stanydale also has six apses, but distributed evenly across the rear of the chamber. Viewed from the front, the similarity between the two temples is apparent. Both have a concave facade; both use large orthostats to frame entrances that rise above paved ground. Each of the two curved facades ends with orthostats. In Mnajdra, they are notched to align with the horizontal courses of drystone masonry. Both temples are constructed with massive masonry set vertically and horizontally; both use rubble-filled double-wall construction, with corbelling in the apse walls. A visitor approaching the temples from the rear will notice that the backwall casing in both structures consists of uneven boulders carefully fitted together to form the back of the heel-shape. A long-short

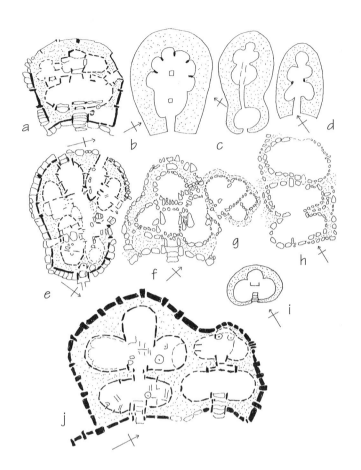

building technique is apparent in both although it is not as consistently applied at Stanydale (PLATES 62 & 63). The apses at Stanydale are comparable in size to Rooms 2, 3 and 4 of Mnajdra South. Mnajdra South is in a much better state of preservation than Stanydale, and the stones used in the interior were cut and dressed. Stanydale lacks this last feature so it is not easy to perceive all the structural similarities, especially from photographs. Mnajdra South had a more elaborate internal structural arrangement than Stanydale. The oracle holes, oracle chambers, pubic triangles, various types of altars, pillar niches and pit-marked decorations — all suggestive of highly evolved religious practices — have no parallels or analogues at Stanydale. Though both temples are assumed to have had roofs laid over horizontal beams, at Stanydale, two vertical beams provided additional support. They would have given the temple a tent-like appearance. Vertical beams are not present in Mnajdra South or in any of the Maltese temples.

Fig. 95
Plans of Maltese and Scottish temples

a) *Mnajdra South, Malta*
b) *Stanydale, Shetland*
c) *Yoxie, Shetland*
d) *Tarxien Far East, Malta*
e) *Hagar Qim, Malta*
f) *Ta Hagrat South, Malta*
g) *Ta Hagrat North, Malta*
h) *Korbin II, Malta*
i) *Mnajdra East, Malta*
j) *Ggantija South and North, Malta*

Stanydale and Mnajdra South both give the visitor a distinct sense of their internal spatial layout. The difference is striking. At Stanydale, the interior is clearly defined and open with the six near-symmetrical apses along the back wall creating regular lines of tension that converge at a central point in the interior space. Mnajdra South differs markedly in that the 'waist' or entry between Room 1 and Room 2 precludes any sight of Rooms 3 and 4 by a visitor positioned centrally in Room 1. In addition, the farther wall (i.e., the west wall) of Room 1 lacks the cleanness of line or symmetry noted at Stanydale. Altars, niches and standing orthostats disrupt the line of vision. This subdivision of the space makes for a protective intimacy, a sense of being enclosed within a small space made safe by the megalithic masonry that defines it. This complicated spatial arrangement heightens the sensation of movement and the passage of time. Simultaneously, the curvilinear quality of the interior space, repeated over and over again by the various circular apses and niches, creates a feeling of cyclical repetition. The use of dressed blocks of globigerina stone for most of the interior work at Mnajdra South adds to the sense of intimacy; at Stanydale, the visitor looks out on rougher, harsher walls of sandstone blocks of generally similar size. However, neither Mnajdra's nor Stanydale's simple, unarticulated exterior appearance hints at their awe-inspiring internal spatial arrangement.

Comparison of Stanydale with Mnajdra East and Ta Hagrat North, which like Stanydale are built from undressed stones, will be useful. The photographs show the same use of orthostats at the ends of apses and the courses of uneven stones in the apse walls (PLATES 64 & 65).

SPACE

Both Mnajdra South and Stanydale face east; both are located in a hollow, have a hill behind them, are near the sea and are close to other religious structures. Despite the difference in climate, both share similar landscapes: bleak, rocky, treeless, and seemingly limitless beneath the open skies. This vista was probably much the same during the Neolithic as the trees had already mostly gone in both places — by 3800 B.P. in Scotland and probably later in Malta.[14] However, Trump claims that "We could argue that [during the Temple Period] timber must have been readily available."[15]

Mnajdra South is about 100 m southeast of the sea, overlooking it; Stanydale is about 0.5 km northeast of the sea, which is not visible from the temple. In all, Mnajdra enjoys the more spectacular setting; it shares the cyclic drama of the sea. Stanydale, more sheltered by rolling hills, possesses a feeling of tranquillity. The basic inland structure of the Maltese islands cannot have altered much from the initial human colonization — 5200 B.P. However, the Maltese coastline must have been somewhat different because the entire island has been tilting higher on the west and lower on the east, resulting in many bays and inlets of the north and east coast becoming drowned valleys. Also, as a result of karsic erosion (chemical dissolution in which the rock is dissolved by water and is carried away) many new caves must have been formed by the sea or existing ones enlarged, altering the coastline.[16] In contrast, the coastline of the Orkneys and probably that of the Shetlands has changed dramatically over the last six thousand years; " . . . gradual submergence and cliff erosion have combined to destroy the fringes of the early landscape."[17] Because of this, we know very little about the forebears of early Neolithic farmers who probably settled on shores now submerged, or of "the foraging visits by Mesolithic fishermen that may have created a store of knowledge about the islands many years before colonization began."[18]

ARTIFACTS

Mnajdra South has yielded a significant number of artifacts: Impressed Ware pottery, tools, statues, phallic pendants, votive offerings, a lobed object (see Fig. 40) and a rough clay figurine that resembles a north Syrian example of the 7th millennium B.P. No human bones or skeletal remains have been found. Stanydale has yielded pottery, tools, small adze pendants, and quartz cores. In design, the pottery appears to be related to that of Whalsay and includes large and small pots, some of which are very fine and one of which has *pit marks*.[19]

Yoxie and Tarxien Far East

Comparison of the Yoxie and Tarxien Far East temples is difficult. Both structures are severely deteriorated with the ratio of fallen stone to standing stone heavily favoring the former. However, recourse can be made to the excavation reports of Calder[20] and Evans.[21] In both cases, these professional archaeologists did careful work and compiled exhaustive notes on their findings. They saw the structures in a better state of repair than they are in now. The similarities between the two temples are impressive. Both structures use a double-wall and rubble construction. In each temple, the stones used for both the outer and inner walls are undressed boulders and megaliths. Both have a concave facade pierced by a center entrance leading into the first chamber. Both the passage and the chamber were originally paved. In each case, the temples had two inside chambers, the innermost of which was trefoil. Though the passageway at Yoxie is considerably longer than that at Tarxien Far East, the chambers are close in size. The central apse at Tarxien Far East is 1.20 m in diameter; at Yoxie about 1.50 m. The ratio between the sizes of the chambers is similar, with those at Yoxie being the larger. In both facades, orthostats flank the entrance to the chambers.

The degree of curvature and the extent of the facades differ greatly. Tarxien Far East broadly follows the characteristic Maltese pattern but without any excessive lateral extension. At Yoxie, the concave facade extends laterally into a pair of almost meeting horns enclosing a space nearly as big as the main chamber. It is worth noting that the concave facades of Vementry and Punds Water are closer in curvature and extent to that of Tarxien Far East than is the powerful and distinctive Yoxie facade. Tarxien Far East offers a unique feature. Under its ruined eastern section lies a subterranean chamber, *suggesting that the temple also incorporated a tomb*.

Space

Yoxie temple on the lower slopes of a hill overlooks the sea, only 30 m distant. Some 90 m east is the Benie Hoose, on a small cliff. Tarxien Far East, on the other hand, is located inland in Malta, about 2 km from the sea. Its site is cramped by the later Tarxien Central complex built close by. Today, the growth of the town of Pawla has virtually enclosed the site. Beyond Pawla, the landscape is hilly and stark, typically dry and barren.

Yoxie and Tarxien Far East are both too much in ruins to allow for extensive or easily validated comparisons. Both temples have distinctive but different coloration. At Tarxien Far East, the coralline stone is a pinkish-cream color tinged with patches of greenish-grey lichen while at Yoxie a more greenish rock with flecks of white and black predominates. Though the stone used in the building of both the temples was neither cut nor dressed, enough pieces were of suitable size for drystone construction methods. Today, however, the state of disrepair at Yoxie and Tarxien Far

East make definitive comment on their internal configuration difficult. In both cases, the internal space appears to have been axial and loosely symmetrical, suggestive of organic growth rather than of a rigid construction plan.

ARTIFACTS

No artifacts or skeletal remains have been found at Tarxien Far East, but the Yoxie site has yielded some fragments of pottery. Two types were found: one was hard, coarse and dark; the other, finer with incised patterns similar to those on the Beaker-style sherds found at the nearby Ness of Gruting House.

CHAPTER THREE

HOUSES: SACRED AND SECULAR HABITATIONS

Other investigations into dwelling places, the first at the Skara Brae, Gruting and the Benie Hoose sites, the second at Ghar Dalam, provide findings that support and strengthen the case for the recognition and worship of the Great Goddess. Though we will address houses in detail later, a number of overall or shared characteristics should be mentioned here. Analysis of these Orcadian and Shetland Neolithic dwelling places suggest that they served as more than simple basic shelter (FIG. 96). A habitation, more than any other structure, is the most intimate shelter of human beings because, besides providing for the needs of the body, it is a reflection of the soul — what people feel about themselves, their relationship with the land, with the flora and fauna, with the forces of nature, and their place in the world among other human beings. Judging from their form and location, the Maltese and Scottish peoples shared a respect for the forces of nature and a concern for the productivity of the land. The proximity of houses to temples and tombs shows that people had a desire to live in harmony with seen and unseen forces. The character and context of the finds associated with Maltese and Scottish houses suggest that within them certain areas may have been reserved for ritual use.

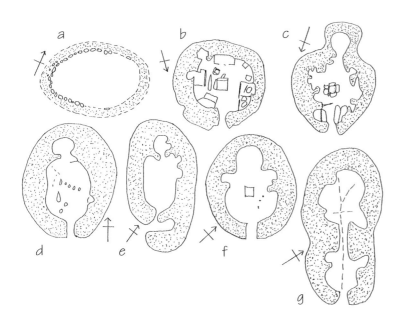

Fig. 96
Plans of Maltese and Scottish houses

a) Ghar Dalam, Malta
b) Hut 7, Skara Brae, Mainland, Orkney
c) Hut 8, Skara Brae
d) Gruting School House, Mainland, Shetland
e) Stanydale School House, Mainland, Shetland
f) Gairdie House, Mainland, Shetland
g) Benie Hoose, Whalsay Island, Shetland.*

*The Benie Hoose appears with houses on this page for purposes of comparison.

The proximity of these dwellings to tombs and temples suggests that the living did not consider death to be final. Rather, bonds existed between the living and the dead, with the dead held in esteem as having a measure of power over life and over the fertility of land and sea that sustained it. This regard for the dead and concern for their influence harks back to the dawn of humankind. It is entirely in keeping with the findings deduced from examination of burial sites as early as those at Shanidar (c. 60,000 B.P.).

FORM

In a number of cases, the houses themselves have characteristics that suggest a close relationship with religion — or at least with the underlying concern expressed through religion. The huts at Skara Brae, the Gruting School House and the Benie Hoose all reflect the essential ovoid or womb-like shape common to all the Maltese tombs and temples. As Michael Dames has noted, the Gruting School House can be considered as a physical embodiment of the Great Goddess, with her nurturing womb represented by the interior space of the hut.[22] The incised pillars lying alongside the hearth of Huts 7 and 8 at Skara Brae, the hidden inscriptions and some of the objects found in the huts suggest that religious ceremonies or rituals were held in the dwellings. Cells inside the house walls may have served as meditation areas. The small drains running from the cells to the interior of the houses may have had a symbolic purpose (a "spirit way") as well as the practical one of carrying away libations.

Hut 8, set apart as it is from the other huts of the settlement, differs markedly from them (see Fig. 64). It shares the anthropomorphic configuration of the Gruting School House, but it lacks the beds, dressers, benches, and utensils found in huts serving as homes. Hut 8 may have been a public building primarily used for religious and political functions. There is no evidence that these activities were separate from daily life in Neolithic times as they are today in Caucasian cultures.

The shapes of the Shetland houses and the associated finds suggest a hieratic as well as a domestic function. The location of the Benie Hoose and its proximity to and relationship with the Yoxie temple suggest that it too served as more than a dwelling place. It may well have been the site of religious observations and rituals. Prehistorians offer different hypotheses on its origins. These include: (1) The Benie Hoose represents an amalgamation of Late Neolithic Beaker elements combined with local invention;[23] (2) like the cairns to which it is related, it was built by people who came from the European continent c. 3000 B.P.,[34] and (3) its form and special association with Yoxie suggest its derivation from Maltese temples[25] (PLATES 66, 67, 68, 69).

Artifacts

Finds at Ghar Dalam include *the bone fragments of two children,* four and seven years old, a small clay cow muzzle, and Grooved Ware sherds with a red ochre wash.[26] The Skara Brae finds include the *skeletal remains of four women, intentionally buried within the hut walls,* ox bones, Grooved Ware pottery, stone balls, bead pendants, a whalebone dish full of red pigment, a star-shaped object, implements and masses of clay.[27] To inter the remains of human beings in dwelling areas as both the Neolithic Maltese and the Scottish islanders did indicates the importance the living conferred upon the dead. The children's and women's bones at the base of the wall implies that the hut builders meant them to be part of the foundation of the houses — to bless and support them. The fact that the four Skara Brae skeletons were those of women could indicate that the community believed women possessed special powers which they could employ benevolently in life and death or it could mean that *only women* were thought worthy of burial inside houses, as was the case at Çatal Hüyük during the 7th millennium.

The artifacts found at Benie Hoose include 1800 implements; pottery sherds, some plain, some decorated with *pit marks,* others with *hobnail decoration (both of which are found in Malta)*, stone disks, round balls of quartz and one star-shaped object. To date, *hobnail decoration has been found only on Whalsay.*[28]

The possible functions of the Benie Hoose raise questions. In shape it relates to other house sites although it is larger, more elaborate and has a horned forecourt. This suggests ritual use; however, the fact that no human bones were discovered in it discourages the idea that it might have been a tomb. The artifacts associated with the Benie Hoose, most of which were tools, suggest a non-religious use, but miniature axes and stone balls often present in temples and tombs were also found.[29] However, because most artifacts were tools, Calder surmised that the Benie Hoose was a habitation. And because of its size, shape and relationship to Yoxie, he postulated that it was a house for priests. I believe that the Benie Hoose could have been a temple that functioned also as a sacred storage space for votive offerings or it may have been a communal dwelling place or both.

CHAPTER FOUR

THE MEANING OF THE MALTESE AND SCOTTISH STRUCTURES

An overall assessment of the meaning of the physical evidence — structures, sculpture, artifacts and other remains — requires consideration of what led to their construction and use. We must attempt to let the physical evidence we have considered project — or speak to us — within its total context. What, then, can we conclude about the tombs and temples of the Orkney and Shetland Islands? With what degree of confidence can we talk of the worship of the Great Goddess in these northern islands, bleak beneath their cool skies?

Anyone who has visited both the Maltese and the Scottish sites has an immediate sense that the same considerations governed the location of tombs and temples in these distant and different settings. The form, location and finds, but most of all the sheer number of tombs, both Maltese and Scottish, convey an impelling religious belief in an afterlife, in a cult of the dead and in a chthonic deity. In both cases the tombs reflect a burial of the dead in either natural hollows in the earth or in hollows created in gentle, almost non-invasive additions to the landscape — the barrow or cairn, made of the rock of the area and largely turf-clad or hidden by the flora indigenous to the setting. The burial chambers or cells in the tombs reflected the curvilinear, bean- or womb-shaped lines of the Xemxija tombs which in turn echo the curvilinear quality of the human body as it rests in a fetal position. Similarly, the bones found in the Orkney and Shetland tombs, as at Taversoe Tuick, showed signs of excarnation, of having been cleaned of flesh (probably by carnivorous animals or by the slower action of the elements) before being placed in the tombs. This practice was widespread in the late Paleolithic Age and was a common element in the Mediterranean Neolithic world, the home of the Great Goddess. And, of course, the proximity of houses and temples to tombs suggests that the living considered the dead to be important, serving as links to the deity.

Other similarities the Orkney and Shetland tombs share with the Maltese are persuasive. The predilection for building in stone may have been dictated as much by recognition of and respect for the durability of this elemental substance as by the comparative scarcity of timber. In many cultures of the ancient world, stones were considered sacred, the bones of the earth. All the Scottish and Maltese structures are in somewhat remote settings of great natural harmony; all are close to open water. Surely, as in the case of Malta, this can only represent a conscious effort to place the dead where the great cycles of nature, both on land and sea, were most fully experienced.

The grave goods found in the Orkney and Shetland tombs are a significant factor. The practice of burying objects of adornment and beauty — which obviously had a value for the living — dates back to the earliest Paleolithic burials and has been met with in Jericho, throughout Mesopotamia, in Çatal Hüyük and in Malta.

The tombs themselves offer other points of comparison that reinforce the sense of a shared tradition and shared rituals. Red ochre was found on the floors of the Xemxija tombs; red pebbles were used to form the floor at the Punds Water tomb. These pebbles were not indigenous but were brought from outside the area. In some cases, the bones found in the Xemxija tombs clearly indicate that the dead had been placed in a fetal position inside the tombs and smeared with red ochre. The symbolism to be evoked from these two actions is evident: the dead were placed in a fetal position in the cave or womb of the earth and smeared with blood, the fluid of life, in order that they might be reborn. The same position can be inferred from the much sparser skeletal remains in several Scottish tombs and from the female skeletons at Skara Brae. Given that in the great majority of cases — and the Hypogeum provides many — the use of red ochre was clearly associated with the Goddess and the belief in rebirth, the red pebbles carefully brought from distant places in the Shetlands surely had the same religious meaning.

I have emphasized that the association of grave goods with the Great Goddess has been constant and strong. In some notable cases, particularly that of the Folkton Drums on which the eye motif of the Goddess is powerfully presented, the evidence for the worship of the Goddess in Neolithic Britain becomes suddenly immediate, powerful and palpable. The Folkton Drums image has been compared with the Ruginosa Vase and the oculi motif from the southeast wall of the Holm of Papa Westray tomb. The viewer has the distinct sense that all three examples constitute a coding, identification or "trademarking," so clearly defined is the underlying symbol that appears on all these artifacts.

Similarly, a pottery sherd found at Skara Brae whose oculi motif reflects that of the stone screens of Tarxien Center offers as clearcut and meaningful an image as does the contemporary dove of peace (see Fig. 71). I believe that the far fainter and less easily discerned bull's head represented by the O engraving in the main chamber of the Holm of Papa Westray belongs to a taurine tradition long associated with the Goddess, one which we saw in all its exuberant power in the shrines of Çatal Hüyük (see Fig. 56).

If we consider all of the carvings of the Holm of Papa Westray as incised symbols, make a determination as to what they represent, and then interpret them within the established traditions of the Goddess, Her chthonic associations and above-ground avatars, we shall be faced with a rich array of parallels and associations.

The inscriptions at the Holm of Papa Westray include oculi motifs, schematic bull motifs, the butterfly, vulvas, the snake, and cup marks. All these incriptions are found at Malta but executed with greater precision, in greater depth and with greater sophistication. There are three oculi motifs at the Holm of Papa Westray, and at Tarxien Center the oculi motif is finely exemplified in the magnificent carved screens. At Tarxien, the motif achieves its most perfect and fully finished form while the oculi motifs at the Holm of Papa Westray are crudely executed with the immediacy of magic intent.

I provided a description and interpretation of the Holm of Papa Westray inscriptions in Book Two, Chapter Two. I believe that the Papa Westray inscriptions are of great importance in establishing a link of belief between southern and northern Goddess-worshipping areas.

Like the Holm of Papa Westray, Taversoe Tuick has certain features that reveal the survival of archaic usage and ancient ritual which were still considered powerful and necessary when the Neolithic islanders built the tombs. What other explanation can there be for two rock-cut chambers, one of which has been completely relined with drystone masonry? This rock section, relined with masonry to make it conform with tomb-building customs, revitalizes the ancient symbolic connection between the cave and the tomb. Another feature that suggests a symbolic or ritual purpose is the drain that connects the lower rock-cut chamber with the miniature chamber. It starts out as an exit from the lower chamber to the outside of the cairn, then becomes a channel that leads directly to the miniature chamber, like an umbilical cord between mother and embryo.

Other features also suggest Great Goddess symbolism: the *three* tomb chambers, the fact that the upper chamber has *three* lobes and that there are *three* stalls in the miniature chamber. Moreover, the finds are suggestive. Thirty-five disk beads of grey shale were found; they are possibly schematic vulvas alluding to rebirth. A star-shaped object was also found, apparently a schematic image of the chthonic deity in the birth-giving position (see Fig. 68).

The Dwarfie Stane's tripartite interior space also suggests the Great Goddess' triune symbolism. Maes Howe's shape and structure hark back to its derivation from older tombs with their tellurian focus while other aspects indicate an involvement with the new sky religion.

Vementry and Punds Water have special features that suggest an indirect relationship with Maltese temples and with the Goddess: the long-short building technique which could have had a symbolic as well as a practical function; the concave facades which recall bulls' horns; the heel-shaped cairns which could represent a highly schematized bull's head—like the O in the Holm of Papa Westray inscriptions; and the two triangular end stones at the outer points of the facade which could have had a practical as well as a symbolic function — as schematized horns.

The basically trefoil shape of Vementry and Punds Water suggests a triune emphasis. This shape, humanoid when considered with the entrance passage, must have been considered symbolically powerful. It was used for the majority of Shetland cairns.

While the broad similarities between Maltese and Scottish tombs are too general to suggest other than a common origin, specific features shared by these structures suggest like religious beliefs and practices in honor of the same chthonic deity.

In commenting on the similarities between the Yoxie and Stanydale temples and Tarxien Far East and Mnajdra South, we face the same problem as with the tombs. The Maltese structures are in a better state of preservation than the Shetland ones and also exist within a fuller and richer context. The Shetland temples are two among only a few scattered structures, almost all uncared for and in a poor state of preservation.

To understand fully the meaning of a temple, we have to know what its creators were trying to communicate about their religious beliefs and their deity. Temples whose function is to preserve and glorify the religious beliefs of a society are designed to evoke strong emotional responses in the faithful, kindling in them a sense of spiritual tranformation and creating the feeling of becoming one with the deity. A temple is not only the place where the deity is worshipped, it is the habitation of the deity, and as such, it is an extension of the deity. It is meant to embody the deity.

But, whether standing in a chamber of a Maltese temple beneath the serene skies of the Mediterranean or amid the tumbled walls of Yoxie or Stanydale beneath the cloudier skies of the north, the visitor is moved by the same pervasive sense of the numinous. The settings of the temples; the long views they give onto; the nearness of the sea; and the protective backdrop of distant hills — all heighten the sense of the sacredness of structures. It is not difficult when within the temples to feel — if not share — this palpable sense of the sacred with which our forebears imbued their places of worship. The concept that we considered when discussing the Maltese temples — that the temple reflected and was the body of the Goddess — seems just as forcefully real in the encompassing, intimate chambers of Yoxie and Stanydale, roofless and windswept though they be. And if we visualize the temples as the central meeting places of

Neolithic society, it becomes easy to accept that religion — the belief in a deity presiding over the cycles of life, death and rebirth — would indeed be a powerful binding force in the remote communities of these islands, isolated in the northern Atlantic or central Mediterranean as they were.

The canal-like entry passages into the temples, the womb-like shape of the inner chambers, their trefoil configuration (in the great Maltese temples becoming five, six and seven-lobed) all reinforce the sense of tomb and temple being way-stations in the great cycle of life, death, and rebirth over which the Goddess presided. The monumentality of megalithic architecture and the durability of stone both emphasize the centrality of the belief in the Goddess to the Neolithic peoples of Malta and of the northern archipelagoes. In Her honor they built structures that could not be mistaken and would outlast time.

In conclusion, we can accept that the similarities between the Shetland temples and those of Malta are individually striking and collectively persuasive. The concave forecourts with their horn-shaped retaining orthostats at the outer ends certainly suggest a sheltered meeting place where the community could gather; the relatively small chambers at Yoxie emphasize a shared intimacy through which the community could jointly experience the comforting power of religion. However, in strong contrast to Yoxie, Stanydale has a very large central chamber and the apses are, in comparison, both small and shallow. If we accept that the concave forecourts of tombs such as Vementry and Punds Water and the appearance of this feature at Stanydale and at Yoxie (in this case in modified form) represent in symbolic form the sweep of the bull's horns and the lunar crescent, then the most striking features of these stone structures speak to us of the Goddess. This interpretation of the forecourts gains in strength when we recognize that the retaining orthostats at the ends of the forecourts are themselves clearly horn-shaped.

Preliterate societies speak to us through symbol and structure, through the greater or lesser evidences of artifacts — whether formal and finished or incidental and abandoned. An engraving on a tomb wall, a statuette, beads from a grave all provide clues, whether forceful or fragmentary, from which we must make our conclusions about the lives of peoples.

In Malta, in the Orkneys and Shetlands, the same question arises: what do we know of the people who built the tombs and temples? What other remains have they left through which we can recreate and evaluate the challenges and conditions of their lives? Here, in a reversal of roles, it is the Orkneys rather than the Maltese islands that yield the richest rewards.

The locations of the Maltese and Scottish structures evoke in the visitor a similar feeling that their builders had a sensitivity for the land and its potential and had a desire to live in harmony with nature. Specific similarities are found in certain Maltese tombs and temples and in some Orcadian and Shetland tombs, temples and houses, indicating that they possessed a ritual and symbolic meaning in addition to their function as dwellings. Gairdie's anthropomorphic shape is found in several contemporary and later houses (FIG. 97) and suggests that this shape may have been considered especially magical and apt for a dwelling. (I was not able to visit this site and so I have relied on Calder's drawings and description. Since his careful excavation, the site has suffered neglect and is apparently entirely in ruins.)

One further connection between Scotland, Malta and the Mediterranean area should be mentioned. This is the bone plaque (see Fig. 59) found in Jarlshof, an Iron Age settlement on Mainland, Shetland. The plaque (which might belong to the Late Neolithic or the Bronze Age) shows definite affinities to Neolithic plaques found in Portugal, Spain and Cyprus. The influence of the Goddess appears to have survived into later ages, reflected by the unexpected appearance of surprising artifacts.

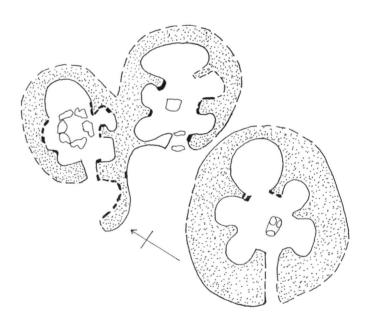

Fig. 97
Late Neolithic houses at Jarlshof, Mainland, Shetland (early 1st millennium B.P.). House on right is 13.3 m long.

CHAPTER FIVE

THE INHABITANTS OF MALTA AND SCOTLAND: COMPLEX ORIGINS

Opinions about the inhabitants of Maltese and Scottish structures differ and are necessarily in large part conjectural. The Ghar Dalam hut, chronologically very early, has revealed remains that are too sketchy to allow us to theorize with confidence on the physical types of its inhabitants. But the substantial finds at Skara Brae have inspired a number of theories about the settlement's inhabitants: (1) the Skara Brae population represented one of the two groups of ethnically distinct people living simultaneously in Orkney; this group of people was ethnically and culturally similar to the folk that built Maes Howe, Stenness, the Ring of Brodgar; these builders, in turn, had close connections with the henge builders of southern England;[30] (2) the Skara Brae skeletal remains are those of dolichocephalic people, the same ethnic type as the people who built the chambered tombs found along the Mediterranean littoral;[31] and (3) the Skara Brae inhabitants were an elite group supported by tributes of food from the local rural population; Hut 8 was a communal kitchen and work room where imported meats and grain were cooked.[32]

In the Shetlands, the inhabitants of Gruting School, the Benie Hoose and the other houses were probably the same folk that built the tombs and temples to which the houses are geographically and morphologically related.[33] It is probable that the Knap of Howar settlement site, which has yielded Unstan Ware, represents a distinct and apparently separate cultural tradition from the Skara Brae settlement, which yielded Grooved Ware. However, these people were not necessarily an ethnically separate group.[34]

There is still disagreement as to what sort of society of peoples both the Maltese and Scottish structures served. Did the tombs and temples serve *all* the members of an egalitarian society? Or did two ethnically distinct groups of people co-exist in a contiguous space? Perhaps two societies with different religious beliefs and practices co-existed both in Malta and Scotland for much of our period. This could account for some of the anomalies found among the artifacts and in the structures themselves.

CONCLUSION

In conclusion we can confidently say that the evidence points to an indirect but undeniable relationship between the Maltese and the Scottish structures — the habitations of the Goddess — either through an intermediary Neolithic group or through an older common source, perhaps through the diffusion of archetypes throughout the Paleolithic and Neolithic worlds. The former possibility seems more likely for several reasons. While in Malta there is evidence of developing forms, in Scotland, especially in the Shetland Islands, the forms appear already evolved. We do not find a continuing series from the more primitive to the more sophisticated. Because they were probably the first structures in the Shetlands and because their primary function was to serve as shelter, the houses seem organic rather than rigid in design. Tombs, similar to Maltese temples in their concentric facades and chambered or lobed interiors, appear next, and then temples. In the Shetland temples, the builders incorporated the earlier tomb and house forms in evolved and perfected shapes. The result is a much larger, symmetrically disposed internal space.

Malta and the Orkneys and Shetlands offer a rich array of structures that have largely retained their initial physical shape. When change has occurred, it appears to have been a process of sympathetic, organic expression within the style and layout of the core structure. Though the evolution of the Maltese temples suggests a change in ideology and perhaps even religious conflict, the Shetland temples are too few and supportive evidence is too sparse to provoke similar inferences. Malta's archaeological record suggests a very religious, somewhat hermetically sealed civilization which, when it collapsed, spread its seeds to the European mainland, perhaps through settlers escaping the problems of a disrupted civilization. In contrast, the Orkneys and Shetlands, much bigger and closer to the mainland than Malta, were therefore subject to more frequent and consistent outside influence. Their monuments do not suggest the rise and fall of an isolated insular civilization as Malta's do. Certainly the physical isolation of both these Mediterranean and North Atlantic islands and the very limited resources and raw materials they offered contributed to the survival of their structures.

Oceans are trackless, seas unmarked. We do not know the number, the business or the frequency of visits of those who came by water to Malta or to the Orkneys and Shetlands. We can identify shared characteristics in architecture and in engraved designs, and we can evaluate the signs of a common worship of the Great Goddess.

Chief among these — and beyond the scope of the present book — is the movement of like-minded peoples and the transmission of the archetypes and practices of megalithic architecture from Malta to the northern archipelagoes. Many prehistorians and archaeologists will point out that the route is clearly marked and that the clues are many. Both statements are true.

In broad general terms we can speak of an advance of megalithic architectural design and practice along the Atlantic seaboard of western Europe. Sicily, Sardinia, Corsica, the French and Spanish littorals (both Mediterranean and Atlantic), Brittany, Ireland, Scotland — all boast extensive and impressive megalithic remains. Rock-cut tombs, chambered cairns, menhirs, dolmens, stone circles, standing stones, stones engraved with Goddess motifs — all are found. Certain structures predominate in certain places; others abound in other areas.

Brittany, for example, offers an unrivalled array of standing stones. Carnac, where the Neolithic inhabitants arranged them in immense rows, is particularly impressive. The Boyne Valley of central Ireland has magnificent chambered cairns such as New Grange and Knowth; and western Scotland provides powerful examples of engraved rock faces. Many sites throughout western Europe and the British Isles have yielded the symbols associated with the Great Goddess — the spiral, the zigzag, the bull's head, the meander and others.

Nothing is definitely known about what happened to the Neolithic Maltese Temple Builders. However, I believe that there is some evidence of out-migration of people and beliefs — some possible colonization, or at least cultural fertilization, in nearby territories such as Sicily, Sardinia and southern France. From these areas, there is an easy progression north by sea or by land. The reappearance of classic Maltese temple design in the Orkneys, and especially in the Shetlands, in structures built over a millennium later, highlights several major questions: Was there a connection between the two cultures? Why did the architectural forms "incubate" for so long before appearing in the north? By what routes or by what agencies did the religious beliefs and the architectural forms travel? What signs of passage remain along the routes? Are there any other similar structures in Europe that would signal the passage of "colonists" or "spreaders of ideas"?

We can argue convincingly that the Maltese tomb and temple culture did not disappear without a trace. Rock-cut tombs that recall earlier Maltese and Italian examples are found in abundance in Spain, Portugal and France and in the later Neolithic and Bronze Age Italy, with the oldest rock-cut tombs in the Mediterranean near Bari.[35] In the early rock-cut tombs, there is the indication of collective burial, evidence of an egalitarian society. There are also hypogea. While rock-cut tombs are numerous, hypogea are relatively few. However, their size and the mass interments made in them suggest that their builders held strong religious beliefs. Hypogea, later in date than Malta's great Hal Saflieni labyrinth, have been excavated in Sicily, Sardinia, Portugal and France.[36] Lately, an earlier Hypogeum-type structure has been excavated in Gozo — the Brochtorff Circle.[37] Some of these structures have features that unmistakably recall the earlier Hal Saflieni Hypogeum.

The Castelluccio culture of Sicily (2000 B.P.) produced tombs that have components similar to those of the Hypogeum. Although they are much smaller, the tombs of Cava Lavazzo, which I visited, are surprisingly like the Hypogeum in their use of engaged pilasters, concave jambs, and low kerbstones, all carved out of the living rock (see Fig. 41). Collective burial was practiced by the Castelluccio people as it was in the Temple Culture of Malta, indicating a generally egalitarian type of society.

In the south of France, apparently some 21 km from Montpellier, Provence, small hypogea from approximately 2000 B.P. have been discovered. They are similar in type to the Hal Saflieni Hypogeum.

What is important about the rock-cut tombs and hypogea of Sicily and mainland Europe that reflect local variations in style and structure is that many of them are more recent than those of Malta. Given the tremendous range of gallery and passage graves and the widespread presence of dolmens, it is of great interest that these two distinctive Maltese forms are found so far afield. The Dwarfie Stane, with its incised jambs and lintels reflecting the decorative architectural motifs of the Hal Saflieni Hypogeum, may suggest some deeply hidden, mysterious march of influence from the Mediterranean cradle up the western seaways to the distant Orkneys and Shetlands. The designs found in Malta — the spiral, meander, bull's head, oculus, etc. — some of which hark to the Paleolithic and which suggest the presence of the Great Goddess, are also found in Scotland. Another Maltese feature, the porthole, is found in a chamber in a megalithic structure at San Baulo in the Balearic Islands. Though these examples are few and only lightly touched upon, they are tantalizing and could be significant.

One final question will serve to highlight the nature and extent of the problems discussed above. Why are there so few clear representations of the human form surviving from the British Neolithic period? I have arrived at four possible conclusions: (1) northern people, because they had a less consistent light source than did Mediterranean people, preferred to celebrate their deity in myths told by special myth-tellers in the warmth and glow of the fire; (2) northern people created their human figures out of perishable materials, therefore, survivals are few; (3) the Neolithic peoples of the British Isles (and northern peoples in general) considered it dangerous to depict their deity in recognizable form and created a tabu against the practice; (4) they depicted the human figure in ways so highly stylized or abstracted that few images or symbols can, with any confidence, be termed representations of the deity in anthropomorphic form.

Many other problems could be identified and discussed. Even if the

Maltese and Orkney and Shetland people had been literate, we would still have unanswered questions. To assume that the written records of a literate society will provide the evidence needed to support confident statements on the lives, values and religious thought of those who wrote them is to make a dangerous assumption. The earliest hieroglyphic and cuneiform records can be interpreted in a number of different ways, depending on the orientation of who is interpreting them, and every new cache yields information that requires prehistorians to modify earlier beliefs and pronouncements.

In order to arrive at the most balanced and complete vision of a society, one must pay at least as much attention to the archaeological record and its context, and to the mythological, anthropological, folkloric and linguistic record as to the contemporary written record. In preliterate societies, where no written records assist the researcher, even greater sensitivity must be brought to the interpretation of other forms of evidence.

I believe the archaeological record, together with other forms of non-literate evidence, will help us understand more of what we seek to know about the Great Goddess. To enter Her habitations and to consider what they suggest and evoke is to open our minds and hearts to the reality of a long-lost world in which gynocentric values prevailed and in which a matristic society may have been the natural order. Recognition of the Goddess is the first step in an exploration and understanding of the Neolithic world. To enter Neolithic tombs, temples and even houses is to enter the habitations of the Goddess: it is to enter Her body.

NOTES AND REFERENCES

APPENDIXES

ILLUSTRATIONS: SOURCES AND CREDITS

PLATES

BIBLIOGRAPHY

155

Notes and References

Introduction

1. I have a book in preparation that will deal with the significance of early images of the Goddess.

Glossary

1. Aubrey Burl, *Rings of Stone*, New York: Ticknor & Fields, 1980, 276.
2. *Ibid.*
3. *Webster's Third International Dictionary*, 3 vols., Chicago: G. & C. Merriam Co., 1971, Vol. I, 265.
4. Graham Clark, *World Prehistory*, Cambridge: At the University Press, 1977, 129-130.
5. Alistair Service and Jean Bradbery, *Megaliths and their Mysteries*, New York: Macmillan Publishing Co., Inc., 1979, 227.
6. Euan Mackie, *The Megalith Builders*, New York: Dutton, 1976, 13.
7. Service and Bradbery, 264.
8. Leon E. Stover and Bruce Kraig, *Stonehenge, the Indo-European Heritage*, Chicago: Nelson-Hall, 1978, 195.
9. *Ibid.*
10. Marija Gimbutas, *The Civilization of the Goddess,* San Francisco: Harper San Francisco, 1991, 432.
11. Colin Renfrew, *Problems of European Prehistory*, Edinburgh: At the University Press, 1979, 195.
12. Webster's, I, 669.
13. *Ibid.*, 783.
14. Service and Bradbery, 265.
15. John Davies Evans, *Malta,* London: Thames and Hudson, 1959, 33.
16. Audrey Shore Henshall, *The Chambered Tombs of Scotland*, 2 vols., Edinburgh: At the University Press, 1963-1972, II, 185.
17. Gimbutas, *Civ.*, 432.
18. Gloria Feman Orenstein, *The Reflowering of the Goddess*, New York: Pergamon Press, 1990, xvi.
19. Colin Renfrew, *Before Civilization*, New York: Penguin Books, 1976, 3.
20. Stover and Kraig, 197.
21. Gimbutas, *Civ.*, 433.
22. *Ibid.*
23. *Ibid.*, 432.
24. *Ibid.*, 24.
25. Webster's II, 1402.
26. Robert Graves, *New Larousse Encyclopedia of Mythology,* New York: Prometheus Press, 1972, v.
27. Gimbutas, *Civ.*, 434.
28. Service and Bradbery, 265.
29. Gimbutas, *Civ.*, 434.
30. *Ibid.*
31. *Ibid.*
32. Ruth Whitehouse, "The Rock-cut Tombs of the Central Mediterranean," *Antiquity*, December 1972, XLVI:184, 275-281.

33. Evans, *Malta*, 136-137.
34. Stover and Kraig, 200.
35. Webster's, III, 2233.
36. Stover and Kraig, 201.
37. Siegfried Giedion, *The Eternal Present: The Beginnings of Art*, New York: Bollingen Foundation, 1964, 79.
38. Gimbutas, *Civ.*, 435.
39. Whitehouse, "Rock-cut Tombs," 276-280.
40. Henshall, *C.T.*, II, 177.

BOOK ONE: MALTA: AN ISLAND OF MYSTERY

1. Even though there is a considerable array of Neolithic figurines from many parts of the world, it is beyond the scope of this book to cover all those areas.

Chapter One

2. All measurements are given in meters. For a conversion table, please turn to Appendix B.
3. Renfrew, *B.C.*, 252.
4. In conversation with me in Malta in 1985, Renfrew agreed that there is no hard evidence of such a hierarchical society in Malta.
5. Service and Bradbery, 86.
6. Patrick Brydone, *Tour through Malta and Sicily*, London, 1773, Letter XV, 130.
7. D.H. Lawrence, *Collected Letters*, Cambridge: At the University Press, 1984,Vol. III, 533, letter to Catherine Carswell.
8. Colin Renfrew, *The Megalithic Monuments of Western Europe*, London: Thames and Hudson, 1983, 64.
9. Colin Renfrew, "New Configurations in Old World Archaeology," *World Archaeology*, October, 1972, 2:2, 208.
10. Evans, *Malta*, 45.
11. *Ibid.*, 47.

Chapter Two

12. Sybille von Cles-Reden, *The Realm of the Great Goddess*, Englewood Cliffs, New Jersey: Prentice-Hall, 1962, 72, 95.
13. John Davies Evans, *The Prehistoric Antiquities of the Maltese Islands*, London: Athlone Press, 1971, 18.
14. Evans, *Malta*, 35.
15. *Ibid.*, 36.
16. von Cles-Reden, 73.
17. Evans, *Malta*, 62.
18. *Ibid.*

Chapter Three

19. *Ibid.*, 133.
20. *Ibid.*, 136.
21. Luigi M. Ugolini, *Malta: origine della civiltà Mediterranea*, Roma: La Libreria dello Stato, 1934, 114.

22. *Ibid.*, 134.

23. David H. Trump, *Malta: An Archaeological Guide,* London: Faber and Faber Ltd., 1972, 25.

24. Gertrude Rachel Levy, *The Gate of Horn,* London: Faber and Faber Ltd., 1946, 135.

25. Michael Dames, *The Silbury Treasure,* London: Thames and Hudson, 1976, 61.

26. Mimi Lobell, "Spatial Archetypes,"*Quadrant, Journal of the C.C. Jung Foundation for Analytical Psychology,* Winter 1977, 10:2, 18.

27. von Cles-Reden, 78.

28. Evans, *Prehistoric*, 179-181.

29. *Ibid.*, 180.

30. *Ibid.*, 179.

31. *Ibid.*, 175.

32. Trump, *Malta*, 29.

33. Ramona and Desmond Morris, *Men and Snakes*, New York: McGraw-Hill, 1965, 11.

34. von Cles-Reden, 82.

35. See Caroline Malone, Anthony Bonanno, Tancred Gouder, Simon Stoddart, and David Trump, "The Death Cults of Prehistoric Malta," *Scientific American*, December 1993, 269:6, 110-117. Also see p. 55 of this text.

Chapter Four

36. Levy, 14, 22, 127, 215.

37. John E. Pfeiffer, *The Creative Explosion*, Ithaca, New York: Cornell University Press, 1982, 111.

38. Evans, *Malta*, 148.

39. Trump, *Malta*, 29.

40. I could not ascertain whether this tree was modeled after local vegetation. The plant could have thrived in Malta during the early Neolithic, before the Temple Culture, as Malta was significantly more forested then. This could be an interesting area of investigation.

Chapter Five

41. Evans, *Malta*, 142.

42. James Mellaart, *Excavations at Hacilar,* 2 vols. Edinburgh: At the University Press, 1970, Vol. 1, 168-178.

43. Ian F.G. Fergusson, "New Views on the Hypogeum and Tarxien," in Bonnano, ed. *Archaeology and Fertility Cult in the Ancient Mediterranean*, Amsterdam: B.R. Grüner Publishing Co., 1986, 152.

44. Gimbutas, "The 'Monstrous Venus' of Prehistory or Goddess Creatrix," *Comparative Civilization Review*, No. 7, Fall 1981, 10:3, 18.

45. Themistocles Zammit, "Neolithic Representations of the Human Form from the Islands of Malta and Gozo," *Journal of Royal Anthropological Institute of Great Britain and Ireland*, 1924, Vol. LIV, 77.

46. Raffaelo Battaglia, "Le statue neolitiche di Malta e l'ingrassamento muliebre presso i Mediterranei," *IPEK*, 1927, Vol. II, 159.

47. Barbara Walker, *The Woman's Encyclopedia of Myths and Secrets,"* San Francisco: Harper & Row Publishers, 1988, 218.

48. Cristina Biaggi, "The Significance of the nudity, obesity and sexuality of the Maltese Goddess figure," in A. Bonanno, ed., *Archaeology and Fertility Cult in the Ancient Mediterranean*. Amsterdam: B.R. Grüner Publishing Co., 1986, 135.

49. Zammit, "Neolithic Representations," 74.

50. Christopher Kininmonth, *Malta and Gozo,* London: Jonathan Cape, 1970, 54.

51. Biaggi, "Significance . . . ," 137.

Chapter Six

52. von Cles-Reden, 94.
53. *Ibid.*
54. *Ibid.*
55. *Ibid.*
56. Trump, *Malta*, 64.
57. This would make an interesting investigation. It is possible that ancient societies placed special emphasis on vocal training to produce effective theatrical presentations in their religious ceremonies and rituals.
58. Cristina Biaggi, "The Priestess Figure of Malta," *The Meaning of Things*, Ian Hodder, ed., London: Unwin Hyman, 1989, 120. For information on Maltese Bormlizas, see McLeod & Herndon, 87-88.
59. Marija Gimbutas, *The Language of the Goddess*, San Francisco: Harper & Row, 1989, 323.
60. Trump, *Malta*, 61.
61. Service and Bradbery, 98.
62. A. J. Agius, *The Hal-Saflieni Hypogeum*, Rabat, Malta: Vexillina Printing Press, 1978, 23.
63. von Cles-Reden, 95.
64. Mackie, *M.B.*, 151.
65. *Ibid.*
66. Zammit, T. "Neolithic Hypogeum at Hal Saflieni, Malta," 1983, cited in Levy, *The Gate of Horn*, 131.
67. von Cles-Reden, 73-74.
68. Merlin Stone gives a fine explanation of this in her book, *When God Was a Woman*, New York: Dial Press, 1976, 212-213.

Chapter Seven

69. Evans, *Prehistoric*, 116.
70. Trump, *Malta*, 68.
71. Evans, *Prehistoric*, 130.
72. This is the first appearance of the Great Goddess sheltering Her believers. We will see this image 4000 years later in Piero della Francesca's *Madonna della Misericordia*.
73. See Zammit in Evans, *Malta*, 158.
74. Michael Ridley, *The Megalithic Art of the Maltese Islands*, Poole, England: Dolphin Press, 1976, 64.
75. *Ibid., 20.*
76. *Ibid.*
77. *Ibid.,* 20-22.
78. Renato La Ferla, *A New Look at the Old Temples*, Malta: The Malta Chamber of Architects and Civil Engineers, 1968, 5-6.
79. Ridley, 23-24.
80. *Ibid.*
81. Although in Malta there are indications that in some instances the animal presented is male—a bull—in other cases a cow seems to be depicted, as in the Tarxien relief (see Plate 35). There is no clear indication in the literature whether bone remains are those of bulls or cows.
82. Mackie, *M.B.*, 154.
83. Buffie Johnson, *Lady of the Beasts: Ancient Images of the Great Goddess and Her Sacred Animals.*

New York: Harper & Row, 1988, 320.

84. *Encyclopedia of Organic Gardening*, Emmaus, Pa.: Rodale Press, Inc., 1978, 745.

85. Service and Bradbery, 101.

86. Marija Gimbutas believes that pit marks symbolize amniotic fluid (conversation with the author, November 2, 1988).

87. Ridley, 84.

88. E. O. James, *The Cult of the Mother Goddess*, New York: Frederick A. Praeger, 1959, 22.

89. James George Frazer, *The Golden Bough*, 1912, London: Macmillan & Co., Ltd., 1955, Part IV, Book I, 106 *et seq*.

90. Dorothy Cameron, *Symbols of Birth and Death in the Neolithic Era*, London: Kenyon-Deane Ltd. 1981, 7.

91. James Mellaart, *The Neolithic in the Near East*, New York: Charles Scribner's Sons, 1975, 61.

92. Cameron, *Symbols*, 13, 27-32.

93. Evans, *Prehistoric*, 238-240.

94. Evans, *Malta*, 153.

95. Ridley, 103.

96. Evans, *Prehistoric*, 93.

97. von Cles-Reden, 102, 105.

98. Kininmonth, *Malta and Gozo*, revised edition, London: Jonathan Cape, 1979, 52-53.

99. Biaggi, "The Priestess Figure of Malta," 21.

Chapter Eight

100. Trump, *Malta*, 20-21.

101. Service and Bradbery, 97.

102. Mackie, *M.B.*, 150.

103. *Ibid.*, 151.

104. *Ibid.*

105. *Ibid.*, 158.

106. *Ibid.*, 162.

107. von Cles-Reden, 70.

108. Kininmonth, 1979, 40.

109. Service and Bradbery, 90.

110. von Cles-Reden, 71.

111. H. N. Savory, *Spain and Portugal*, London: Thames and Hudson, 1968, 88-89.

112. Evans, *Malta*, 45-48.

113. von Cles-Reden, 108.

114. Colin Renfrew, "Malta and the Calibrated Radiocarbon Chronology," *Antiquity*, June 1972, XLVI:182, 141-145.

115. Evans, *Malta*, 108.

116. *Ibid.*

117. David Trump, *Skorba*, London: Oxford, 1966, 51.

118. Renfrew, "New Configurations," 208.

119. Unless one believes that these were female figures.

120. Kininmonth, 1970, 60-61.

121. *Ibid.*

122. Biaggi, "The Priestess Figure of Malta," 1986.

123. Biaggi, "Significance . . . ,"138.

124. Biaggi, "Priestess," 120.

125. *Ibid.*

126. *Ibid.*

BOOK TWO: THE ORKNEYS AND SHETLANDS: SCOTLAND'S ISLANDS OF CHALLENGE

Chapter One

1. Dionise Settle in Richard Hakluyt, *Principal Navigations of the English Nation, 1598-1600*, Vol. VII., New York: AMS Press, 1965, 213.

2. Henshall, *C.T.*, I, 57-58 and 136-137.

3. William Lithgow, *Rare Adventures and Painful Peregrinations*, 1614-1642, Glasgow: James MacLehose, 1906, xx.

4. Colin Renfrew, "British Prehistory: Changing Configurations," in Renfrew, ed., *British Prehistory*, London: Duckworth, 1974, 32.

5. *Ibid.*

6. Gordon Childe, *The Prehistory of Scotland*, London: Kegan Paul, Trench, Trubner & Co., Ltd., 1935, 22.

7. I.F. Smith, "The Neolithic," in Renfrew, *British Prehistory*, 101.

8. Colin Renfrew, *Investigations in Orkney*, London: Society of Antiquaries, 1979, 209.

9. Henshall, *C.T.*, II, 286.

10. Euan Mackie, *Scotland: An Archaeological Guide*, Park Ridge, New Jersey: Noyes Press, 1975, 25.

Chapter Two

11. Renfrew, *Orkney*, 201.

12. Henshall, *C.T.*, I, 78.

13. *Ibid.*, 86.

14. Renfrew, *Orkney*, 66-68.

15. Renfrew, *B.C.*, 155.

16. David H. Trump, "Megalithic Architecture in Malta," in Renfrew, ed., *Megalithic Monuments of Western Europe*, 72.

17. Renfrew, *Orkney*, 216.

18. *Ibid.*, 214.

19. Henshall, *C.T.*, I, 61.

20. Henshall, "Scottish Chambered Tombs and Long Mounds," in Renfrew, *British Prehistory*, 155.

21. Henshall, *C.T.*, I, 234.

22. *Ibid.*, 195.

23. *Ibid.*, II, 177.

24. *Ibid.*, I, 113.

25. Water gathered in cupmarks is to this day considered to have healing properties (Gimbutas, *Civ.*, 432). Cupmarks and "shields" are frequently found symbols in Paleolithic iconography and seem to symbolize vulvas.

26. Horns are important in Paleolithic iconography and seem to symbolize growth and fertility. See the "Venus" of Laussel.

27. von Cles-Reden, 279.

28. Henshall, "Scottish Tombs," 155.

29. *Ibid.*

30. Renfrew, *Orkney*, 214.

31. Charles S. T. Calder, "Neolithic Structures in Scotland," in F.T. Wainwright, ed., *The Northern Isles*, Edinburgh: Thomas Nelson and Sons, Ltd., 1962, 18.

32. Renfrew, *B.C.*, 151.

33. In the Paleolithic, the trapezoid is a symbol for the vulva.

Chapter Three

34. Mackie, *M.B.*, 86.

35. Gordon V. Childe, *Ancient Dwellings at Skara Brae*, Edinburgh: Her Majesty's Stationery Office, 1977, 9.

36. Childe, *Skara Brae*, London: Kegan Paul, Trench, Trubner and Co., Ltd., 1931, 23.

37. Could some of these huts have been used as ritual houses - as bleeding huts?

38. *New York Times*, 11/17/87, C-1

39. Renfrew, *Orkney*, 214-217.

40. Robert Wernick, *The Monument Builders*, New York: Time-Life Books, 1973, 73

41. E.A.S. Butterworth, *The Tree at the Navel of the Earth*, Berlin: Walter de Gryter & Co., 1929, 22.

42. Childe, *S.B.*, 107.

43. Dorothy N. Marshall, "Carved Stone Balls," *PSAS,* 1976, Vol. 108, 63.

44. *Ibid.*

45. *Ibid.*, 63.

46. *Ibid.*, 64.

47. *Ibid.*

48. Charles S. T. Calder, "Report on the Discovery of Numerous Stone Age House-sites in Shetland," *PSAS*, 1956, Vol. LXXXI, 391.

49. Childe, *S.B.*, 144.

50. Aubrey Burl, *Rites of the Gods*, London: J.M. Dent & Sons, Ltd., 1981, 77.

51. Henshall, *C.T.*, 149.

52. Aubrey Burl, *Prehistoric Avebury*, New Haven: Yale University Press, 1979, 100.

53. Henshall, *C.T.*, II, 177.

54. *Ibid.*, 181.

55. Childe, *S.B.*, 131.

56. *Ibid.*, 132.

57. O.G.S. Crawford, *The Eye Goddess*, New York: The Macmillan Co., 1956, 107.

58. Stuart Piggott, *Neolithic Cultures of the British Isles*, 1954, Cambridge: At the University Press, 1970, 345.

59. Calder, "House Sites," 383.

60. *Ibid.*, 381.

61. Charles S.T. Calder, "Excavations at Whalsay, Shetland, 1954-5," *PSAS*, 1961, Vol. XCIV, 42.

Chapter Four

62. Mackie, *M.B.*, 38.

63. Henshall, *C.T.*, II, 277.

64. *Ibid.*, 278.

65. *Ibid.*, 279.

66. *Ibid.*

67. *Ibid.*, 280.

68. *Ibid.*, 281.

69. *Ibid.*, 283.

70. Service and Bradbery, 191.

71. Mackie, *M.B.*, 81.

72. *Ibid.*

73. *Ibid.*, 161-162.

74. *Ibid.*

75. *Ibid.*, 166.

76. *Ibid.*, 167-168.

77. *Ibid.*, 168.

78. *Ibid.*, 184-185.

79. *Ibid.*, 175-176.

80. *Ibid.*, 177-178.

81. Gordon V. Childe, "The Earliest Inhabitants," in F.T. Wainwright, ed., *The Northern Isles*, 16.

82. Evan Hadingham, *Circles and Standing Stones*, Garden City: Doubleday, 1976, 24-25.

83. Renfrew, *B.C.*, 160.

84. *Ibid.*

BOOK THREE: THE SHETLAND ISLANDS: THE NORTHERNMOST HOME OF THE GODDESS

1. Charles S.T. Calder, "Cairns, Neolithic Houses and Burnt Mounds in Shetland," *PSAS,* 1964, Vol. XCVI, 69-71.

2. Henshall, *C.T.*, I, 139.

3. *Ibid.*

Chapter One

4. *Ibid.*, 282-286.

5. *Ibid.*, I, 143.

6. Mackie, *M.B.*, 85.

7. Henshall, *C.T.*, I, 58.

8. *Ibid.*, 151.

9. *Ibid.*, 140-146.

10. *Ibid.*, 172.

Chapter Two

11. Calder, "Whalsay," Fig. 30, 30.

12. *Ibid.*, 29.

13. *Ibid.*

14. *Ibid.*, 31.

15. *Ibid.*

16. *Ibid.*

17. Charles S.T. Calder, "Report on the Excavation of a Neolithic Temple at Stanydale in the Parish of Sandsting, Shetland," *PSAS*, 1950, Vol. LXXXIV, 198.

18. *Ibid.*, 186.

19. *Ibid.*, 189.

20. *Ibid.*, 191.

21. *Ibid.*

22. *Ibid.*, 194-197.

23. *Ibid.*, 196-197.

24. *Ibid.*, 196.

25. *Ibid.*, 202.

Chapter Three

26. Calder, "Whalsay," 35.

27. I believe that it has to do with the ancient Pillar Cult, prevalent in the Neolithic, and which had its orgins in the Paleolithic.

28. Calder, "Whalsay," 40.

29. Calder, "House Sites," 340.

30. Dames, *Silbury*, 62-63.

31. *Ibid.*, 62.

32. Henshall, *C.T.*, I, 4.

33. Levy, 129.

34. Dames, *Silbury*, 62-63.

35. *Ibid.*, 61.

36. Henshall, *C.T.*, I, 137.

37. Claire O'Kelly, *Passage Grave Art in the Boyne Valley*, Cork: Eire: Houston & Son, 1978, 15-22.

38. Elizabeth Balneaves, *The Windswept Isles*, London: John Gifford, 1977, 40.

39. *Ibid.*

40. *Ibid.*

Chapter Four

41. Levy, 146.

42. Andrew Fleming, "The Myth of the Mother Goddess," *World Archaeology*, October 1969, 1:2, 258-259.

43. Hadingham, *Circles*, 145.

44. *Ibid.*, 145.

45. Evan Hadingham, *Ancient Carvings in Britain: A Mystery*, London: Garnstone Press, 1974, 80.

46. Glyn Daniel, "Megalithic Monuments," *Scientific American*, July 1980, 243:11, 89.

47. R.A.S. Macalister, "The Goddess of Death in Bronze Age Art and the Traditions of Ireland," *IPEK*, 1926, Vol. II, 255.

48. Daniel, "Megalithic Monuments," 89.

49. Macalister, 260.

50. *Ibid.*

51. Charles F. Herberger, *The Thread of Ariadne*, New York: The Philosophical Library, 1972, 19.

52. Dames, *Silbury*, 67.

53. O'Riordain and Daniels, cited by Dames, *Silbury*, 67.

54. Service and Bradbery, 40.

55. Levy, 146.

56. Déchelette, Joseph, "Une Nouvelle interpretation des gravures de New Grange et de Gavr'inis," *L'Anthropologie*, 1912, Vol., XXIII, 51.

57. Service and Bradbery, 39.

58. Hadingham, *Carvings*, 20.

59. *Ibid.*, 79.

60. Piggott, *Neolithic Cultures*, 219, 254.

61. Hadingham, *Carvings*, 79.

62. Levy, 65 and Peter Lancaster Brown, *Megaliths, Myths and Men*, New York: Harper Colophon Books, 1978, 287.

63. Burl, *Rites*, 170.

64. *Ibid.*, 171.

65. Hadingham, *Carvings*, 28.

66. Rainbird Clark, *Grimes Grave*, London: Her Majesty's Stationery Office, 1963, 21.

67. *Ibid.*, 22.

68. Calder, "Whalsay," 40.

69. Calder, "Stanydale," 196.

BOOK FOUR: COMPARISON: THE ARCHITECTURAL LEGACIES OF MALTA AND SCOTLAND

Chapter One

1. Whitehouse, "Rock-cut Tombs," 276.

2. Service and Bradbery, 188, 202.

3. Henshall, *C.T.*, II, 283.

4. *Ibid.*, 192-193.

5. *Ibid.*, I, 122.

6. Renfrew, *Orkney*, 1.

7. Whitehouse, "Rock-cut Tombs," 276-277.

8. Henshall, *C.T.*, II, 282, 286.

9. *Ibid.*, 157.

10. F.T. Wainwright, ed., *The Northern Isles*, Edinburgh: Thomas Nelson and Sons, Ltd., 1962, 26.

11. Levy, 131.

12. Calder, "Cairns, Neolithic Houses," 69.

13. Renfrew, *B.C.*, 151.

Chapter Two

14. Renfrew, *Orkney*, 34.

15. Trump, *Malta*, 18.

16. *Ibid.*

17. Anna Ritchie, "The First Settlers," in Colin Renfrew, ed., *The Prehistory of Orkney*, Edinburgh: At the University Press, 1985, 36.

18. *Ibid.*

19. Calder, "Stanydale," 196.
20. Yoxie in 1950
21. Tarxien Far East in 1955.

Chapter Three

22. Dames, *Silbury*, 62 and 65.
23. Henshall, *C.T.*, II, 286.
24. *Ibid.*
25. Calder, "Stanydale," 201.
26. Trump, *Skorba*, 11, 12, and 22.
27. Childe, *S.B.*, 23, 52, and 193.
28. Calder, "Whalsay," 40.
29. Calder, "Neolithic Structures," in Wainwright, 41.

Chapter Five

30. Renfrew, *Orkney*, 206-207, 214-217.
31. Childe, *S.B.*, 192-193.
32. Mackie, *M.B.*, 176. In my estimation this is the least likely of the possibilities.
33. Henshall, *C.T.*, II, 286.
34. Renfrew, *Orkney*, 51.

CONCLUSION

35. Whitehouse, "Rock-cut Tombs," 279.
36. Jean-Pierre Mohen, *The World of Megaliths*, New York: Facts on File, 1990, 155.
37. See Caroline Malone, Anthony Bonnano, Tancred Gouder, Simon Stoddard and David Trump, "The Death Cults of Prehistoric Malta," *Scientific American*, December 1993, 269:6, 110-117.

APPENDIXES

Appendix A-1

Table of Maltese and Scottish Tomb Sizes*

Tomb	Exterior Plan Size	Interior Plan Size
Xemxija average Tomb 5	———	3.5 x 1.2 x 1 6 x 5 x 1.6
Hypogeum x 2	———	600 sq m lowest point: 10.6 average room size: 1.5 x 1.5 x 1 to 6 x 5
Taversoe Tuick	cairn diam: 9.15 height: 3 m	lower chamber: 3.74 x 1.6 x 1.59 upper chamber: 4.5 x 3 x 1.6 miniature chamber: 1.52 x 1.16 x .86
Holm of Papa Westray	cairn: 35 x 16.8 x 3	chamber: 20 x 1.53 x 2 average cell: 1 x .80 x 1.10
Dwarfie Stane	stone: 8.5 x 4.5 x 2	passage and cell: 2.5 x 2.8 x .90 largest cell: 2.3 x .86 x .90
Maes Howe	cairn diam.: 35 height: 73	chamber: 4.7 x 4.7 x 4 largest cell: 2.1 x 1.4 x 1.1
Vementry	cairn diam.: 7.93 height: 1.80 facade length: 10.98 facade height: 1.22	chamber: 2.74 x 3.2 x 1.2
Punds Water	cairn diam.: 9.76 height: 2 facade length: 15.25 facade height: 1.3	chamber: 2.05 x 1.76 x 1.2

*Exterior and interior sizes are widest measurements in meters; the last number is the height.

Based on Calder, "Cairns," 43; Henshall, *Chambered Tombs*, I, 177, 195, 201, 223, 237; Trump, *Malta*, 59; and Evans, *Prehistoric*, Plans 14a and 14b.

Appendix A-2

Table of Maltese and Scottish Temple Sizes*

Temple	Exterior Plan Size	Interior Plan Size
Mnajdra South	18 x 17.64 x 4	14 x 13 x 4
Stanydale	19.11 x 13.23 x 3.66	11.89 x 6 x 71 apses: 2.44 x 1.22
Tarxien Far East	13 x 10	10 x 7
Yoxie	18.75 x 10.98	15 x 4.4
Mnajdra East	9 x 7	7 x 5
Ta Hagrat South	18 x 15	15 x 12
Ta Hagrat North	8.3 x 6	7 x 5
Hagar Qim	30 x 25 x 5	25 x 2 x 5
Korbin	20 x 12	——
Ggantija South	30 x 30 x 5	25 x 25 x 5

*Exterior and interior sizes are widest measurements in meters; those not listed were unavailable.

Based on: Calder, "Stanydale," 190; Calder, "Whalsay," 29-33; Evans, *Prehistoric,* Plans 8 and 16; and Trump, *Malta,* 67, 94, 99, 154.

Appendix A-3

Table of Maltese and Scottish House Sizes*

House	Exterior Plan Size	Interior Plan Size
Ghar Dalam	4.9 x 6.7	6.7 x 4.2
Skara Brae		
Hut 7	8 x 7.3 x 2.5	5 x 4.8 x 2
Hut 8	11.7 x 8.8 x 2.5	6 x 4.8 x 2
Gruting School		
House	18 x 14 x 2.5	14 x 10 x 2
Gairdie House	14.6 x 12 x 2.5	10 x 8 x 2
Benie Hoose	24.4 x 12.8 x 3	18 x 7 x 2.5

*Exterior and interior sizes are widest measurements in meters. No size was available for the exterior and interior height of the Ghar Dalam house.

Based on: Calder, "House Sites," 353; Calder, "Whalsay," 32; Childe, *Skara Brae*, 37-41, 49-52; and Trump, *Skorba*, 10-11.

Appendix B

Table of Conversion
(metric to non-metric)

1 centimeter	=	0.3937 inches
1 meter	=	3.28 feet
1 kilometer	=	0.621 miles

Appendix C

List of Abbreviations

B.C.	*Before Civilization,*	Colin Renfrew
C. H.	*Çatal Hüyük,*	James Mellaart
Civ.	*The Civilization of the Goddess,*	Marija Gimbutas
C.T.	*The Chambered Tombs of Scotland,*	Audrey Henshall
M. B.	*The Megalith Builders,*	Euan Mackie
PSAS	Proceedings of the Society of Antiquaries of Scotland	
S. B.	*Skara Brae,*	Gordon Childe

Illustrations: Sources and Credits

(See Bibliography for full title and author listings.)

Figures

1	Ridley, *Megalithic Art,* p. 10.
2	Based on: Renfrew, "Malta,"*Antiquity,* pp.141-145; Service and Bradbery, *Megaliths,* Macmillan, pp. 86-103; Trump, *Malta* , pp. 26, 28, 40; Gimbutas, *Civ.,* p. 471.
3	Trump, *Malta,* p. 26.
4a	Evans, *Prehistoric,* plans 31-35.
4b	Author's drawing.
5	Courtesy of National Museum of Archaeology, Malta.
6a,b	Author's drawing.
7a,b	Courtesy of National Museum of Archaeology, Malta.
7c	Author's drawing based on Mellaart, *Hacilar,* Vol. I, p. 521.
8	Author's drawing based on Evans, *Prehistoric,* plan 8.
9	Courtesy of National Museum of Archaeology, Malta.
10	Trump, *Malta*, fig. 22, p. 154.
11	Author's drawing based on Ridley, *Megalithic Art*, p. 48.
12	Trump, *Malta*, p. 99.
13a,b	Courtesy of National Museum of Archaeology, Malta.
14	Author's photograph.
15	Trump, *Malta*, fig. 16, p. 94.
16	Courtesy of National Museum of Archaeology, Malta.
17a	Courtesy of Naturhistorisches Museum, Vienna.
17b	Mellaart, *Çatal Hüyük*, fig. 50, p. 182.
17c,d	Courtesy of National Museum of Archaeology, Malta.
17e	Courtesy of Plovdiv Archaeological Museum, Plovdiv, Bulgaria; photograph from Gimbutas, *Gods*, plate 147, p. 160.
18a	Courtesy of National Museum of Archaeology, Malta.
18b	Gimbutas, "The Temples of Old Europe," *Archaeology*, p. 42.
19	Courtesy of National Museum of Archaeology, Malta.
20	Mellaart, *Çatal Hüyük*, fig. 52, p. 184.
21	Courtesy of National Museum of Archaeology, Malta.
22	*Ibid.*
23	Derived from Trump, *Malta*, p. 59 and Evans, *Prehistoric,* plans 14a and14b.
24	Photograph by Diana Green.
25a,b	Courtesy of National Museum of Archaeology, Malta.
26a,b	*Ibid.*
27a,b	*Ibid.*
27 c	Author's drawing based on Renfrew, *Problems of European Prehistory*, p. 63.
27d	Author's drawing based on Marshack, *Roots*, fig. 164, p. 291.
27e	Author's drawing. Courtesy of National Museum of Archaeology, Malta.
28	Courtesy of National Museum of Archaeology, Malta.
29	Trump, *Malta*, fig. 12, p. 66.
30	Ugolini, *Malta,* fig. 66, p. 116.
31a	Evans, *Prehistoric*, plate 22, No. 4.
31b	McMann, *Riddles of the Stone Age*, plate 30.
31c	*Ibid.*, plate 117.
31d	*Ibid.*, plate 65.
32	Courtesy of National Museum of Archaeology, Malta.

33 Author's drawing based on Ridley, pp. 21-23.

34a Evans, *Prehistoric*, plate 18, No. 1.

34b Author's photograph.

35 Courtesy of National Museum of Archaeology, Malta.

36 *Ibid.*

37a Cameron, *Symbols of Birth and Death*, p. 13.

37b Photo by Jean Mazenot, *L'art de L'ancienne Égypte*, Éditions Citadelle & Mazenod, Paris.

38a-d Courtesy of National Museum of Archaeology, Malta.

39a *Ibid.*

39b Fleming, "The Myth of the Mother Goddess," *World Archaeology,* fig. 31h, p. 250.

40 Courtesy of National Museum of Archaeology, Malta.

41a Bernabó Brea, *Sicily before the Greeks*, plate 37.

41b Courtesy of National Museum of Archaeology, Malta.

42 Author's drawing.

43 Author's drawing based on Henshall, *C.T.*, Vol. I, p. 57, map 9.

44 *Ibid.*, p. 137, map 10.

45 Based on: Renfrew, *Orkney*, pp. 208-209, 217, 218; Mackie, *Scotland*, 23; Mackie, *Science and Society in Prehistoric Britain*, fig. 36, p. 224; and Gimbutas, *Civ.*, p. 487.

46a Author's drawing based on Henshall and Davidson, *C.T.*, plan 49, p. 160.

46b *Ibid.*, plan 22, p. 121.

46c *Ibid.*, plan 13, p. 115.

46d *Ibid.*, plan 36, p. 142.

46e, f Burl, *Rings of Stone*, pp. 92 and 113 (in Ticknor and Fields edition), courtesy of Francis Lincoln, Ltd., publisher.

47a Courtesy of The Society of Antiquaries of Scotland (henceforth:Soc Ant Scot for all Calder's work); drawing from Calder, "Cairns," p. 48.

47b Henshall, *C.T.*, Vol. I, p. 177.

47c *Ibid.*, p. 171.

48a Courtesy Soc Ant Scot, from Calder, "Neolithic Structures in Shetland," in Wainwright, *Northern Isles*, p. 34.

48b Courtesy Soc Ant Scot, from Calder, "Neolithic Structures," p. 33.

49 Based on Henshall, "Scottish Chambered Tombs and Long Mounds," in Renfrew, *British Prehistory*, pp. 154, 161-162; and Henshall, *C.T.*, Vol I, pp. 77-78, 84, 122, 125 and 189.

50 Author's drawing based on Renfrew, *Orkney*, p. 221; Henshall, *C.T.*, Vol. I, pp. 185, 187, 201, 223, 239 and 245.

51 Author's drawing based on Henshall and Davidson, *C.T.*, plan 49, p. 160.

52 *Ibid.*, plan 22, p. 121.

53 Author's drawing.

54 *Ibid.*

55 *Ibid.*

56a Mellaart, *Çatal Hüyük*, fig 23, p. 109.

56b *Ibid.*, fig. 32, p. 120.

56c Gimbutas, *Gods*, plate 178, p. 188; courtesy of Archaeological Museum, Cracow, Poland.

56d Author's drawing.

56e Childe, *Skara Brae*, plate LII, No. 3.

57a Gimbutas, *Gods*, plate 119, p. 138; Publ. V. Dumitrescu, *L'art de Roumanie*, No. 80.

57b Courtesy of British Museum.

57c Author's drawing.

57d Author's drawing based on Mallowan, "Excavations at Brak...," *IRAQ*, cited by Crawford, *Eye Goddess*, fig. 2, p. 26.

58a Courtesy of Musée Nationale de Préhistoire, Les Eyzies de Tayac.

58b Courtesy of Musée Nationale de Belgrade.

58c Author's drawing based on Morris, *The Prehistoric Rock Art of Galloway*, p. 55.

58d Author's drawing.

59a Courtesy of National Museum of Scotland, Edinburgh.

59b,c   Crawford, *Eye Goddess*, fig. 16d, e, p. 53.

59d   *Ibid.*, fig. 16a, p. 53.

59e   *Ibid.*, fig. 16g, p. 53.

60a   Courtesy of Tankerness House Museum, photograph by John Brundle.

60b,c   Henshall, *C.T.*, Vol. I, plate 54, p. 134.

61   Henshall and Davidson, *C.T.*, plan 13, p. 115.

62   Author's drawing based on Henshall and Davidson, plan 36, p. 142.

63a   Burl, *Rings of Stone*, New Haven: Ticknor and Fields, 1980, p. 113; reprinted by courtesy of Francis Lincoln, Ltd., London.

63b   *Ibid.*, p. 92.

64a   Author's drawing reproduced with the permission of the Controller of Her Britannic Majesty's Stationery Office; from the Royal Commission of the Ancient Monuments of Scotland, Twelth Report, Vol. III, 1946, fig. 268, p.182.

64b   Childe, *Skara Brae*, plan of Skara Brae.

65a   *Ibid.,* plate LIII; located in Skara Brae Museum.

65b   *Ibid.,* plate LII; located in Skara Brae Museum.

65c,d   *Ibid.,* plate LIV; located in Skara Brae Museum.

65e   Author's drawing.

66a   Author's photograph; located in Skara Brae Museum.

66b   Childe, *Skara Brae*, plate LIV, located in Skara Brae Museum.

66c   Author's drawing based on Clark, *The Neolithic Village of Skara Brae*, p. 21.

67a   National Museum of Antiquities of Scotland cited by Childe, *Skara Brae*, plate XXXVII, No. 1.

67b   *Ibid.,* Plate XXXVIII, No. 4.

67c   *Ibid.,* Plate XXXVIII, No. 2.

67d   Author's photograph; located in National Museum of Antiquities of Scotland.

67e   Author's photograph.

68a   Childe, *Skara Brae*, plate LII, No. 3.

68b   Author's drawing derived from Savory, *Spain and Portugal*, fig. 24b, p. 91.

69a   Author's drawing based on Marshack, *Roots*, fig. 168h, p. 295.

69b   Author's drawing based on Calder, "House Sites," p. 394.

70a,c   Author's drawing based on Childe, *Skara Brae*, p. 154; located in Skara Brae Museum.

70d   Author's drawing based on Gimbutas, *Gods*, fig. 103, p. 159.

71a   National Museum of Antiquities, Edinburgh, cited and photographed by Childe, *Skara Brae*, plate XLV.

71b   Photograph from archives of National Museum of Antiquities, Edinburgh, cited by Clarke, *The Neolithic Village of Skara Brae*, plate 7, p. 20, located in Skara Brae Museum.

71c,d   National Museum of Antiquities, Edinburgh, cited and photographed by Childe, *Skara Brae*, plate XLVIII.

72a   Henshall, *C.T.*, Vol. I, p. 177.

72b   *Ibid.*, p. 171.

72c   Calder, "Neolithic," from Wainwright, fig. 11, p. 34; courtesy of Soc Ant Scot..

72d   *Ibid.*, fig. 12, p. 35; courtesy of Soc Ant Scot.

72e   *Ibid.*, fig. 11, p. 34; courtesy of Soc Ant Scot.

72f   Calder, "House Sites," fig. 9, p. 365; courtesy of Soc Ant Scot.

73   Henshall, *C.T.*, Vol. I, fig. 11, p. 177.

74   *Ibid.*, fig. 8, p. 171.

75   Calder, "Excavations . . . Whalsay," p. 29; courtesy of Soc Ant Scot.

76a   Calder, "Stanydale," p. 189 ; courtesy of Soc Ant Scot.

76b   *Ibid.*, p. 187; courtesy of Soc Ant Scot.

77   *Ibid.*, fig. 6, p. 193; courtesy of Soc Ant Scot.

78a   Author's drawing based on Trump, *Skorba*, fig. 10, p.12.

78b,c   Childe, *Skara Brae*, plan of Skara Brae.

78d   Calder, "House Sites," p. 365; courtesy of Soc Ant Scot.

78e,f   *Ibid.*, p. 370; courtesy of Soc Ant Scot.

78g   Calder, "Whalsay," p. 32; courtesy of Soc Ant Scot.

79a   *Ibid.*, p. 28; courtesy of Soc Ant Scot.

79b   *Ibid*., p. 32; courtesy of Soc Ant Scot.

80   Calder, "House Sites," p. 365; courtesy of Soc Ant Scot.

81   *Ibid*.

82   O'Kelly, *Passage Grave Art in the Boyne Valley*, Cambridge, England: Proceedings of the Prehistoric Society, 1973, pp. 39, 354-82.

83   Author's drawing based on Balneaves, *The Windswept Isles*, plate 17, p. 41.

84a   Courtesy of National Gallery of Art, Washington D.C., derived from Giedion, *Eternal Present,* fig. 293, p. 442.

84b   Author's drawing based on Déchelette,"Gravure's de New Grange," p. 36; courtesy of Masson Editeur, Paris.

84c   Author's drawing based on Morris, *Prehistoric Art*, p. 135.

84d   Author's drawing based on Henshall, *C.T.*, Vol. I, plate 24, p. 134.

85   Courtesy of British Museum.

86   *Ibid*.

87a   Gimbutas, *Gods*, plate 119, p. 138.

87b   Author's drawing based on von Cles-Reden, fig. 49, p. 224.

87c   Fleming, "The Myth of the Mother Goddess," fig. 31h, p. 250.

87d   Courtesy of British Museum.

87e   National Museum of Antiquities, Edinburgh, cited and photographed by Childe, *Skara Brae*, plate XLVIII.

87f   Author's drawing.

88a   Childe, *Skara Brae*, plate XLV.

88b   Evans, *Prehistoric*, plate 22, No. 2.

89a-c   Author's drawings, courtesy of National Museum of Archaeology, Malta.

89d   Author's drawing.

89e   Mellaart, *Çatal Hüyük*, fig. 32, p. 120.

90a   Author's drawing based on Evans, *Malta*, plate 85.

90b   Author's drawing based on Childe, *Skara Brae*, fig. 18, p. 148.

91   Derived from Renfrew,"Malta," pp. 141-145; Trump, *Malta*, pp. 26, 28, 40; Renfrew, *Orkney*, pp. 208, 209, 211, 218; Mackie, *Scotland*, p. 23; and Mackie, *Science and Society in Prehistoric Britain*, fig. 36, p. 224.

92a   Calder, "House Sites," p. 365; courtesy of Soc Ant Scot.

92b   Calder, "Neolithic," in Wainwright, p. 34: courtesy of Soc Ant Scot.

92c   Calder, "House Sites," p. 365; courtesy of Soc Ant Scot.

92d   Childe, *Skara Brae*, Plan of Skara Brae.

92e   Calder, "House Sites," pp. 365, 370; courtesy of Soc Ant Scot.

92f   Calder, "Cairns," pp. 47-48; courtesy of Soc Ant Scot.

92g   Trump, *Malta*, p. 99.

92h   Author's drawing.

92i   Evans, *Prehistoric*, plan 8.

92j   Henshall, *C.T.*, Vol. I, p. 177.

93a   Author's drawing.

93b   Calder, "Cairns," p. 43; courtesy of Soc of Ant Scot.

93c   *Ibid*., p. 49; courtesy of Soc Ant Scot.

93d   Henshall, *C.T.*, Vol. I, p. 177.

93e   *Ibid.*, p. 195.

93f,g   *Ibid.*, p. 237.

93h,i   *Ibid.*, p. 223.

93j   *Ibid.*, p. 201.

93k   Evans, *Prehistoric*, plans 14A and 14B.

94   Derived from Renfrew, "Malta," pp. 141-145; Service and Bradbery, pp. 86-103; Trump, *Malta*, pp. 26, 28, and 40; Renfrew, *Orkney*, pp. 208-209; Mackie, *Scotland*, p. 23; Mackie, *Science and Society*, p. 224.

95a   Trump, *Malta*, p. 99

95b-d   Calder, "Neolithic," in Wainwright, p. 34; courtesy of Soc Ant Scot.

95e   Evans, *Prehistoric*, plan 18A.

95f,g   *Ibid.*, plan 8.

95h   *Ibid.*, plan 16.

95i   Trump, *Malta*, p. 99.

95j   *Ibid.*, p. 154.

96a   Author's drawing based on Trump, *Skorba*, fig. 10, p. 12.

96b,c Childe, *Skara Brae*, plan of Skara Brae.

96d-f Calder, "House Sites," p. 365; courtesy of Soc Ant Scot.

96g   Calder, "Whalsay," p. 32; courtesy of Soc Ant Scot.

97   Calder, "Stanydale," p. 201; courtesy of Soc Ant Scot.

Plates

All plates are photographs by the author except:

1) Plates 22b, 38a, and 39a, which are drawings by the author.

2) Plate 3c from Trump, *Malta*, Fig. 32, p. 154.

3) Plates 24, 25, 27, and 28 which are photographs by A. Micallef, by courtesy of the Museum Department, Malta.

BIBLIOGRAPHY

Abelanet, Jean. *Signes Sans Paroles.* Paris: Hachette, 1986.

Abramova, Z.A., "Paleolithic Art in the U.S.S.R.," *Arctic Anthropology*, Fall, 1967, IV:2, 1-179.

Agius, A.J. *The Hal-Saflieni Hypogeum.* Rabat, Malta: Vexillina Printing Press, 1978.

Allen, Max. *The Birth Symbol in Traditional Women's Art From Eurasia and the Western Pacific.* Toronto: The Museum for Textiles, 1981.

Allione, Tsultrim. *Women of Wisdom.* London: Routledge & Kegan Paul, 1984.

Ammerman, Albert J. and Cavalli-Sforza, L.L. *The Neolithic Transition and the Genetics of Populations in Europe.* Princeton: At the University Press, 1984.

Amiet, Pierre. *The Art of Ancient Near East.* New York: Harry N. Abrams Inc., 1977.

Arnheim, Rudolf. *The Dynamics of Architectural Form.* Berkeley: University of California Press, 1977.

The Art of Lepenski Vir. Catalogue to Exhibition, Southampton Art Gallery, 30 August - 5 October, 1986. Portsmouth: Directorate of Leisure, Tourism and Amenities, 1986.

Aubarbier, Jean-Luc and Binet, Michel. *Prehistoric Sites in the Perigord.* Translated by Angela Moyon. Rennes: Ouest France, 1985.

Balneaves, Elizabeth. *The Windswept Isles.* London: John Gifford, 1977.

Battaglia, Raffaelo. "Le statue neolitiche di Malta e l'ingrassamento muliebre presso i Mediterranei," *IPEK, Jahrbuch für Prähistorische und Ethnographische Kunst*, 1927, Vol. II, 131-156 and Tables 44-51.

Bates, Daisy. *The Passing of the Aborigines.* London: John Murray, 1938.

Bazin, Germain. *The History of World Sculpture.* Translated by Madeline Grey. Greenwich, Connecticut: New York Graphic Society, 1968.

Beltrán, Antonio. *Rock Art of the Spanish Levant.* Translated by Margaret Brown. London: Cambridge University Press, 1979.

Berger, Pamela. *The Goddess Obscured.* Boston: Beacon Press, 1985.

Bernabó Brea, Luigi. *Sicily Before the Greeks.* London: Thames and Hudson, 1959.

Bernardini, Enzo. *La Prehistoria in Liguria.* Genova: Sagep Editrice, 1977.

Biaggi, Cristina. "Megalithic Sculptures that Symbolize the Great Goddess." Unpublished dissertation, New York University, School of Education, 1983.

_____. "The Priestess Figure of Malta," in Ian Hodder, ed. *The Meaning of Things, Material Culture and Symbolic Expression.* London: Unwin Hyman, 1989.

Biaggi, Cristina. "The Significance of the Nudity, Obesity and Sexuality of the Maltese Goddess Figure," in A. Bonanno, ed. *Archaeology and Fertility Cult in the Ancient Mediterranean.* Amsterdam: B. R. Grüner Publishing Co., 1986.

Biaggi, Cristina and Lobell, Mimi. "The Goddess Mound," unpublished pamphlet, 1985.

Bible. King James Authorized Version.

Boardman, John. *Athenian Black Figured Vases.* New York and Oxford: Oxford University Press, 1974.

Bord, Janet and Colin. *A Guide to Ancient Sites in Britain.* London: Granada Publishing, 1979.

Bordes, François. *The Old Stone Age.* New York: McGraw-Hill Book Co., 1973.

Boulton, J.T. and Robertson, A. eds. *Letters of D.H. Lawrence.* Cambridge: At the University Press, 1984.

Bouton, Katherine, "A Reporter at Large, the Dig at Cnidus," *The New Yorker,* July 17, 1978, 33-69.

Braidwood, Robert J. *Prehistoric Men.* Chicago: Natural History Museum, 1951.

Breasted, James Henry, Jr. *Egyptian Servant Statues.* New York: Bollingen Foundation, 1948.

Brennan, Martin. *The Stars and Stones.* London: Thames and Hudson, 1983.

Briard, Jacques et Fediaevsky, Nicholas. *Mégalithes de Bretagne.* Rennes: Ouest-France, 1987.

Briffault, Robert. *The Mothers.* 1927. Abridged by Gordon Rattray Taylor. New York: Atheneum, 1977.

British Museum Guide. London: British Museum Publications Ltd., 1976.

Brodrick, Alan Houghton. *Father of Prehistory.* New York: William Morrow & Co., 1963.

Brown, Peter Lancaster. *Megaliths, Myths and Men.* New York: Harper Colophon Books, 1978.

Brown, Mackenzie C. *The Triumph of the Goddess.* Albany: The State University of New York Press, 1990.

Brydone, Patrick. *Tour Through Malta and Sicily.* London. 1773.

Burl, Aubrey. *Megalithic Brittany.* London: Thames and Hudson, 1985.

_____. *Prehistoric Avebury.* New Haven: Yale University Press, 1979.

_____. *Rings of Stone.* New York: Ticknor & Fields, 1980.

_____. *Rites of the Gods.* London: J.M. Dent & Sons Ltd., 1981.

Burney, Charles. *The Ancient Near East.* Ithaca, N.Y.: Cornell University Press, 1970.

Butterworth, E.A.S. *The Tree at the Navel of the Earth.* Berlin: Walter de Gryter & Co., 1929.

Calder, Charles S.T. "Cairns, Neolithic Houses and Burnt Mounds in Shetland," *PSAS,* 1964, Vol. XCVI, 37-86.

_____. "The Dwarfie Stane, Hoy, Orkney: Its Period and Purpose," *PSAS,* 1936, Vol. LXX, 217-236.

Calder, Charles S.T. "Excavations at Whalsay, Shetland, 1954-5," *PSAS*, 1961, Vol. XCIV, 28-45.

_____. "Neolithic Structures in Scotland," in F.T. Wainwright, ed., *The Northern Isles*. Edinburgh: Thomas Nelson and Sons, Ltd., 1962, 26-43.

_____. "Report on the Discovery of Numerous Stone Age House-sites in Shetland," *PSAS*, 1956, Vol. LXXXI, 340-397.

_____. "Report on the Excavation of a Neolithic Temple at Stanydale in the Parish of Sandsting, Shetland," *PSAS*, 1950, Vol. LXXXIV, 185-205 and Plates XVI, Vol. XXIII.

Cameron, Dorothy O. *The Ghassulian Wall Paintings*. London: Kenyon-Deane Ltd., 1981.

_____. *Symbols of Birth and Death in the Neolithic Era*. London: Kenyon-Deane, Ltd., 1981.

Campbell, Joseph. *The Masks of the Gods: Creative Mythology*. New York: The Viking Press, 1971.

_____. *The Masks of the Gods: Occidental Mythology*. New York: The Viking Press, 1972.

_____. *The Masks of the Gods: Oriental Mythology*. New York: The Viking Press, 1970.

_____. *The Masks of the Gods: Primitive Mythology*. New York: The Viking Press, 1972.

_____. *The Mythic Image*. Princeton: At the University Press, 1974.

_____. *The Way of the Animal Powers*. Vol. I. San Francisco: Harper & Row, 1983.

Caponigro, Paul. *Megaliths*. Boston: Little, Brown and Co., 1972.

Castleden, Rodney. *The Stonehenge People: An Exploration of Life in Neolithic Britain 4700-2000 B.C.* London and New York: Routledge & Kegan Paul, 1987.

Chicago, Judy. *The Dinner Party, a Symbol of Our Heritage*. Garden City, N.Y.: Anchor Books, 1979.

Childe, Gordon V. *Ancient Dwellings at Skara Brae*. Edinburgh: Her Majesty's Stationery Office, 1977.

_____. *The Dawn of European Civilization*. New York: Alfred A. Knopf, 1925.

_____. "The Earliest Inhabitants," in F.T. Wainwright, ed., *The Northern Isles*, 9-25.

_____. *The Prehistory of Scotland*. London: Kegan Paul, Trench, Trubner & Co., Ltd., 1935.

_____. *Skara Brae*. London: Kegan Paul, Trench, Trubner and Co., Ltd., 1931.

Christ, Carol P. *Laughter of Aphrodite*. San Francisco: Harper & Row, 1987.

Clark, D.V. *The Neolithic Village of Skara Brae*. Edinburgh: Her Majesty's Stationery Office, 1976.

Clark, Graham. *World Prehistory*. Cambridge: At the University Press, 1977.

Clark, R.T. Rundle. *Myth and Symbol in Ancient Egypt*. London: Thames and Hudson, 1978.

Clark, Rainbird. *Grimes Grave*. London: Her Majesty's Stationery Office, 1963.

Clarke, D.V., Cowie, T.G.; and Foxon, A. *Symbols of Power: At the Time of Stonehenge.* Edinburgh: Her Majesty's Stationery Office, 1985.

Coburn, Thomas B. *Encountering the Goddess.* New York: State University of New York Press, 1991.

Condren, Mary. *The Serpent and the Goddess.* San Francisco: Harper & Row, 1989.

Constable, George and the editors of Time-Life Books. *The Neanderthals.* N.Y.: Time-Life Books, 1973.

Crawford, O.G.S. *The Eye Goddess.* London: Phoenix House Ltd., 1957.

Culican, William, "Arts of Stone Age European Peoples," in *The New Encyclopedia Britannia,* Macropaedia, Chicago; 1974, Vol. 17, 702-703.

Dahlberg, Frances, ed. *Woman the Gatherer.* New Haven: Yale University Press, 1981.

Dames, Michael. *The Avebury Cycle.* London: Thames and Hudson, 1977.

_____. *Mythic Ireland.* London: Thames and Hudson, 1992.

_____. *The Silbury Treasure.* London: Thames and Hudson, 1976.

Daniel, Glyn. *The Megalithic Builders of Western Europe.* Baltimore, Md.: Penguin Books, 1962.

_____. "Megalithic Monuments," *Scientific American,* July,1980, 243:11, 78-90.

Daniel, Glyn and Bahn, Paul. *Ancient Places: The Prehistoric and Celtic Sites of Britain.* London: Constable, 1987.

Davidson, H.R. Ellis. *Gods and Myths of Northern Europe.* Harmondsworth, England: Penguin Books Ltd., 1964.

Davidson, J.L. and Henshall, A.S. *The Chambered Cairns of Orkney.* Edinburgh: The University Press, 1989.

Déchelette, Joseph. "Une nouvelle interprétation des gravures de New-Grange et de Gavr' inis," *l'Anthropologie,* 1912, Vol. XXIII, 29-52.

Dexter, Miriam Robbins. *Whence the Goddess: A Source Book.* New York: Pergamon Press, 1990.

Diner, Helen. *Mothers and Amazons.* New York: Julian Press, 1965.

Doumas, Christos. *Early Cycladic Art.* New York: Frederick A. Praeger, 1969.

_____. *The N.P. Goulandris Collection of Cycladic Art.* London: British Museum Publications Ltd., 1986.

Downing, Christine. *The Goddess: Mythological Images of the Feminine.* New York: Crossroads, 1984.

Dragoo, Don W. *Mounds of the Dead.* Pittsburgh: Annals of the Carnegie Museum, Vol. 37, 1989.

Düerr, Hans Peter. *Dreamtime.* Translated by Felicitas Goodman. New York: Basil Blackwell, 1985.

Edwards, Carolyn McVickar. *The Storyteller's Goddess.* San Francisco: Harper and Row, 1991.

Eisler, Riane. *The Chalice and the Blade.* San Francisco: Harper & Row, 1987.

Eisler, Riane and Loye, David. *The Partnership Way*. San Francisco: Harper & Row, 1990.

Eliade, Mircea. *Patterns of Comparative Religion*. Cleveland: Meridian Books, 1965.

Eliot, Alexander. *Myths*. New York: McGraw-Hill, 1976.

Encyclopedia of Organic Gardening. Emmaus, Pennsylvania: Rodale Press, Inc., 1978.

Evans, Arthur. *The Palace of Minos at Knossos*. 1921. 7 vols. New York: Biblo and Tannen, 1964.

Evans, John Davies. *Malta*. London: Thames and Hudson, 1959.

_____. *The Prehistoric Antiquities of the Maltese Islands*. London: Athlone Press, 1971.

Fagan, Brian M. *People of the Earth: An Introduction to World Prehistory*. Boston: Little, Brown and Co., 1986.

Farrar, Janet and Stewart. *The Witches' Goddess*. Custer, Washington: Phoenix Publishing Co., 1987.

Fergusson, Ian F.G. "New Views on the Hypogeum and Tarxien," in *Archaeology and Fertility Cult in the Ancient Mediterranean*, Amsterdam: B.R. Grüner Publishing Co., 1986.

Fisher, Elizabeth. *Woman's Creation: Sexual Evolution and the Changing of Society*. New York: McGraw-Hill, 1979.

Fleming, Andrew. "The Myth of the Mother Goddess," *World Archaeology*, October, 1969, 1:2, 247:261.

Flood, Josephine. *Archaeology of the Dreamtime*. Honolulu: University of Hawaii Press, 1983.

Forde-Johnston, J. *Prehistoric Britain and Ireland*. New York: W.W. Norton and Co., 1976.

Forte, Elizabeth Williams. *Ancient Near Eastern Seals: A Selection from the Collection of Mrs. William H. Moore*. New York: The Metropolitan Museum of Art, 1976.

Frazer, George James. *The Golden Bough: A Study in Magic and Religion*. Parts 1-9. 1912. London: Macmillan & Co., Ltd., 1955.

_____. *The New Golden Bough*, 1890. Abridged and edited by Theodore A. Gaster. New York: Mentor Books, 1964.

French, Marilyn. *Beyond Power*. New York: Summit Books, 1985.

Gadon, Elinor W. *The Once and Future Goddess*. San Francisco: Harper & Row, 1989.

Galland, China. *Longing for Darkness: Tara and the Black Madonna*. New York: Penguin, 1990.

Gardner, Louise. *Art through the Ages*. Seventh edition. Revised by Horst de La Croix and Richard G. Tansey. New York: Harcourt Brace Jovanovich, Inc., 1976.

Giedion, Siegfried. *The Eternal Present: The Beginnings of Art*. New York: Bollingen Foundation, 1964.

Gimbutas, Marija. *The Civilization of the Goddess*. San Francisco: Harper San Francisco, 1991.

_____. *The Earth Fertility Goddess of Old Europe*. Besançon: Centre National de la Recherche Scientifique, 1987.

Gimbutas, Marija. *The Goddesses and Gods of Old Europe*. Berkeley and Los Angeles: University of California Press, 1982.

_____. *The Gods and Goddesses of Old Europe—7000-3500 B.C.* London: Thames and Hudson, 1974.

_____. *The Language of the Goddess*. San Francisco: Harper & Row, 1989.

_____. "The 'Monstrous Venus' of Prehistory or Goddess Creatrix," *Comparative Civilization Review #7*, Fall, 1981, 10:3,1-26.

_____. "Old Europe c. 7000-3500 B.C. : The Earliest European Civilization before the Infiltration of the Indo-European Peoples,*The Journal of Indo-European Studies*, I:1, 1973, 1-20.

_____. "The Temples of Old Europe," *Archaeology*, November/December, 1980, 33:6, 41-50.

_____. "The Three Waves of the Kurgan people into Old Europe, 4500-2500 B.C." *Archives Suisses d'anthropologie générale*, Genève, 43:2, 1979, 113-137.

_____. "Vulvas, Breasts and Buttocks of the Goddess Creatrix," in Speroni, Charles and Buccellati, Giorgio eds., *The Shape of the Past*, Los Angeles: Institute of Archaeology and Office of the Chancellor, 1981.

Gimbutas, Marija; Winn, Shan; and Shimabuku, Daniel. *Achilleion: A Neolithic Settlement in Thessaly, Greece, 6400-5600 B.C.* Los Angeles: Institute of Archaeology, University of California, 1989.

Gleason, Judith. *Oya, in Praise of the Goddess*. Boston & London: Shambhala, 1987.

Goldman, Bernard. "Typology of the Mother Goddess Figurines," *IPEK*, 1963, Vol. 20, 8-15.

Gomez-Tabanera. "Les Statuettes Feminines Paléolithiques dites 'venus'," Asturies, Perigord: *Rencontre Internationale pour L'Étude des Civilizations Préhistoriques*, 1978.

Goode, W.J. *Religion Among the Primitives*. Glencoe, Ill.: Free Press, 1951.

Goodrich, Norma Lorre. *Priestesses*. New York: Franklin Watts, 1989.

Gootner-Abendroth, Heide. Translated by Maureen T. Krause. *The Dancing Goddess: Principles of a Matriarchal Aesthetic*. Boston: Beacon Press, 1991.

Graves, Robert, "Introduction," in *New Larousse Encyclopedia of Mythology*, v-viii.

_____. *The White Goddess*. 1948. New York: Farrar Straus Giroux, Inc., 1973.

Gregg, Susan Alling. *Foragers and Farmers*. Chicago: At the University Press, 1988.

Grigson, Geoffrey. *The Painted Caves*. London: Phoenix House Ltd., 1957.

Guido, Magaret. *Sardinia*. New York: Frederick A. Praeger, 1964.

Hadingham, Evan. *Ancient Carvings in Britain: A Mystery*. London: Garnstone Press, 1974.

_____. *Circles and Standing Stones*. Garden City: Doubleday, 1976.

_____. *Early Man in the Cosmos*. London: William Heinemann, Ltd. 1983.

Hadingham, Evan. *Secrets of the Ice Age.* New York: Walker and Co., 1979.

Hakluyt, Richard. *Principal Navigations of the English Nation, 1598-1600.* Vol. VII. New York: AMS, 1965.

Hamilton, J.R.C. *Excavations at Jarlshof, Shetland.* Edinburgh: Her Majesty's Stationery Office, 1956.

Harrison, Jane Ellen. *Prolegomena to the Study of Greek Religion.* 1903. Cleveland and New York: The World Publishing Company; Meridian Books, 1966.

_____. *Themis.* 1911. London: Merlin Press, 1977.

Hawkes, Jacquetta. *The Atlas of Early Man.* New York: St. Martin's Press, 1978.

_____. *Dawn of the Gods.* London: Chatto & Windus, 1958.

Hawkes, Jacquetta and Woolley, Leonard. *History of Mankind, Vol. I, Prehistory and the Beginnings of Civilization.* New York: Harper & Row, 1963.

Heidel, Alexander, transl. *The Babylonian Genesis.* Chicago: At the University Press, 1972.

Henshall, Audrey Shore. *The Chambered Tombs of Scotland.* 2 vols. Edinburgh: At the University Press, 1963-1972.

_____. "Scottish Chambered Tombs and Long Mounds," in Colin Renfrew, ed., *British Prehistory,* 137-163.

Herberger, Charles F. *The Thread of Ariadne.* New York: The Philosophical Library, 1972.

Herity, Michael. *Irish Passage Graves: Neolithic Tomb-builders in Ireland and Britain, 2500-2000 B.C.* Dublin: Irish University Press, and New York: Barnes and Noble, 1974.

Hitti, Philip Khuri. *History of the Arabs.* Fifth edition. London: Macmillan, 1951.

Hole, Frank and Heizer, Robert. *An Introduction to Prehistoric Archaeology.* Third edition. New York: Holt, Rinehart and Winston, Inc., 1973.

Hood, M.S.F. "The Home of the Heroes," in Piggott, ed. *The Dawn of Civilization,* New York: McGraw-Hill Book Company, 1967.

James, E.O. *The Ancient Gods.* London: Weidenfeld and Nicolson, 1960.

_____. *The Cult of the Mother Goddess.* New York: Frederick A. Praeger, 1959.

Jayakar, Pupul. *The Earth Mother.* New Delhi, India: Penguin Books, 1980.

Johnson, Buffie. *Lady of the Beasts: Ancient Images of the Great Goddess and Her Sacred Animals.* New York: Harper & Row, 1988.

Joukowsky, Martha. *A Complete Manual of Field Archaeology.* Englewood Cliffs, New Jersey: Prentice-Hall, Inc., 1980.

Joussaume, Roger. *Des Dolmens Pour Les Morts.* Paris: Hachette, 1985.

Kininmonth, Christopher. *Malta and Gozo.* London: Jonathan Cape, 1970.

_____. *Malta and Gozo.* Rev. ed. 1970. London: Jonathan Cape,1979.

Koltur, Barbara Black. *The Book of Lilith.* York Beach, Maine: Nicholas Hays, Inc., 1987.

La Ferla, Renato. *A New Look at the Old Temples.* Malta: The Malta Chamber of Architects and Civil Engineers, 1968.

Lantier, Raymond. *Man Before History.* Translated by Unity Evans. New York: Walker and Co., 1965.

Leach, Maria, ed. *Standard Dictionary of Folklore, Mythology and Legend.* San Francisco: Harper & Row, 1972.

Lederer, Wolfgang. *The Fear of Women.* New York: Harcourt Brace Jovanovich, Inc., 1968.

Lee, Richard B. and Devore, Irven, eds. *Man the Hunter.* Chicago: Aldine Publishing Company, 1977.

Lerner, Gerda. *The Creation of Patriarchy.* New York and Oxford: Oxford University Press, 1986.

Leroi-Gourhan, André. *Treasures of Prehistoric Art.* New York: Harry N. Abrams, n.d.

le Scouezec, Gwenc'hlan. *Bretagne Mégalithique.* Paris: Seuil, 1987.

Levy, Gertrude Rachel. *The Gate of Horn.* London: Faber & Faber Ltd., 1946.

L'Hélgouach, Jean. *Les sépultures mégalithiques en Armorique.* Rennes: Imprimerie Alençonnaise, 1965.

Lithgow, William. *Rare Adventures and Painful Peregrinations.* Glasgow: James MacLehose, 1906.

Lobell, Mimi. "The Goddess Temple," *Journal of Architectural Education,* Sept. 1975, XXIX:1, 20-23.

_____. "Spatial Archetypes," *Quadrant, Journal of the C.C. Jung Foundation for Analytical Psychology,* Winter, 1977, 10:2, 5-44.

_____. *Spatial Archetypes: The Hidden Patterns of Psyche and Civilization.* London and Boston: Shambhala Archetypes Press, forthcoming.

McKay, J.G. "The Deer Cult and the Deer-Goddess Cult of the Ancient Caledonians," *Folklore,* June, 1932, 43:1, 144-174.

McLeod, Norma and Herndon, Marcia. "The Bormliza, Maltese Folksong Style and Women," *Journal of American Folklore,* 1975, 88:347, 81-100.

McMann, Jean. *Riddles of the Stone Age.* London: Thames and Hudson, 1980.

McNeill, Marian F. *The Silver Bough.* 1957. 4 vols. Glasgow: William MacLellan, 1959.

Macalister, R.A.S. "The Goddess of Death in the Bronze Age Art and the Traditions of Ireland," *IPEK,* 1926, Vol. II, 255-264 and Plate II.

Mackenzie, Donald A. *The Migration of Symbols.* London: Kegan Paul, Trench, Trubner & Co., 1926.

_____. *Scottish Folklore and Folklife.* London: Blackie & Son Ltd., 1935.

Mackie, Euan. *The Megalith Builders.* New York: Dutton, 1976.

_____. *Science and Society in Prehistoric Britain.* New York: St. Martin's Press, 1977.

Mackie, Evan. *Scotland: An Archaeological Guide*. Park Ridge, New Jersey: Noyes Press, 1975.

Malinowski, Bronislaw. *The Father in Primitive Psychology*. New York: W.W. Norton & Co., 1927.

Mallowan, M.E.L. "Excavations at Brak and Chagar Bazar," *IRAQ*, Autumn, 1947, IX:2, 89-259.

Malone, Caroline; Bonnano, Anthony; Gouder, Tancred; Stoddart, Simon; and Trump, David. "The Death Cults of Caroline Prehistoric Malta," *Scientific American*, December 1993, 269:6, 110-117.

Manley, John. *Atlas of Prehistoric Britain*. Oxford: Phaidon, 1989.

Maringer, Johannes. *The Gods of Prehistoric Man*. London: Weidenfeld and Nicolson, 1956.

Markey, T.L., and Greppin, John A.C. *When Worlds Collide: The Indo-Europeans and the pre-Indo-Europeans*. Ann Arbor, Michigan: Karoma Publishers, 1990.

Marshall, Dorothy N. "Carved Stone Balls," *PSAS,* 1976, Vol. 108, 40-72.

Marshack, Alexander. "Ice Age Art," catalogue to the exhibition, May 24, 1978 - January 15, 1979, New York: Museum of Natural History.

_____. *The Roots of Civilization*. New York: McGraw-Hill, 1972.

Matthews, Caitlin. *The Elements of the Goddess*. Shaftesbury, Dorset: Element Books Ltd., 1991.

Mellaart, James. *Çatal Hüyük*. London: Thames and Hudson, 1967.

_____. *Excavations at Hacilar*. 2 vols. Edinburgh: At the University Press, 1970.

_____. *The Neolithic in the Near East*. New York: Charles Scribner's Sons, 1975.

Mellaart, James; Hirsch, Udo; and Balnipar, Belkis. *The Goddess from Anatolia*. 4 volumes. Milan: Eskenazi, 1989.

Meyerowitz, Eva L.R. *The Divine Kingship of Ghana and Ancient Egypt*. London: Faber & Faber Ltd., 1960.

Michalowski, Kazimierz. *Art in Ancient Egypt*. New York: Harry N. Abrams, n.d.

Miklouho-Maclay, N. *Travels to New Guinea*. Moscow: Progress Publishers, 1982.

Mohen, Jean-Pierre. *The World of Megaliths*. New York: Facts on File, 1990.

Mookerjee, Ajit. *Kali: The Feminine Force*. London: Thames and Hudson, 1988.

Moon, Beverly, ed. *An Encyclopedia of Archetypal Symbolism*. Boston & London: Shambhala, 1991.

Morris, Ramona and Morris, Desmond. *Men and Snakes*. New York: McGraw-Hill, 1965.

Morris, Ronald W.B. *The Prehistoric Rock Art of Galloway and the Isle of Man*. Poole, Dorset: Blandford Press Ltd., 1979.

Murray, Margaret A., "Female Fertility Figures," *Journal of the Royal Anthropological Institute of Great Britain and Ireland*. 1934, Vol. LXIV, 93-100 and plates VIII-XII.

Neil, Nigel R.J. "A Newly Discovered Stone in Orkney," *Antiquity,* July 1981, LV:214, 129-131 and plate XXIV.

Neumann, Erich. *The Great Mother.* 1955. Princeton: At the University Press, Bollingen Foundation, 1972.

Noble, Vicki. *Shakti Woman: The New Female Shamanism.* San Francisco: Harper San Francisco, 1991.

O'Kelly, Claire. *Passage Grave Art in the Boyne Valley.* Cork, Eire: Houston & Son, 1978.

_____. *Passage Grave Art in the Boyne Valley.* Cambridge: Proceedings of the Prehistoric Society, 1973, 354-382.

Olson, Carl, ed. *The Book of the Goddess: Past and Present.* New York: Crossroads, 1983.

Orenstein, Gloria Feman. *The Reflowering of the Goddess.* New York: Pergamon Press, 1990.

Papathanassopoulos, G. *Neolithic and Cycladic Civilization.* Athens: Melissa Publishing House, 1981.

Parrott, André. *Sumer.* London: Thames and Hudson, 1960.

Parrot, J. "Le Gisement Natufien de Mallaha (Eynan), Israël, *L'Anthropologie,* 1966, 70:5-6, 437-483.

Patai, Raphael. *The Hebrew Goddess.* New York: Avon Books, 1978.

Pereira, Sylvia Brinton. *Descent of the Goddess: A Way of Initiation for Women.* Toronto: Inner City Books. 1981.

Pericot-Garcia, Luis; Galloway, John; and Lommel, Andreas. *La Prehistoria e i Primitivi Attuali.* Florence: Sansoni Editore, 1967.

Pfeiffer, John E. *The Creative Explosion.* Ithaca, New York: Cornell University Press, 1982.

Phillips, Patricia. *The Prehistory of Europe.* Harmondsworth, Middlesex, England: Penguin, 1981.

Piggott, Stuart, ed. *The Dawn of Civilization.* New York: McGraw-Hill Book Company, 1967.

Piggott, Stuart. *Neolithic Cultures of the British Isles.* 1954. Cambridge: At the University Press, 1970.

_____. *Scotland Before Prehistory.* Edinburgh: At the University Press, 1982.

Pittman, Holly. *Ancient Art in Miniature: Near Eastern Seals from the Collection of Martin and Sarah Cherkasky.* New York: The Metropolitan Museum of Art, 1978.

Powell, T.G.E. *Prehistoric Art.* New York: Frederick A. Praeger, Publishers, Co., 1966.

Prideaux, Tom. *Cro-Magnon Man.* New York: Time-Life, 1973.

Pritchard, James B. *Palestinian Figurines.* New Haven: American Oriental Society, 1943.

Rand McNally International Atlas. Chicago: Rand McNally & Co., 1969.

Reed, Evelyn. *Woman's Evolution.* New York: Pathfinder, 1950.

Reis, Patricia. *Through the Goddess.* New York: Continuum, 1991.

Reiter, Rayna R., ed. *Towards an Anthropology of Women.* New York and London: Monthly Review Press, 1975.

Renfrew, Colin. *Archaeology and Language.* New York: Cambridge University Press, 1987.

_____. *Before Civilization.* New York: Penguin Books, 1976.

_____. "British Prehistory: Changing Configurations," in Renfrew, ed., *British Prehistory*, London: Duckworth, 1974, 1-40.

_____. "The Development and Chronology of Early Cycladic Figurines," *American Journal of Archaeology,* January, 1969, 73:1, 1-32.

_____. *Investigations in Orkney.* London: Society of Antiquaries, 1979.

_____. "Malta and the Calibrated Radiocarbon Chronology," *Antiquity,* June, 1972, XLVI:182, 141-145.

_____. "New Configurations in Old World Archaeology," *World Archaeology,* October, 1972, 2:2, 201-202.

_____. *Problems of European Prehistory.* Edinburgh: At the University Press, 1979.

Renfrew, Colin, ed. *The Megalithic Monuments of Western Europe.* London: Thames and Hudson, 1983.

_____. *The Prehistory of Orkney.* Edinburgh: At the University Press, 1985.

_____. *British Prehistory.* London: Duckworth, 1974.

Renfrew, Colin; Gimbutas, Marija; and Elster, Ernestine S. *Excavations at Sitagroi.* Los Angeles: The Institute of Archaeology, The University of California, 1986.

Ridley, Michael. *The Megalithic Art of the Maltese Islands.* Poole, England: Dolphin Press, 1976.

Ritchie, Anna and Ritchie, Graham. *The Ancient Monuments of Orkney.* Edinburgh: Her Majesty's Stationery Office, 1978.

Ritchie, Anna, "The First Settlers," in Renfrew, ed., *The Prehistory of Orkney*, 36-54.

Ritchie, Graham, "Ritual Monuments," in Renfrew, ed., *The Prehistory of Orkney* 118-131.

Rouse, Irving. *Migrations in Prehistory.* New Haven: Yale, 1986.

Royal Commission on the Ancient Monuments of Scotland — Twelfth Report — With an Inventory of the Ancient Monuments of Orkney and Shetland. 2 vols. Edinburgh: His Majesty's Stationery Office, 1946.

Saccacyn-della Santa, E. *Les figures humaines du Paléolithique Superieur Eurasiatique.* Antwerp: De Sikkel, 1947.

Salmonson, Jessica Amanda. *The Encyclopedia of Amazons: Women Warriors from Antiquity to the Modern Era.* New York: Paragon House, 1991.

Sanders, N.K. *Prehistoric Art in Europe.* Harmondsworth, Middlesex, England: Penguin Books Ltd., 1985.

Sanders, N.K. transl. *Poems of Heaven & Hell from Ancient Mesopotamia.* Harmondsworth, Middlesex, England: Penguin Books,1971.

Savory, H.N. *Spain and Portugal.* London: Thames and Hudson, 1968.

Schwenck, Theodor. *Sensitive Chaos*, transl. by Oliver Whicher and Johanna Wrigley, New York: Schocken Books, 1976.

Service, Alistair and Bradbery, Jean. *Megaliths and their Mysteries.* New York: Macmillan Publishing Co., Inc., 1979.

Settle, Dionise in Richard Hakluyt, ed. *Principal Navigations of the English Nation, 1598-1600.* Vol. VII. N.Y. : AMS Publishers, 1965.

Sjöö, Monica and Mor, Barbara. *The Great Cosmic Mother.* San Francisco: Harper & Row, 1987.

Smith, I.F. "The Neolithic," in Colin Renfrew, ed., *British Prehistory*, 100-136.

Sollas, W. J. *Bushmen.* 1911. Third edition. New York: Macmillan & Co., 1924.

Spence, Magnus. *Standing Stones of Stenness and Maes Howe.* Crawley, Sussex: Research into Lost Knowledge Organization, 1974.

Srejovíc, Dragoslav. *Lepenski Vir.* New York: Stein and Day, 1972.

Stoddard, Simon; Bonnano, Anthony; Gouder, Tancred; Malone, Caroline; and Trump, David. "Cult in an Island Society: Prehistoric Malta in the Tarxien Period," *Cambridge Archaeological Journal,* 1993, 3:1, 3-19.

Stone Merlin. *Ancient Mirrors of Womanhood.* 2 vols. New York: New Sibylline Books, 1979.

_____. *When God Was a Woman.* New York: Dial Press, 1976.

Stover, Leon E. and Craig, Bruce. *Stonehenge, the Indo-European Heritage.* Chicago: Nelson-Hall, 1978.

Teubal, Savina J. *Hagar the Egyptian: The Lost Traditions of the Matriarchs.* San Francisco: HarperSan Francisco, 1990.

Thom, Alexander. *Megalithic Sites in Britain.* Oxford: At the Clarendon Press, 1976.

Thomas, David Hurst. *Archaeology.* New York: Holt, Rinehart and Winston, 1979.

Thompson, George D. *Studies in Ancient Greek Society: The Prehistoric Aegean.* 2 vols., London: Lawrence & Wishart, 1949-1955.

Trump, David H. *Malta: An Archaeological Guide.* London: Faber and Faber Ltd., 1972.

_____. "Megalithic Architecture in Malta," in Renfrew, ed., *The Megalithic Monuments of Western Europe*, 64-76.

_____. *The Prehistory of the Mediterranean.* New Haven and London: Yale University Press, 1980.

_____. "Radio-carbon, Malta and the Mediterranean," *Antiquity,* December, 1963, XXXVII:148, 302-303.

_____. *Skorba.* London: Oxford, 1966.

Twohig, Elizabeth Shee. *The Megalithic Art of Western Europe.* Oxford: At the Clarendon Press, 1981.

Ucko, Peter J. *Anthropomorphic Figurines of Predynastic Egypt and Neolithic Crete with Comparative Material from the Prehistoric Near East and Mainland Crete.* London: Andrew Szmidla, 1968.

Ucko, Peter J. "The Interpretation of Prehistoric Figurines," *Journal of the Royal Anthropological Institute of Great Britain and Ireland,* 1962, vol. 92, 38-54.

Ucko, Peter J. ed. *Form in Indigenous Art.* London: Gerald Duckworth and Co., 1977.

Ucko, Peter J. and Rosenfeld, Andrée. *Paleolithic Cave Art.* New York: McGraw-Hill, 1967.

Ugolini, Luigi M. *Malta: origine della civiltà Mediterranea.* Roma: La Libreria dello Stato, 1934.

Van Buren, Elizabeth Douglas. *Clay Figurines of Babylonia and Assyria.* New Haven: Yale University Press, 1930.

_____, "New Evidence concerning an Eye-Divinity," *IRAQ,* Autumn, 1955, XVII:2, 164-174.

von Cles-Reden, Sibylle. *The Realm of the Great Goddess.* Englewood Cliffs, New Jersey: Prentice-Hall, 1962.

Wainwright, F.T., ed. *The Northern Isles.* Edinburgh: Thomas Nelson and Sons, Ltd., 1962, 26-43.

Wainwright, Geoffrey. *The Henge Monuments: Ceremony and Society in Prehistoric Britain.* London: Thames and Hudson, 1990.

Walker, Barbara G. *The Woman's Dictionary of Symbols and Sacred Objects.* San Francisco: Harper & Row, 1988.

_____. *The Woman's Encyclopedia of Myths and Secrets.* San Francisco: Harper & Row, Publishers, 1983.

Wasson, Gordon R.; Kramrisch, Stella; Ott, Jonathan; and Puck, Carla A.P. *Persephone's Quest: Entheogens and the Origin of Religion.* New Haven: Yale University Press, 1986.

Webster's Deluxe Unabridged Dictionary. Second Edition. Revised by Jean L. McKechnie. New York: Dorset & Barber, 1979.

Webster's Third International Dictionary. 3 vols. Chicago: G. & C. Merriam Co., 1971.

Wendorf, Fred and Schild, Romuald. "The Earliest Food Producers," *Archaeology,* October, 1981, 34:5, 30-36.

Wernrick, Robert. *The Monument Builders.* New York: Time-Life Books, 1973.

Wheeler, Mortimer, "Ancient India," in Piggott, ed., *The Dawn of Civilization.* New York: McGraw-Hill Book Co., 1967.

White, Randall. *Dark Caves, Bright Visions.* New York & London: The American Museum of Natural History in association with W.W. Norton & Co., 1986.

Whitehouse, David and Ruth. *Archaeological Atlas of the World.* London: Thames and Hudson, 1975.

Whitehouse, Ruth, "The Rock-cut Tombs of the Central Mediterranean," *Antiquity,* December, 1972, XLVI:184, 275-281.

Whitmont, Edward C. *The Return of the Goddess.* New York: Crossroads, 1984.

Whittle, Alasdair. *Neolithic Europe: A Survey.* New York: Cambridge University Press, 1985.

Wilshire, Donna. *Virgin, Mother, Crone: Mysteries of the Triple Goddess.* Rochester, Vermont: Inner Traditions, 1994.

Witt, R.E. *Isis in the Graeco-Roman World.* Ithaca: Cornell University Press, 1971.

Woods-Martin, W.G. *Traces of the Elder Faiths of Ireland.* 2 vols. London: Longmans, Green, and Co., 1902.

The World Atlas of Archaeology. Boston, Massachusetts: G.K. Hall & Co., 1985.

Zammit, Themistocles, "Neolithic Representations of the Human Form from the Islands of Malta and Gozo," *Journal of the Royal Anthropological Institute of Great Britain and Ireland,* 1924, vol. LIV 67-100 and Plates V-XX.

INDEX

Goddess, statues of, 25, 38-39, 43, 48. *See also* Figurines, female

Gozo, 13-14, 42; location and description, 3; woman with magic beans, creator of temples, 14. *See also* Ggantija temples

Grave goods, 9, 10, 33, 35-36, 56, 72, 88, 119-120, 142. *See also* Artifacts; Pottery

Great Goddess of Tarxien, 24-25, 38-39, 48

Great Hall, Hypogeum, 34, 80

Great Pyramid, 6

Greece, 7, 27

Grimes Grave Goddess. *See* Chalk Goddess of Grimes Grave

Grooved ware, 86, 93, 139, 147

Gruting School House, 92, 99, 109, 111, 138-139, 147

Gynocentric values, 153

Habitation sites. *See* Dwelling places

Hacilar, 2, 23, 24, 28, 47, 88

Hadingham, Evan, 96, 116

Hagar Qim temples, 12, 15, 20-22, 34, 39, 42, 43, 45, 47, 49, 107, 133; external shrine, 21; figurines, 12, 23-24, 34; Phallus stone, 22

Hal Saflieni, Hypogeum, 29, 55, 151-152. *See also* Hypogeum

Hal Tarxien, 49

Hatched lozenges, 87

Heads, figurines, separate and movable, 24, 34

Healing power of Goddess, 19

Hebrides, 94

Hebridean Neolithic pottery, 93-94

Heel-shaped tombs or cairns. *See under* Cairns; Tombs, shape of

Henges, 6, 79, 82, 92, 127. *See also* Stone circles; Stones of Stenness

Henshall, Audrey, 70, 79, 95, 99, 100, 111, 112, 127

Herberger, Charles F., 115

Hobnail decoration, 47, 140

Holm of Papa Westray tomb, 66, 72-76, 87-88, 90, 95, 112, 113, 120, 121, 127, 128, 142-143

Holy of Holies, Hypogeum, 31-32, 34, 80

Houses. *See* Dwelling places

Hoy, Island of, 61, 76

Human form or humanoid shapes in structures, 85, 86, 109, 111, 135, 144, 146; lack of in British Isles, 152. *See also* Temples, shape of; Tombs, shape of

Hypogeum, 11, 14, 29-36, 43, 47, 48, 49, 55, 72, 79, 80, 120, 126, 127, 128-131; description of, 29-34; animal avatars, 35-36; artifacts, 19, 34-35, 48; double-bead pendant, 35-36; figurines, 23, 25; grave goods, 35-36; ritual features, 34; snake pits, 36; tombs, 32-33, 56. *See also* Brochtorff Circle; Cava Lavazzo; Great Hall; Holy of Holies

Iberia, 9, 54, 76, 95, 112, 117, 118, 119, 131; Slate idols, 76

Incubatio; Incubation. *See* Dream incubation

Inhumation, 95

Inscriptions. *See* Carvings

Shanidar, 138

Sheep, 44, 51, 55

Shetland Islands, 46, 98; inhabitants of, 64, 98, 112, 147; location and environment, 62-64; inhabitants of, 64

Shetland Islands, tombs and temples, 66, 100-102, 103-108; evaluation of, 108-109, 111-112. See also Benie Hoose; Gruting School House; Ness of Gruting house; Punds Water tomb; Stanydale Temple; Vementry tomb; Yoxie temple

Siberia, Paleolithic figurines, 24

Sicily, 3, 4, 7, 43, 54, 55, 56, 57, 58, 67, 152

Silbury Hill, 111

Skara Brae, Orkneys, 83, 84, 85-89, 120, 138, 139, 142, 147; carvings, 87-89, 113; Hut 4, 85; Hut 7, 85, 87, 139; Hut 8, 85, 86, 112, 139, 147; inhabitants, 86, 95-96; pottery, 93, 96

Skeletal remains, 10, 32-33, 54, 55, 85, 86, 118, 119, 139, 141, 142. *See also* Bones and bone fragments; Burial practices

Skorba shrine, 10, 11, 51, 55; figurines, 11, 28

Skorba temple, 10, 11

Sleeping Priestess figurines, 28, 30, 38, 39, 43

Sleeping Priestess of Malta, 43

Snakes, 15, 36, 74, 88, 143. *See also* Chthonic deity

Sow-and-piglets images, 42, 51

Spain, 60, 64, 67, 115, 117, 146, 151

Spherical object from Malta, 53. *See also* Stone balls

Spheres. *See* Stone balls

Spiral motifs, 16, 30, 31, 40-41, 45-46, 47, 90, 93, 112, 113, 116; interpretations of, 45-46; as representation of Goddess, 116; relationship to plants, 47

Stalactites, 8, 19

Stalagmites, 8, 19

Standing stones, 105, 113, 151, 152

Stanydale temple, Shetlands, 66, 94, 99, 102, 103, 105-107, 108, 110, 111, 112, 120, 128, 132; comparison to Mnajdra, 133-135, 144

Star-shaped objects, 72, 90-91, 120, 128, 139, 140, 143

Stentinello pottery, 7, 55, 57

Stone balls from Scotland, 53, 90-91, 93, 120, 139, 140; theories on use of, 90, 120

Stone circles, 81-82, 83-84, 103, 105, 113, 152. *See also* Henges; Ring of Brodgar; Stones of Stenness

Stone disks, 91-92, 140

Stone of Prayer. See Hagar Qim

Stonehenge, 6, 92

Stones of Stenness, 66, 79, 81-83, 103, 127, 147

Ta Hagrat temples, 11, 15, 38, 48, 55, 133, 134-135

Tarxien Cemetery Culture, 56-57, 58

Tarxien Goddess, 25-26

Tarxien period, 11, 20, 37

Tarxien temples, 15, 20, 24, 25, 34, 37-42, 43-44, 45, 47, 48, 51-52, 55, 120, 135-137; Center temple, 40-42, 47, 48, 50, 58, 136, 142, 143; East temple, 42; Far East temple, 38, 104, 128, 136-137, 144; West temple, 38-40, 48, 49